# Smokefree

# Smokefree

## A Social, Moral and Political Atmosphere

## SIMONE DENNIS

Bloomsbury Academic
An imprint of Bloomsbury Publishing Plc

B L O O M S B U R Y
LONDON • OXFORD • NEW YORK • NEW DELHI • SYDNEY

**Bloomsbury Academic**

An imprint of Bloomsbury Publishing Plc

| | |
|---|---|
| 50 Bedford Square | 1385 Broadway |
| London | New York |
| WC1B 3DP | NY 10018 |
| UK | USA |

**www.bloomsbury.com**

**BLOOMSBURY and the Diana logo are trademarks of Bloomsbury Publishing Plc**

First published 2016

**British Library Cataloguing-in-Publication Data**
A catalogue record for this book is available from the British Library.

ISBN: PB: 978-1-4725-6919-6
HB: 978-1-4725-6920-2
ePDF: 978-1-4725-6922-6
ePub: 978-1-4725-6921-9

**Library of Congress Cataloging-in-Publication Data**
A catalog record for this book is available from the Library of Congress.

Typeset by Deanta Global Publishing Services, Chennai, India
Printed and bound in India

# Contents

List of Figures viii
Foreword ix
Acknowledgements xi
Acknowledgements of persons xii

Orienting notes: Ethnographic vignettes from a fascinating
atmosphere 1

A fascinating atmosphere 1
Ethnographic vignettes 2
The strength (or weakness) of vignettes 7
A note on Australian specificity and broader relevance 8

Introduction: There's something in the air 11

Examining smoking in the era of smokefree: Public health and
anthropology 11
The anthropology of smoking (a smokefree anthropology) 12
Anthropology's smoker 16
A new approach to smoking and smokefree 17
An argument for inchoateness 19
The structure 22

PART ONE The lay of the smokefree land 27

1    The difference between tobacco and tomatoes 29

Introduction 29
On 'atmospheres' 31
Some thoughts on an uninsurable monkey 33
Public health interventions and the construction of the smoker 36
The Benson and Hedges World Series Cricket, 1988 39
Smokefree places 42
The nuances of public place legislation 43
Legislating the air 47

**2**  Oppositionary pairings and ruinous smoke 48

Introduction 48
Oppositionary pair: Right and wrong 48
Oppositionary pair: Public health and tobacco companies 50
Oppositionary pair: A long life or an untimely death 53
Oppositionary pair: The time of smoking and the time free of smoking 60
Oppositionary pair: Two spatial states 67

**3**  Reimagining the smoker 70

Introduction 70
The smoker, doubly constructed 72
Public health's rational agent 78
Anthropological reformulation of the smoker? 82
Michelle the rational smoker 86
Michelle, reanalysed 88
Putting things that are meant to be held apart, together: The internal inconsistency of smoking 90
Come off the veranda 93

**PART TWO** First, second, third and fourth hand smoke 95

**4**  Breathing in smoke(free), firsthand 97

Introduction 97
The theoretical backgroundedness of the air itself 99
Air as agent 101
Explicating the (firsthand) air for the ignorant agent 104
Take a big breath in 109

**5**  Miasmatic exhalation: Breathing out (secondhand) 114

Introduction 114
Explicating the secondhand air 115
The nose knows danger 118
Jennifer, defender of the air 120
Public air 122
An illness-inducing stench: Cancer is catching 124
There is difference in the air 127
Colonial anthropology: Eradicating smoke and mosquitoes 128
Protecting the infinite and pure air 130

**6**  Abject thirdhand smoke 133

Introduction 133
Thirdhand smoke 135

'Mobile tobacco contamination packages' 137
Smell and the thirdhand trickster 138
Touch: How to deal with witches in the family 144
The air has a history 146
The second law of thermodynamics 148

**7  Fourthhand smoke: Going to Flavor Country** 151

Introduction 151
Explicating the air in cigarette advertising 152
Come on, come to Flavor Country 152
Small t taste 155
Capital T taste 156
Olive Brown is *Not* classy 157
All flights to Flavor Country have been grounded 160
The bitter taste of a gangrenous foot 161
Smoking to remember the air 163
Come breathe on me, honey 164
The rational agent and the travel agent 166

Conclusion 169
Notes 173
References 179
Index 193

# List of Figures

**Figure 1**   Image of a clogged artery  57

**Figure 2**   Set A health warnings  63

**Figure 3**   Set B health warnings  64

**Figure 4**   'Indigenous Woman'  82

**Figure 5**   Michelle, just as I first encountered her, and her friend Sam, also pregnant, also 16, also smoking (author's original drawing)  87

**Figure 6**   A caricature of Megan in action (author's original drawing)  165

# Foreword

**S**mokefree is both the title of Simone Dennis's book and its central preoccupation. She employs the term to characterize not only the specific legislation that bears its name, but also the current atmosphere surrounding smoking – not just smoking as a practice, but also as a field of inquiry. One only needs to watch a film from the 1980s – the 1990s, even – to realize that Smokefree is a recent phenomenon (although many of the gases that constitute its atmosphere have been present for centuries). Take Leaving Normal, an American film I first saw in 1993 and recently watched again. Located in the road trip genre, it focuses on the journey to Alaska undertaken by two relative strangers: Darly (Christine Lahti) and Marianne (Meg Tilly). Marianne is a peripatetic dreamer with a string of broken marriages. Darly is a waitress and former stripper; loud and caustic, she smokes like a chimney throughout the film – in bars and restaurants, in cars and homes.

If all that indiscriminate smoking isn't jarring enough to the contemporary viewer, one scene particularly stands out. Darly and Marianne have arrived at the house of Marianne's resolutely middle-class sister, who is married with two young children. Darly, whose tolerance for kids is clearly limited, has been tasked with telling them a 'Huggie bear' bedtime story. After recounting a highly abbreviated version in which the forest burns down, the trappers sell Huggie to the zoo, and he dies of hardened arteries, she informs the children that she is going to have a smoke. Sarah (all of 8) immediately says, 'Cigarettes are bad.' Darly responds, 'No, Sarah, cigarettes are good. And you know something? When you grow up, you should smoke. Mmm. Good. Cigarettes.' The scene is played for laughs, but it reads somewhat differently twenty-two years later. Certainly not everywhere, but in Australia, the site of Dennis's ethnographic work, and Canada, where I reside, these kinds of moments immediately date the film. Why? Because the atmosphere has changed. Viewers might still be moved to laughter, but it's now slightly uneasy. 'These are innocent children,' we think to ourselves; 'she is corrupting them'.

It's precisely these barometric changes in atmosphere that Dennis explores in Smokefree. This is not the oft-told narrative in which the current social, political and legislative environment is the result of scientific advances in our knowledge of smoking and successful efforts to curb the practices of a morally bankrupt industry. Nor is it a libertarian fable about the consequences of a growing degree of public health paternalism and its concomitant erosion of individual rights. Both of these tales – equally presentist, equally narrow – have been told before. Dennis shows that they, too, are a product of the atmosphere of Smokefree, in which we are presented with an image of two oppositional forces – tobacco control and the tobacco industry – straining against each other. Instead, she paints a rather different picture, one where these forces are never quite so opposed as they imagine. They bleed together at the edges; they mirror each other curiously; they construct their object (the smoker) in ways that obscure other possibilities of seeing.

Here, Dennis offers us another way of imagining this atmosphere, one not grounded in the instrumentalism that has become part and parcel of how tobacco research is increasingly approached. Without setting herself up as the detached observer with privileged access to truth, she explores the affective, spatial and temporal dimensions of smoking and smokefree, threading her account with rich ethnographic vignettes from her fieldwork in Australia (undoubtedly one of the more interesting countries in which to be conducting research on this topic). In many respects her agenda shares much in common with Richard Klein in his seminal book Cigarettes are Sublime, and she exhibits the same talent for weaving together theory and illustration, with equally provocative and engaging results.

Although in many respects Smokefree is the intellectual successor to Klein's work, it nevertheless poses an important corrective as well. After all, Klein predicted that the prevailing anti-smoking climate was merely a symptom of America's long-standing love–hate relationship with tobacco and that the pendulum would soon swing back. In 1993, the same year that Klein published his book and Darly puffed her way through Leaving Normal, that still seemed like a possibility. More than two decades later, with the atmosphere of Smokefree continuing to thicken, it looks increasingly unlikely.

Unapologetically phenomenological in orientation, Dennis shows us the untapped possibilities of this kind of approach. Whether you agree with Bourdieu's characterization of phenomenology or not, Dennis gives us irrefutable proof that it is compatible with an interest in structure and capital (in all the senses that Bourdieu describes), and can dramatically enrich our understanding of these phenomena. In this respect, her perspective provides a critical intervention into prevailing approaches to smoking, because they have been so utterly overdetermined by the political economy of tobacco use.

Judith Butler once observed that feminist critique should remain self-critical with respect to the totalizing gestures of feminism itself. Dennis's book reminds us that this remains true of many fields of inquiry. While I have no doubt that some readers will be challenged by the ideas and arguments she presents, I am equally convinced that it is an extremely important book, one that demands engagement, if not agreement.

Kirsten Bell, University of British Columbia

# Acknowledgements

## Acknowledgement of informing works

This book is derived in part from the following published journal articles:

Dennis, S. (2011), 'Smoking Causes Creative Responses: On State Antismoking Policy and Resilient Habits', *Critical Public Health* 21 (1): 25–35, doi: 10.1080/09581596.2010.529420. Available online: http://tandfonline.com/doi/abs/10.1080/09/0958596.2010.529420.

Dennis, S. (2013), 'Golden Chocolate Olive Tobacco Packaging Meets The Smoker You Thought You Knew: The Rational Agent and New Cigarette Packaging Legislation in Australia', *Contemporary Drug Problems* 40 (1): 71–97, doi: 10.1177/009145091304000105. Available online: http://cdx.sagepub.com/content/40/1/7.full.pdf+html.

Dennis, S. (2014), 'Explicating the Air: The New Smokefree (And Beyond)', *The Australian Journal of Anthropology*, forthcoming doi:10.1111/taja.12103. Pre-publication version available online: http://onlinelibrary.wiley.com./doi/10.1111/taja.12103.

# Acknowledgements of persons

I am grateful to Kirsten Bell, who generously discussed ideas and drafts, and wrote the excellent Foreword to this book. I thank my anthropology colleagues at the Australian National University, The University of Melbourne and Macquarie University, who gave feedback on sections of the book given at each of their seminar series. Many thanks to Dianne, for reading drafts of the manuscript, and to Don for listening to spoken-word versions. I am grateful too, to Keaka for his interest in this ongoing project and his continued support of it. Finally, I wish to acknowledge the smokers who have generously given of their time in interviews and discussions that form the ethnographic basis of this work. Thank you for talking with me.

# Orienting notes: Ethnographic vignettes from a fascinating atmosphere

## A fascinating atmosphere

This book examines a captivating and pervasive atmosphere – 'smokefree'. I've been enthralled by its development across the decade-long period I've spent anthropologically immersed in researching smoking. I've been equally fascinated by how anthropologists working specifically on smoking have, by and large, disattended some of the more interesting aspects of smoking and the 'smokefree' context in which it occurs in favour of supporting the public health goal of winning the war on smoking. While laudable, academic alignment to this goal limits what we can know about smoking to within the confines of a cessation agenda. This book presents a view from outside of public health and offers up another, different way to think about smoking and the atmosphere of smokefree.

This work is informed by a range of Australian materials, including specific pieces of legislation that have figured particularly prominently in the smokefree atmosphere. These have generated much media interest and lively debates have ensued in face-to-face contexts, on television shows and radio talkback, and in internet discussions. This was particularly the case following reportage of Australia's decision to adopt plain packaging, implemented in 2012. Smokefree public place legislation also prompts energetic discussion. On 12 January 2015, the Queensland state government announced it was considering banning smoking on the balconies of apartment buildings. On the morning of 13 January, a commercial television station's morning show panel was discussing the proposal in the most animated of ways. It was a discussion that rapidly became concerned with the issue of whether or not the state should be allowed to prohibit people from engaging in a legal activity in their own homes. To me, debates about smoke drifting from the site of one's own home and into the spaces occupied by non-smoking others centrally concern *the air itself*. I will dedicate much of this book to bringing this backgrounded atmospheric to the fore in order to usher in my own contribution to the anthropology of smoking, and of 'smokefree'.

Far from being the backdrop against which action (like smoking or attempts to reduce its prevalence) occurs, the air itself is central to the production of the smokefree atmosphere. It is also the accomplice of the state in asserting the force of the smokefree atmosphere, and in bringing it to bear on smoking bodies. It is a double agent, working just as willingly for tobacco companies in making manifest the appeal of cigarettes. I focus throughout on the air itself, bringing it to the fore in my analysis of the smokefree atmosphere in Australia, to reveal something new about how the atmosphere is shaped and sustained, and about smoking itself.

In the book, I make use of the nation's principal online public health resource on tobacco. Produced by the Cancer Council and edited by public health and tobacco experts Scollo and Winstanley, *Tobacco in Australia: Facts and Issues* (2012) is updated as national survey data on smoking is produced and analysed. I draw also on Australia's formally issued National Tobacco Strategy (NTS). The current strategy covers the years 2012–18, and sets the tone for tobacco control in Australia, describing the desired prevalence rate reduction, the suite of anti-smoking messaging that is to be used, the particular groups of people who will be its main targets, and what will be the most important aims to accomplish. I draw, too, mostly silently and reflexively, on my own positionedness as, variously and vacillatingly, a smoker and a non-smoker over the ten-year period in which I have attuned my ethnographic antennae to tobacco smoking and to the developing era of smokefree. In the main, though, I draw on ethnographic data collected in several Australian locations over the last ten years.

# Ethnographic vignettes

The data pressed into service in this book comprises ethnographic vignettes drawn from smokers I have interviewed since 2004. My initial research, carried out in the South Australian capital city of Adelaide between 2004 and 2005, when I was then and there resident, consisted of interviews with some sixty smokers whom I accessed using the ethnographic technique of snow-balling. After encountering initial informants in the street, or in other public contexts where they were smoking, I would often be introduced to other smokers known to them. Informal interviews, which usually lasted from thirty minutes to an hour, took place wherever the interviewee suggested – most commonly, in a café, park or bar when it was possible to smoke in such places, as it was in 2004. Smoking in an enclosed public bar is unthinkable now anywhere in Australia, but it was commonplace ten years ago.[1] It was there I met Megan, who features in Chapter 7 of this book.

Outgoing and, by her own description, 'sexy' and 'fun', twenty-five-year-old Megan was in the bar to hook up. She was, at that time, new to the city, having moved to Adelaide from Sydney in late 2003, only a few months before I interviewed her. So, she told me, she had 'no reputation to lose', and her aim was to 'have sex, and often'. Smoking was incorporated into her flirtatious regime – she smoked mostly when she was out, not so much when she was at home, and often began her coquettish encounters with men by asking strangers whom she fancied for a light. 'Yep, he wants to Flick my Bic, alright!', she remarked after having secured a light from a man who winked at her as he lit her cigarette, right at the start of our interview. Later, as I left the bar, they were ensconced together there, he on the seat I'd vacated. The smoke from their cigarettes entwined together in the air above Megan's blonde head and his dark one, a smoky forerunner, Megan would certainly have hoped, of more intimate entwining to come.

I met Michelle in Adelaide, too, quite by good fortune as she stepped outside of a takeaway with some friends and promptly lit up. She caught my eye not least because she was so young, but probably more because she was heavily pregnant. The interview I conducted with her, perhaps more than any other I've done, crystallized and clarified my approach to, and thoughts about, smoking and those who do it. As I explain in Chapter 3, I now think this crystallization and clarification entirely erroneous. Of course, as seems always to be the way, I only came to this conclusion after having rather excitedly published what I (wrongly) considered my ultimate position piece on the matter in a prominent social science journal. I've never managed to live it down, and I feel very grateful when fellow researchers contact me to ask about it – because then I have a chance to explain how dead wrong I think I was. I have drawn on my own published embarrassment herein, and contrasted my premature conclusions with what I now think about that interview with sixteen-year-old pregnant Michelle, and how my rethinking has, I fervently hope, better crystallized and clarified my thinking about smokers.

As I moved around, from the University of Adelaide to a post in Queensland in 2006, I kept pursuing my interest in smoking, continuing to access smokers by the same technique as I had utilized in Adelaide. The smokers in my family and immediate circle of friends, aware of my academic, and on-again-off-again participatory, interest in smoking, would frequently engage me in conversations on the topic, often informing my sense of what questions might be good to pose in ethnographic interviews with smokers on the street. Sometimes, then, data collection has proceeded along the lines of informal ethnography, where the lines between life and fieldwork are blurred (see Katz 2006).

This was the case with twenty-something Marley, whom I introduce in Chapter 7. I knew Marley through a friend and, as she wrestled with domestic violence, homelessness and unemployment, she'd often give voice to her various frustrations from the safety of the sofa of my friend, who had generously taken her in. She wasn't allowed to smoke indoors, so her stream of mournful woes came out with great pauses in between, when she'd left off talking to go and smoke four or five Holiday cigarettes outside in my friend's garden. A while after Marley's departure, my friend, confronted with the butts that were littered everywhere (despite the old jar she'd supplied for Marley to put them in), dejectedly told me, 'Apparently, there is a certain kind of spider that incorporates the spent butt into its web; they used to use rolled-up leaves. Also, the butts, because of all the chemicals in them, kill off the sparrow mite, when the sparrows use the filter material to line their nests. Just exactly what I need. More spiders, more sparrows.'

The day Marley came home from the shops after having copped an earful of abuse from some 'up themselves' real estate girls, Marley's fury was truly unleashed. I was at the ready, notebook in hand. After recounting the story to her rescuer and me, Marley leapt up from the sofa and chain-smoked outside, coming in only now and again to add a detail she'd left out, or to pronounce new ways she'd thought of to have her revenge on 'those bitches'.[2]

The line between life and fieldwork is also blurred in the sense that, on occasion, I've encountered smokers *because* I have been smoking myself; while this has not been consistently so (especially since I have not been a smoker, at least not much of one, for the last three years or so), it has been increasingly the case that when I approach smokers presently, I am often regarded with suspicion and even trepidation. An approach from someone who is not holding a cigarette towards someone who is holding a lit one, particularly if the person is smoking near a café or other smokefree place on a breezy day, may not have a pleasant outcome for the smoker these days. As one forty-something male smoker in Canberra put it as I approached him for an interview, 'If you'd come up to me twenty or even ten years ago like you just did, I would've thought you were coming to bot a smoke. But nowadays, you expect to be told off – or asked to move on.'

More formally and recently informing this work is ethnographic research carried out with around forty-five smokers living in Australia's capital city, Canberra, in the Australian Capital Territory, between 2012 and 2014. This work corresponded with my appointment to the Australian National University (ANU) (in 2008), in spaces and contexts in which cigarettes were bought and sold (i.e. at checkout counters in supermarkets and small corner stores), in which people were smoking (i.e. in those areas in Canberra city and surrounds where smoking is permitted). Even though I'm describing this portion of my data as more formal, in the sense that it was collected in the main in and through interviews I conducted in Canberra city streets, there were still some occasions when, again, the line between 'fieldwork' and 'life' became blurry and indistinct. One important informant of this work, Olivia, came to be involved in this way.

Just as I made Marley's acquaintance via a shared connection with a friend, I met Olivia from our mutual circulation around the higher education terrain of Canberra city: Olivia and I knew one another, as familiar faces rather than by name, because we moved in the same educational circles. One day, I sat to smoke, and so did she. She smiled at me, and I took the opportunity to ask her for an interview, which I conducted right there and then, as we smoked companionably together on a sunny bench on the campus of the ANU. ANU wasn't a smokefree campus then, in 2012, but it is preparing to be now, in 2015 having already sent out a survey to a random selection of its staff about two options: 1. Go smokefree but retain designated smoking areas; 2. Go completely smokefree. I wasn't among those who received the survey, but a colleague who did receive it recently remarked to me of it:

> It's really best characterized as a survey that asks, 'do you really hate smoking, or do you *really, really,* hate smoking?' Of course, I declined to respond to it because it was so clearly self-interested, i.e. not interested in the views of staff, and particularly not interested in the views of smokers.

The survey itself is indicative of the intolerance for smoking in the Australian Capital Territory more broadly, which, according to 2013 Australian Institute of Health and Welfare (AIHW) figures, has a smoking prevalence rate for adults over 18 under the national average (of around 13 per cent) at just over 10 per cent (Australian Government AIHW 2013). Although a smokefree policy did not exist at the time I interviewed Olivia, back in 2012, it didn't stop another colleague from shouting at us, 'you drug addicts!', as he passed by. Although he laughed as he uttered the words, indicating they were meant in jest, Olivia remarked when he was out of earshot that she was getting tired of being made to feel a pariah, even though she was doing something completely legal. She felt she didn't deserve it, a feeling made plain as she differentiated herself in our interview from people who *might* deserve negative attention: as she named them, 'teenage boys' and 'bums', who didn't care about their image as they smoked, like white, fifty-something, middle-class Olivia definitely did. She made the remarks as Australia readied itself for the introduction of the world's first plain packaging laws, in which Canberra figured prominently.

Canberra is the site from which the national statements on smoking are issued – such as the announcement of the Australian government's legal win on plain packaging. Australia has taken a leading role in tobacco control on the world stage, but, since its recent win over Big Tobacco in the Australian High Court in

November 2011 which ushered in the world's-first plain packaging legislation, its profile in tobacco control has heightened. In the win, the Australian Labor government, with the support of the Federal opposition, moved to prevent tobacco companies from using their trademarks and branding on packaging. There ensued a legal challenge brought against the Commonwealth by Big Tobacco (comprising British American Tobacco, Philip Morris, Imperial Tobacco, Van Nelle Tabak Nederland and Japan Tobacco International SA), on grounds of constitutional invalidity but, on 15 August 2012, the High Court of Australia ruled that the plain packaging laws were constitutionally valid.

On the local stage, the scene was set in the Australian capital for battle lines to be drawn over smoking. In the wake of appearances by the federal health minister and attorney general, who spoke to the public of the win using the language of war and victory, Canberrans took sides. Skirmishes of a sort broke out, that I witnessed as I took to the streets of the capital, field notebook in hand. People in the street felt, it seemed, well within their rights to tell smokers to butt out, and in one case, a serious disagreement broke out at a downtown eatery about where the no-smoking zone began and ended and what a stiff breeze might have to do with it. Isabella, the victim of the wind on that breezy Canberra day, recounted her story to me shortly after she'd been 'verbally abused' by the owner of a café which she'd passed by on foot, cigarette alight, smoke racing ahead of her, making its trouble before she herself even arrived on the scene. I utilize her story in Chapter 2, in which the finer points of smokefree public place legislation reveal themselves as attempts to still and site that which is loath to be still and sited: smoke itself.

Even though smokefree laws had been applied to restaurants and eateries well prior to the final plain packaging decision in the High Court, something seemed to have shifted. Many people with whom I spoke in the street thought the moment ripe for going further, even for making smoking illegal. Others thought, as one man on the street put it, that banning branding on packs was good evidence that 'the Nanny state's gone mad. What'll they do next, mandate the wearing of gumboots every time it rains?!'

In both the Adelaide and Canberra cases, participants in my research, ranged from teenagers like Michelle, to men in their forties, like Haydn, who feared heart disease would be the end result of his smoking and so refused to receive packets with that warning label on them; they came from a range of ethnic, educational and socio-economic backgrounds, like Marley, who 'always hated school', to Olivia, who'd never left the educational environment and taught in a university. Most were revealed to me primarily via their engagement with cigarettes. This, of course, is only one way of identifying smokers in what is indubitably the current climate of tobacco denormalization in Australia (see Chapman and Freeman 2008; Winstanley 2012). As Bell et al. (2010) have pointed out, smoking in public in a climate where stigmatization is common may be difficult or even impossible for some smokers. Thus, identifying smokers by evidence of practice in the public domain is now unlikely to be a reliable method of accessing the full range of members in the category 'smokers'; it only captures those who continue smoking in public under these conditions. These conditions can at times be aggressively anti-smoking.

The conditions didn't stop Judy, in her 70s, and a smoker most of her life, from continuing a pack-a-day relationship with her Peter Jackson Dark Blues. She knew they probably wouldn't kill her, as they had not killed her Dad, who'd been so badly injured in a fall down some stairs that he'd not survived. He'd been a heavy smoker, too, as had her Mum – she'd died of heartbreak after the loss of her husband; Judy reckoned the affliction 'heartbreak' was a terminal one, and certainly one with a more reliable death rate than smoking. In Chapter 3, I utilize Judy's sense of her own lung capacity inherited from her Dad, which made her immune to some of the sure and certain claims of the public health state, about the state of her own lungs.

I've largely interviewed smokers who take up smoking and keep doing it in an environment clearly designed to dissuade the practice. This may cause some readers to draw the presumptive conclusion that I'm going to be sympathetic to the notion that we've got to make sense of smoking, ethnographically, so we can see just why they continue (and henceforth work to stop it).

*But I'm not.*

# The strength (or weakness) of vignettes

This book is liberally peppered with ethnographic vignettes drawn from various times and spaces I've inhabited as a fieldworker over the last decade or so – I've introduced just some of the main characters in the foregoing. I purposely employ the term 'vignette' to describe the ethnographic extracts I make use of in this book, as many anthropologists do when they introduce tone-setting events or happenings drawn from the field. The term 'vignetting' is also used in photographic practice, and in that terrain it refers to any process by which there is loss in clarity towards the corners and sides of an image. In extending this photographic meaning of vignette to metaphorically apply to the cases I use herein, I signal that the specific ethnographic encounters I retell here cannot predict with any clarity the broader responses that smokers have towards legislation in Australia.

While it is certainly true that the bulk of the vignettes I have included in this book come from smokers who have not responded as expected to the public health messages that are intended to stop them from smoking, we must take care not to make too much of this, nor to read into it any predictive force. After all, the ethnographic data I use are very local and particular, and, compared with the populations of the cities from which they are drawn, and to 'Australia', the data are relatively few. They do not constitute anything nearly as certain or grand as an ethnography of Adelaide [or Canberra] smokers. Thus, their predictive force is decidedly weak. The data I use does not permit me to claim that legislation is ineffective, and that smokers will resist it no matter how pointed legal dissuasion becomes (and such a claim is profoundly untrue at a population level in any case).

It might at this point appear as though I have extricated myself from the dangerous mathematical terrain of 'hasty generalization' (a variant of faulty generalization made by reaching an inductive generalization using insufficient evidence) in order to stop critics from committing the opposite fallacy, 'slothful induction'. This would involve them denying the reasonable conclusion of an inductive argument, such as I might claim to have here, on the basis of few but compelling smoker narratives. In this case, slothful induction might take the form of relegating what smokers have told me to the realm of anomalous or aberrant or weak data. As it happens, however *I am not claiming to have the beginnings of a powerful inductive argument issuing from smoker claims about how legislation won't work to change their smoking practices*, nor would I set out to make such a claim – or indeed, its opposite, that legislation *will* work.

To restate: it's important to know from the outset that this book presses data into the service of no agenda, save that which serves to advance our knowledge of smoking practice in the era of smokefree beyond the instrumental. This means I'm equally unaligned to public health and Big Tobacco. And, I'm not particularly wedded to everything about anthropological approaches, either; in fact, I'm very critical of the tradition of medical anthropology that has led to an almost constant interventionist and instrumentalist take on smoking. I'm also critical of much older themes in anthropological approaches, particularly those that assert the rational person and the internal consistency of life. I'm sure I'll make some new enemies but, really, all I'm suggesting is that we step outside some paradigms that dominate research on smoking and smokefree, to see what we can find. Sometimes, that's enlightening. I think it's always necessary.

# A note on Australian specificity and broader relevance

In this book, I talk specifically about the Australian context of smokefree. And, as I've said, this book is based on Australian ethnographic fieldwork conducted under specific conditions of smoking denormalization. However, Australia's smokefree legislation and the analytic claims I make in this book bear more than a passing resemblance to those nations that have crafted their own smokefree atmospheres. While remembering that Australia is not intended in the book to stand metonymically for the rest of the developed world, the first sense in which this is so is that there are aspects of Australia's development of smokefree policies and practices that bear comparison with the other countries included in the Four Country-International Tobacco Control (FC-ITC) Survey, which aims to measure the impact of Framework Convention on Tobacco Control (FCTC) policies in Australia, Canada, the United States and the United Kingdom.

For instance, Australia's development of legislation designed to curtail the practice of smoking in public, outdoor space shares much in common with already developed policy platforms or with those that are still under development in these countries. While this book examines the practice of smoking in a specifically Australian 'atmosphere' intended to discourage it, many of these Australian specificities apply to the experiences of other developed countries with similar socio-economic compositions, and a shared intention to usher in comprehensive smokefree laws. Indeed, as countries with comparatively strong legislation pertaining to smoking, the FC-ITC member countries are already expected to develop policy relationally to one another (see status report on Article 8 of the WHO's) FCTC, the Global Smokefree Partnership (GSP) – in which it is stated that FCTC member countries are expected to refer to one another to learn about the 'best practices [of smokefree] from countries that have successfully implemented smokefree policies' (GSP 2008: 15–16). Thus, Australia's legislative experience is already inextricably intertwined with that of other FC-ITC countries.

Second, despite the fact that the ethnographic claims I make are drawn from specific Australian contexts, the notion that the air itself must be explicated to create the smokefree atmosphere in the first instance is common to those places that have installed it, as is the notion that the air is not a neutral or backgrounded element in its delivery, deep into the lungs of the smoker. Canada, the United States, the United Kingdom and Australia, each invites its smokers to attend to the innards of the body via warnings or graphic images on packages, and each has sought to expertly explicate how smoky air impacts both the internal regions of the smoker's own body and those bodies located in proximity to the smoker (see Haines-Saah, Bell and Dennis 2014). These notions, about how the smallest and most intimate aspects of drawing in and expelling the air permit the entrance into the smoking body of much larger ideas about health, blame, the future, the public and the air itself, are features of the smokefree atmosphere well beyond the Australian bounds to which I am herein ethnographically limited.

# Introduction:
# There's something in the air

## Examining smoking in the era of smokefree: Public health and anthropology

Although tobacco is a legal substance, many governments around the world have introduced extensive legislation to limit and restrict smoking and access to tobacco products. These legislative efforts, which include the designation of increasing amounts and categories of space 'smokefree', point-of-sale presentation rules and packaging legislation together with public education campaigns, have ushered in a new political, temporal and spatial atmosphere of 'smokefree'. This book examines this atmosphere, as it has formed up in an Australian context. What are its key characteristics? Upon what foundational ideas, about smoke, the air itself, the senses, space and time does it depend? What are its effects and consequences, and for whom?

I want to note at the outset that I have written this book in response, and largely in opposition, to how smoking is approached from within the public health paradigm. Indeed, my intention has been to deliberately step outside currently dominant public health framings of smoking. I do so because public health research into smoking is characterized by its instrumental focus: its aim is to minimize tobacco use, and ultimately to bring about its complete cessation. This is certainly laudable, but it also means that the potential for making new discoveries about smoking outside of this agenda is minimal. Despite their obvious, publicly asserted, and antagonistic differences, an equally narrow field of enquiry characterizes research carried out for the tobacco industry, which, of course, is interested in *maximizing* tobacco use. I'm writing in opposition to how smoking is approached from this perspective, too.

In the simplest of terms, my deliberate positionedness outside of a public health framework (and a tobacco industry framework, for all that) might be expressed as my intention to look on smoking neither as a practice that must cease for the public good nor as one that should continue, say, in defence of smokers' legal rights and civil liberties. My approach to smokers and the ways in which they experience legislation designed to curtail smoking is, in other words, without interventionist intention. It's not instrumental, in either direction. I seek instead to observe and analyse practices and environments, and what smokers make of them, as anthropologically interesting phenomena that might yield information about how a dominant and recently emerged political (and moral) atmosphere impacts those who are its targets – smokers in the era of 'smokefree'.

As I will demonstrate, taking an approach that could yield new insights into smoking in the era of smokefree is not a matter of straightforwardly replacing a public health framework that privileges minimization of tobacco use with an anthropological one that might attend to meaning, or power, or embodiment, or some other variety of disciplinary application.

# The anthropology of smoking (a smokefree anthropology)

Smoking has had a presence in a great many anthropological analyses, but it has rarely been a topic of interest in and of itself. In the main, smoking has been mentioned in passing, on the way to – or in the background of – the main topic of interest (see Basil Samson's 1980 work, *The Camp at Wallaby Cross*, as a good example). Anthropologists have been remarking upon its absence since the 1980s. In 1984, Peter Black expressed his astonishment at the dearth of anthropological studies on tobacco use, 'given anthropology's holistic, cross-cultural perspective' (478). Even though he paused to note several weighty contributions to the topic, including Claude Levi-Strauss's examination of the contrast in South American indigenous mythology between honey and tobacco (which Levi-Strauss called a 'culinary paradox' (1973: 303), Black remained stunned that analysts hadn't considered *why people want to smoke*. He noted then that 'special attention' ought to be paid to this question, largely because he was profoundly dissatisfied with the explanatory worth of 'addiction'. He encouraged more investigation, which he felt anthropologists were uniquely qualified to undertake. Specifically, he recommended a focus on the social and economic aspects of tobacco use, and not just on the public health concerns around tobacco use:

> Just as an investigation of Tobian tobacco use may further understanding of the public health situation in the western Carolines, it is also reasonable to expect that such an investigation will help to make sense of economic and intersocietal relations in the area. (1984: 476)

But rather than using tobacco as a lens onto economic and intersocial relations, a good deal of anthropological work has examined how these relations are involved and implicated in smoking uptake and continuance – and thusly these relations have been thoroughly entailed in a public health cessation agenda.

Scant attention was originally paid to calls originally issued in the 1980s to attend anthropologically to tobacco by Black – and others, including Marshall (1981) and Stebbins (1987). Indeed, the continuing lacuna prompted Stebbins to issue another call, in 2001, for anthropologists to recognize 'the global impact of tobacco and its inherently anthropological nature' (2001: 148). These calls were motivated by deep concern for the unequal political–economic aspects of the relations between tobacco companies and smokers.

Since, anthropologists have proffered more reasons for smoking than simply 'addiction' – so addressing Black's lament of its dominance. They have utilized detailed ethnographic data to make their claims – thus attending to his concern about the dearth of ethnographic works on tobacco use. They have also answered Black's question, 'Why do people smoke?' Indeed, a huge range of reasons has been offered up for 'why people smoke'. These include:

- People smoke because cigarettes play a key role in social life, including in patterns of material exchange that maintain one's social position (even if addiction is the foundational explanans – see Glasser (2011); see Strange and McCrory's (1981) analysis of cigarette exchange in prisons[1]).

- People smoke because smoking might soften the stiff rigidity of loneliness, and cigarettes are not so much measured doses of nicotine as they are friends or companions (see Macnaughton 2012).

- People smoke because smoking suspends and implicates them in webs of cultural meaning – which the tobacco industry is adept at exploiting (see Mark Nichter 2003).

- And, people smoke because smoking punctuates long stretches of time, such as those interminable ones spent at a drudgerous job, and opens pathways into the future, as Baer, Singer and Susser note in the 'Up in Smoke' section of their *Medical Anthropology and the World System* volume, of 2003.

The 'why people smoke' question is almost invariably asked in the service of the 'how can it be stopped?' question; the question is, in other words, asked to generate an answer useful to the project of smoking cessation. For Hall, Lopez and Lichtenstein (1999), reducing cancer risk from smoking among Northwest Indian tribes requires an approach of cultural specificity. Nancy

Kauffman and Mimi Nichter (2001) argued that smoking among women has to be disrupted by way of specifically gendered tools. Mark Nichter and Elizabeth Cartwright penned the evocatively titled 'Saving the Children for the Tobacco Industry' in *Medical Anthropology Quarterly* in 1991. Here, they drew attention to how relations of inequity generate and sustain smoking, and how addressing those relations would help liberate smokers from the unequal power relations in which they were ensnared. As smoking is now an activity predominantly practised by the socio-economically and ethnically marginalized,[2] increasing attention is being paid to the unequal relationship between smokers as dependent consumers and the parties responsible for the supply of nicotine in ready-to-smoke form: the big tobacco companies (see Kohrman and Benson 2011).

This intention, to rid the world of the tobacco scourge, is a vigorously pursued one in anthropology. In 2002, Mark Nichter et al. delivered work detailing how qualitative research could be pressed into the service of examining alcohol and drug *dependence*, a characterization of tobacco (and alcohol) use that clearly indicates how smokers are understood – as dependent consumers of tobacco. By 2004, Mark Nichter et al. had produced another informative piece on how qualitative research could contribute to the study of drug use and interventions into the same. This was followed up with a comprehensive review of sixty articles on 'anthropology and smoking cessation' conducted by Goldade et al. in 2012 which sought to answer the question: 'How can lessons learned from anthropological studies of smoking improve the design and effectiveness of smoking cessation interventions?' (2012: 631). Since the 1980s, an interventionist (and instrumentalist) frame has been obviously manifest in these works (and others that I shall mention in due course), as has the characterization of smokers as dependent consumers.

This very clear anthropological alignment to smoking cessation has a good deal to do with the rise of medical anthropology as a distinct disciplinary subfield, and in particular with its early intentions to solve health problems using anthropological insights. To return momentarily to Micronesia, the site of Black's fieldwork, a good example is to be found in the work of medical anthropologist Mac Marshall. In his 2005 'Carolina in the Carolines' piece, he laments the dearth of anthropological attention on tobacco use and attends closely to the (gendered and cultural) meanings associated with smoking in Micronesia. Marshall thus answers calls issued in the 1980s to closely examine tobacco use, but he does so in a particular way typical of the bulk of accounts since the 1980s: with a focus on the dire consequences its consumers might suffer, and what interventions might best stop it.

It is clear that smoking offers up rich pickings for anthropologists; in and through it, one might choose, as I have in this book, to recast the air as more than just the backdrop against which human activity occurs, and to see it instead as being at the heart of political life and relations. One could examine how pollution comes to be established and observed as a category, and how contact with it might come to be dangerous, and how those who are thought to be responsible for spreading pollution are treated – as I am also doing herein. One could attend to the sensory registers in which these elements are evident, as I am also doing. One might make a thoroughgoing analysis of the relations between the person and the state (and/or other powerful parties) made manifest in and through a lens on smoking. One could examine the biopolitics of cigarettes.

Even this very short list indicates that rich pickings are indeed here to be had, but in general these have been harvested in the name of a cessation agenda. Matthew Kohrman's fascinating work on smoking in China, for example, engages the biopolitical but, to quote from his Stanford University website, is ultimately interested in 'analyzing and *intervening* in the biopolitics of cigarette smoking among Chinese citizens' (my emphasis).[3] In Australia, Maggie Brady's work examines relations between the (Indigenous) person and the state (see Brady 2001, 2002). Brady explores the historical and cultural roots of tobacco, and particularly the exploitative relations of power in which it entailed Aboriginal and Torres Strait Islander people – with authoritative parties, like employers who paid in tobacco, and with the state, which failed to attend to the very high morbidity rates of Aboriginal and Torres Strait Islander smokers. Brady advocates for the significance of understanding historical geneses of Indigenous smoking for effective public health interventions into the practice (see, for example, 2001: 120), advice heeded by the Australian government's Taskforce on Indigenous Smoking, which I'll discuss in detail in Chapter 3.

These works express the overriding view and dominant paradigm in research on smoking, namely that research conducted from anthropological perspective is expected to further the goals of tobacco control. Thus, 'tobacco research' might be more properly called 'tobacco control research' (see Mair and Kearins 2007; Bell and Dennis 2013).

As Bell (2013a) has observed, a good deal of the anthropological refusal to deal with smoking outside of a public health-aligned commitment to reducing it, has to do with fears over how any research which produces findings critical of public health aims may be pressed into the service of pro-tobacco interests. Even though Bell has encouraged us to think very carefully about the consequences of an anthropology of tobacco that is limited to agreeing with public health claims,[4] it remains the case that anthropological work specifically on smoking does not offer insight beyond a commitment to ending the global tobacco epidemic.

I have no quibble with the continuation of a medical anthropology tradition, of using disciplinary insights to solve health problems. Nor do I have a quibble with examining the exploitative hierarchies of power that relate smokers and Big Tobacco to one another. Both sorts of enquiry are important, and consequential in that they may provide relief from the injurious effects of relations between tobacco and persons, and tobacco companies and persons. But I *do* have a quibble with this kind of instrumental research being the *only* kind of research that can be *validly* undertaken. As I discuss in Chapter 3, there is a very manifest feeling circulating among anthropologists of smoking that 'you are either with us, or against us': that is, 'with us' in ridding the world of the tobacco scourge, or 'against us' on the side, or even the payroll, of Big Tobacco (see Bell and Dennis 2013). This sort of anthropology of smoking leaves very little room indeed to *understand* tobacco use in the anthropologically fascinating 'atmosphere' of smokefree in which it is now conducted. Instead, there is pressure to actively *intervene* against it. This pressure is an important and thought-provoking part of the atmosphere of smokefree, which manifests not only in public health actions against the scourge of smoke, but also, smoke-like, infiltrates bodies and minds outside that context – anthropological ones included.

# Anthropology's smoker

As Macnaughton et al. have noted, public health conceives of two versions of the smoker: the 'rational smoker' and the 'addict'. The rational smoker is the ignorant smoker. She has been mis- or ill-informed about the practice (usually deliberately, via the tactics of Big Tobacco). Once disabused of her misunderstanding (in and through public health education), this smoker can make a rational decision (to recognize smoking as dangerous and quit). 'Pavlovian manipulation' can be administered to the addict' (Macnaughton et al. 2012: 455). Anthropologists have certainly been critical of this 'doubled' public health subject – they have 'deepened' her with ethnographic detail, so that ignorance or misinformation is not the foundational explanans for her smoking, for instance – (i.e. she might smoke not out of ignorance, but to maintain a social position, or so as not to be lonely). And addiction has been deepened, too, beyond a physical relationship between nicotine and person, to include the unequal (class, social, economic) relationships that might have pushed people into smoking in the first place. But anthropologists have *not*, by and large, gone so far as to question the conceptual bases upon which their own disciplinarily imagined smoker is crafted and this, I think, has very much constrained anthropological enquiry into smoking – in quite a serious way. As I have said, a goodly proportion of the narrowness that characterizes the anthropology of smoking is caused by the alignment of anthropological work with public health goals of cessation. However, narrowness is also produced by long-standing disciplinary notions, about how the discernible 'other', in this case the smoker, is translated, via ethnographic means, into legible terms, to those located outside of her world.[5] In other words, one characteristic of anthropological work undertaken to date on smoking has been its concern with how the curious and apparently inexplicable behaviour of smokers – breathing in gases that could kill, burning up money when they cannot afford to do so – can be explained in terms that make sense to outsiders.

For example, Bruce Knauft's 1987 work reveals smoking to be instrumental to the management of sex and anger among the Gebusi of Papua New Guinea; their smoking is revealed to have a purpose and a rational use in the world, and so becomes more than a senseless inhalation of a burnt substance for no apparent reason. I also have a quibble with this sort of framing of smoking, as the production of smoking as legible in this way depends on the assertion of an internal consistency of the smoker's world (i.e. smoking is 'for this purpose', revealed by anthropological investigation). Such an approach equally fetishizes the long-held anthropological notion that strange worlds can be rendered familiar in rational terms: once the underlying reason is discovered, smoking emerges as a kind of rational response or way of dealing with the world. In Knauft's rendering, it provides a way to manage anger. But smoking might not be best seen in and through the lens of rationality. Anthropologists (like Macnaughton et al.) have already criticized the public health assertion, that smokers are, underneath their ignorance, rational agents. But this is a criticism raised only in form by anthropologists, not in substance, since anthropologists have largely retained the rational smoker in their analyses to date.

In this book, I *don't* retain it. Instead, I propose a new approach that begins with the close examination of the broader atmosphere of 'smokefree' into which smoking and smokers are enfolded. Obviously, given what I've just communicated, that, to my mind, must include the academically produced atmosphere of 'smokefree'.

## A new approach to smoking and smokefree

Smokefree is replete with opportunity for looking at the relations between the state and the (smoking) person – and not just the relations between Big Tobacco and the smoking person. The latter are just as power-laden. In Australia, for instance, we've seen the rapid development of legislation that has ushered in plain packaging, the development and enforcement of extremely strict advertising conditions that limit how cigarettes can appear to persons, the possibility of prohibiting smoking outright, as is currently under consideration in one Australian state, and even the possibility of licensing smokers so that they are bound to limited consumption under very strict conditions. Staunch anti-smoking campaigner and public health Prof Simon Chapman floated this idea in 2012. The proposal, as it was reported on the open access PLoS medicine site under the 'Debate' section, would have involved,

> introducing a smart card license for smokers designed to limit access to tobacco products and encourage cessation. Key elements of the smoker's license include smokers setting daily limits, financial incentives for permanent license surrender, and a test of health risk knowledge for commencing smokers. (Chapman 2012: e1001342)[6]

The relations people have to place in the era of smokefree is also anthropologically interesting but, anthropology's alignment with public health on smoking has permitted scant attention to the fact that smokefree legislation has profoundly changed how and which people can participate in public space. Such legislation shares much, as Brandt (1998) reminds us, with other attempts to segregate one group of people considered polluting and dangerous from another group considered to be at risk from their presence. For instance, Brandt controversially parallels the increasing designation of places 'smokefree' to the Jim Crow era in the American south.

Certainly, it is the case that the atmosphere of smokefree is becoming increasingly prevalent. Many places deemed acceptable to smoke less than a decade ago are now legislatively declared smokefree places; cigarette packages now bear terrifying graphic images of the insides of the smoker's body, and it may well be the case that proposed Tasmanian legislation to ban smoking for anyone born in or after the year 2000 comes to pass. How might this atmosphere be approached and understood, outside the context of harm minimization or its radical industry alternative, the maximization of tobacco consumption? How might it appear, anthropologically, if it were unhindered by a dominant, public health view?

My attempt to differently conceptualize smoking and the atmosphere in which it is conducted is one characterized by attendance to the relations between the 'largeness' of the smokefree atmosphere and the minuteness of bodily processes that a smokefree agenda seeks to influence. Here, I refer to things like the state's concern with protecting the quality of the air itself and the minute and intimate relations this concern produces, namely with the body of the smoker, and with the air in which she is enveloped as she smokes – and particularly with her breath. I am concerned with our relations to the air, and how they can be explicated to foreground understandings of the air that become dominant, and can be put to political use. I am equally concerned with how the air contains ideas, morals, values and hierarchies that can be drawn into and absorbed by bodies just as readily as oxygen. The capacity of the air to circulate ideas and to permeate bodies has been pressed into service in the era of smokefree, and has produced particular sorts of relations with the state and the smoking person. The smoking person, for her part, may not be entirely subject to the dominance of the smokefree air, but she is invariably impacted by its presence, not least because she has the capacity to sully it with her smoke, a dangerous and intimate capacity of breathing out with smoke that is now the focus of legislation.

Some of these relations between the state and the smoker have already been thought of in discursive terms as a sort of violence. Gilbert (2008) for instance, has analysed the medically expert claims utilized in Australian anti-smoking television advertisements from the perspective of psychology. She asserts that such claims are not neutral advisements about harm, but instead represent a powerful form of coercion underpinned by an authoritative definition of 'health'. In health sociology, Haines-Saah (2011) has produced a discursive analysis concerned specifically with the gendered symbolic violence of anti-tobacco messaging – that is, as 'unfeminine' and 'unacceptable'.

Gilbert also argues that these types of expert medical claims might not even work to produce a cessation result in any case, particularly among those who have already proved themselves determined and resilient smokers by continuing to smoke in an environment inhospitable to the practice (as does Haines-Saah 2011, who describes how assertions of 'unfeminine' and 'unacceptable' smoking are actively resisted by female smokers). While I agree with Gilbert's (and Haines-Saah's) assessment of the interestedness of expert medical claims and the power they can exert over the smoker, my own analysis of the smokefree era in Australia is informed much more by phenomenological insights than it is by narrative or discursive analyses. Specifically, I'm interested in how this big, medically authoritative atmosphere gets inside smokers, how it's brought to bear on (and, more accurately *inside*) their bodies – a bearing that is made *whether or not* people decide to give up smoking, or continue it. I make my way into these insights by privileging different sensory registers that make relations between bodies evident.

## An argument for inchoateness

I'm unconcerned in this work with whether advertising, legislation and other elements are effective in reducing smoking prevalence. I am interested instead in how smokers understand, dwell in and *breathe with* the pervasive atmosphere of 'smokefree'. As I will suggest later on in this Introduction, I make this turn away from considering whether the strategies and techniques deployed to limit smoking work, or not, not least because they invariably locate the researcher on one 'side' or the other – anti- or pro-smoking (whether she wishes to be so located or not).

These strategies and techniques utilized to limit smoking include: anti-smoking advertising; point-of-sale rules that require retailers to conceal cigarettes behind solid opaque doors, and forbid them to reveal what is in or out of stock, meaning that the smoker must ask for her brand, by name; the expanding smokefree public place rules that prohibit smoking in more, and more kinds of, places; and rules that govern how cigarettes can appear to us in advertising. These are, we can safely say, resolute and comprehensive strategies and techniques that will indubitably become more numerous – the intention of Australian state and federal governments is to extend the horizon of the smokefree atmosphere, so that it applies to more places, and permits even less exposure to tobacco products.

Smokefree is an all-encompassing and inescapable atmosphere in the terms I've just described. These terms and their expansion have multiple consequences for smokers. Nevertheless, I will argue in this book that, despite its inescapable presence in legislation, anti-smoking advertising, television talkback shows, on the radio, in the newspaper and on the internet, the smokefree atmosphere is, yet, shifting and contingent, not *fully* and *purely* established. The smokefree atmosphere does not quite achieve stability of form largely as a result of the amorphous, wafting non-thing which it attempts to bound and contain: *smoke itself*.

Slipping easily over the spatial, temporal, bodily and legislative bounds made for it in the cases of firsthand and secondhand smoke (respectively, that smoke deliberately draw in by the smoker, and the smoke she expels into the air), tobacco smoke trickily eludes and elides, making a state of 'smokefree' difficult to accomplish in temporal, spatial and corporeal registers. Indeed, smoke has the capacity to bring together spaces, times and persons that are legislatively intended, and certainly, on the part of the state desired, to be held apart.

Even when smoking is legally restricted to designated smoking places, which are legislatively distinguishable from places designated 'smokefree', smoke may refuse to remain therein sited. It harnesses itself effortlessly to the breeze, hitches a lift on air currents, defying legislative barriers designed to keep it within designated smoking (and thus outside of non-smoking) places. It is indeed difficult to contain smoke within spatial parameters, and equally difficult to contend with the capacity of smoke to draw these only conceptually discrete spaces together.

It is equally difficult to restrict smoke within temporal bounds. Thirdhand smoke is smoke that remains after the secondhand smoke has dissipated into the air. This is smoke that has simultaneously assumed a sticky, enduring form. This is a capacity usually not afforded something so wafting and airy as smoke, but it is a capacity nonetheless made manifest in thirdhand smoke's curious ability to affix itself to objects and to stay there, despite efforts (like washing, fanning, scrubbing, etc.) to expunge it. This lingering smoke from the past continues to 'offgas', depositing particles into the surrounding air, making a smokefree time in the future uncertain, unsure and impure, even when its visible and perhaps even, eventually, its odiferous elements have ostensibly departed. In the cases of firsthand, secondhand and thirdhand smoke, and across spaces and times, then, 'smokefree' is not established as a sure and certain and pure presence; all surety is undermined by the wafting, uncontainable omnitude of smoke itself.

This, of course, makes smoke, in Mary Douglas's (1966) language, boundary crosser extraordinaire, and boundary crossers are always dangerous. What is perceived to be ambiguous and marginal is unclean and defiling of established principles. The betwixtness of smoke discharges both power and danger to existing taxonomical and social structures. The Australian state's push for sharp and sure legislative distinctions emerges in response to the defiling capacity of smoke to disrupt boundaries.[7] We see increased demands for the designation of more spaces as smokefree, the introduction of more rules around sales, more stringent laws to govern advertising. But what can contain the uncontainable? It is little wonder that the agenda to diminish smoking in Australia is often referred to as 'The War on Smoking'. The battle is ongoing, the day never quite won, despite the state's continuing twin assertions that if only people knew smoking was so bad for them, they'd quit, and if only people could disrupt the addictive pull of nicotine, they'd quit. Despite the addition of various pharmaco-therapeutic items to the Pharmaceutical Benefits Scheme that provide this disruption, and despite the crafting and dissemination of advertisements described by the state itself as 'graphic' and 'gruesome', the war is still not won – and part of its unwinnability, I suggest, is smoke's capacity to slip beyond the firm conceptual bounds made for it, including those pertaining to the smoker herself.

The crisp, legislative certainty of a smokefree place versus the murky capacity of smoke to infiltrate the same, and the purity of the smokefree air versus the pollution of smoke are, then, I am suggesting, part of an ideal binary taxonomy that is undone by the capacity of smoke to travel.

Smoke is also a boundary crosser in the sense that, as thirdhand smoke, it is both (and neither) air and/nor matter. This liminal material is dangerous – so dangerous in fact that even though there is no evidence, as yet, that it presents harm to humans, several legal cases have already been decided in favour of victims of thirdhand smoke. In 2007, the tobacco control policy and legal resource centre Global Advisors on Smokefree Policy (GASP) reported the outcome of a Lancaster court decision on thirdhand smoke. GASP's website conveyed the information that the Nebraskan county court ruled in favour of a home buyer when it found that the vendor lied about smoking occurring in the home.[8] The complainant was awarded $USD 12 000 in costs related to attempting to mitigate the thirdhand smoke residue during the period in which the buyer lived in the house. While this case actually seems to be more concerned with fraudulent misrepresentation than thirdhand smoke per se, other cases appear to regard thirdhand smoke as *the* matter requiring legal attention.

In 2010, a federal court in the United States, for example, held that a man could advance his case against an employer who refused to reduce his exposure to thirdhand smoke in the workplace, under the Americans with Disabilities Act. In this case, the complainant argued a particular sensitivity to tobacco smoke; such individuals with a particular disease that forms the genetic foundation for the sensitivity are entitled to protection under the act. A very small number of people qualify for such protection under the law. However, Prof of Public Law (and executive director of Action on Tobacco and Smoking) John Banzhaf has noted that a much larger number of people – those with a history of cancer in their families – may be entitled to legal protection. The Tobacco Free Arizona (TFA) website reports that Banzhaf's opinion is that 'judges and regulators may be persuaded that they too are entitled to smoke-free workplaces, restaurants, and other places they frequent'.[9] In a matter in which Action on Smoking and Health was the complainant, the court also directed a university to protect a pregnant employee against exposure to thirdhand smoke in the workplace. In this case, two doctors determined that the smoker's breath and other smoke residue on his clothing endangered the health of the woman and her unborn baby.[10]

Especially in its thirdhand form, as air/matter, smoke is not only liminal, but also abject. Its fouling menace not only destroys boundaries between persons, places and times, but however mammoth the effort to expel the abject, it always returns, 'like a boomerang', says Kristeva, to 'challenge the master' (1982: 2).

# The structure

I've divided this book into two parts. Part I does that foundational intellectual work of giving the lay of the smokefree land, setting out the characteristics of the smokefree atmosphere, and sketching out a kind of recommendation for anthropologically imagining the smoker (or, more properly, not imagining her in the restrictive terms that we presently tend to). This work takes up the first three chapters, which I describe briefly below.

Featuring a recently deceased monkey in a Kmart advertisement, a visit to Alpine country I once took as a teenager, a look at the 1988 Benson and Hedges World Series Cup Cricket, Chapter 1, 'The difference between Tobacco and Tomatoes', provides a sense of the legislative and other foundations upon which Australia's smokefree atmosphere is constructed, and from which it maintains and extends its reach. In this chapter, I provide a sense of the core intention of smokefree that arrays around it all manner of legislation: *the stalwart, unwavering intention to hold things apart – namely that which is smokefree from that which is against it.* This has made for an atmosphere starkly divided into oppositionary pairs, the most obvious of which is the oppositionary pair of public health, on the one hand, and the tobacco companies on the other.

I attend to these oppositionary pairings and ruinous smoke in Chapter 2, titled 'Oppositionary Pairings and Ruinous Smoke'. If I was going to be devotedly structuralist here (which I will not be in this book), I don't think it would be too much of a stretch to say that some of the biggest binary oppositions are here present. Certainly, by the time we get to Chapters 5 and 6 (on secondhand and thirdhand smoke), Levi-Strauss's ultimate binary, between self and other, takes centre stage. Beyond that, the binaries are numerous. Public health is 'good', tobacco companies are 'evil'. They lie; public health tells the truth. Attendance to public health knowledge and the advice it generates means 'life'; getting caught in the thrall of tobacco companies and their deadly little pleasure sticks means, ultimately, death. Smoke itself is the boundary crosser between all these binaries, as well as between those oppositionary couplings that inform the legislative manifestation of smokefree, along spatial and temporal lines: smokefree space as against space in which smoking is permitted; a new (and increasingly striven-for) time of smokefree, as against a past characterized by smoking as a commonplace practice. Having described the poles of the smokefree atmosphere, I turn to a discussion of how smoke tends to sully and blur the boundaries that are so starkly drawn to separate the oppositionary poles of the smokefree atmosphere. The core intention of the smokefree atmosphere, to hold things apart, contrasts very sharply indeed with the capacity of smoke to cross over the boundaries and barriers that keep things – time, spaces, persons, knowledges – at distance from one another.

In Chapter 3, 'Re-imagining the Smoker', I make the claim that the smoking person herself *also* has the capacity to *draw things together that are intended in smokefree to be held apart.* Making this claim allows me to discuss in detail the anthropological attendance to the smoker to date that I've foreshadowed above. This attendance has so far missed the important capacity of smokers to hold together that which is contradictory, or that which issues from oppositionary geneses. It equally permits me to elaborate my own anthropological approach to the smoker. My approach resists claims of assumed rationality and reaches instead towards the undoing and unravelling of an anthropologically purported internal consistency of the smoker's 'world'. Of course, noting that the smoker is capable of drawing together contradictory knowledges ought to be unremarkable, since we might say that this capacity is one shared by all people. But smokers have become so thoroughly defined as certain kinds of people, who will respond in certain kinds of ways to information flowing from either poles, that the power of this ordinary capacity has been overlooked. Reintroducing it, I think, can reorient us, anthropologically, to the smoking person and might generate more productive ways of knowing about smoking in the era of smokefree than we presently have available to us.

Let me pause here to say baldly that I'm not advocating the view that we see smokers as inversely rational – that is, as irrational (read: stupid). This is certainly a popular view to advance. Take Jemma Wayne's *Huffington Post* contribution from early 2014, that includes this:

> Bans and health warnings are entirely the wrong tack. They may go a small way to discourage the habit, but they still focus all efforts on the smoker's sense of logic. On the smoker's reason, their rationale. Thing is – smokers are stupid. (see Wayne 2014)

Public health, as Wayne points out, doubles down on the bet that anti-smoking campaigns will appeal to the smoker's reason. She thinks that public health has lost that bet (because, she says, smokers don't have reason to begin with). Public health blames ignorance – it gets in the way of reason, but can be removed. If the smoker still doesn't quit (the very manifestation of reason), then addiction is to blame – it gets in the way of reason, too, and it's much harder to shift. So is crafted the rational smoker. This is a pretty closed binary: smokers are irrational, smokers are rational. Even though Wayne is writing an opinion piece and can offer her view up however she sees fit, the public health view of smokers is merely the flip side of her offering: Smokers are stupid, she says. Public health says, smokers aren't stupid. They're ignorant and/or addicted. This is blatantly unproductive in terms of advancement of our knowledge of smoking – if anything is stupid, it's probably to continue this sort of intellectual narrow-mindedness. While anthropologists certainly haven't advanced the view that smokers' practice can be characterized as stupidity, they *have* advanced the view that the opposite is true, in their attendance to a cessation agenda (i.e. it's not stupid/irrational; it's to stop loneliness/ be socially engaged/because dependence relations are overwhelmingly powerful).

Having set up the intellectual foundations for this work, I turn to Part II for more substantive ethnographically informed analyses of breathing in smokefree – firsthand, secondhand, thirdhand and fourthhand.

In Chapter 4, 'Breathing in Smoke(free), Firsthand', I consider how an acute awareness of a more usually backgrounded atmospheric, the air itself, has been instrumental to the constitution of the political, moral and social atmosphere known as 'smokefree'. It has been equally instrumental to bearing this atmosphere deep inside the smoker's body. The air is here revealed to be a powerful force that infiltrates bodies to deliver political and moral matter deep within. Taking up a phenomenological tone perhaps more evidently than in other chapters, I look in detail at *how* a sort of medical violence is delivered deep inside the smoker's body (not only *that* it is delivered, after Gilbert's 2008 analysis), in the act of breathing in firsthand cigarette smoke.

In Chapter 5, 'Miasmatic Exhalation: Breathing Out (Secondhand) Smoke', I attend to how exhaled smoky air is explicated in the atmosphere of smokefree. The breath exhaled by the smoker, circulating as it has around the rotted matter of her destroyed lung tissue – a fact that Australians come to know, thanks to graphic anti-smoking advertisements on television and on cigarette packets – comes to be conceptualized as miasmatic in nature. This is an operation by which irresponsible smoking actors, who can be held to account by legislative and socio-moral forces, spread contagious pollution via polluting exhaled suspension. This foul, secondhand, discharge into the air that others must, in their turn, breath into their own lungs, impacts the entirety of the public body, or all breathers. These exhalations are conceived as bearing with them the decayed internal physical, moral and social state of the smoking person, such that they might immediately infect other non-smoking persons in all of these ways, but which are bundled by the state into the '*health* hazard' presented by the passive absorption of environmental tobacco smoke by unwilling bodies.

We are now witnessing the emergence of scientific reports that describe the sinister capacity of smoke toxicants to hide themselves from view in the air, on surfaces, in the clothes the smoker wears. In the sixth chapter, 'Abject Thirdhand Smoke', I do not intend to decide upon the veracity of the science underpinning such claims (the interested reader may consult Bell 2014); rather, I attend to how they circulate in public space, and how they usher in a lurking past that makes claims on the future of the air.

The temporally disrespectful nature of smoke expressed as 'thirdhand smoke' is interesting also because in and through it, smoke assumes an unusual capacity not usually afforded to it: it turns into something enduring, something that cannot be swept away on the breeze, or even with the vigorous wind of a fan. What are the consequences of the newly explicated endurance of a known dissipater, for the smoker to whom it resolutely sticks? And what kinds of insights does thirdhand smoke offer into the air in which smokers and non-smokers circulate?

Having looked closely at how the state explicates the inhaled and exhaled air for smokers, I turn in Chapter 7, entitled 'Fourthhand Smoke: Going to Flavor Country', to examine what smokers themselves might do with smoky breath, and what potentials it might offer to them. One great pleasure of smoking, as theoreticians such as Klein (1993) and Katz (1999) have suggested, comes from its capacity to permit travel outbound from the site of the body, on the strength of an outbound breath (made visible in and through exhaled tobacco smoke) to extend the person outbound from the site of the body. Pleasures of this (or any other sort related to tobacco use) are regarded in public health paradigm as 'ignorance' of the real harms of smoking, but even in the face of expert medical explication of the smoke-filled air, smokers, it seems, take up opportunities to escape the rotting innards of their own sited bodies, and/or to accomplish things, even go places, with their smoky breaths – even to the legendary Flavor Country.

The conclusion to my book invites reflection on the condition of the smoker herself, and anthropological enquiry itself, and the kinds of things we might come to know of them from my analysis which, for the most part, will privilege the air itself. It is the air itself that is bent to the purpose of creating smokefree, the air itself that can offer the smoker a ride to Flavor Country; the air itself that reminds her of the dying condition of her lungs as she engages it in the most intimate of all our connections with the air: in her breath. In a breath, the smoker fouls herself, in a breath she spreads the contagion to others. It is the explication of the air itself that has permitted its protected status, and has ushered in smokefree legislation designed to keep it from being sullied, and in the ejection of smokers from the clean places where the middle classes increasingly dominate. Their presence is in the air, an increasingly middle-class air, devoid of the smell of tobacco burning.

Even as the air becomes less olfactorily reflective of the presence of 'others' outside the middle classes, a state of 'smokefree' is not absolutely accomplished. Smoke, that wafting, cursed, blessed, abject wayfarer, defies categorization in absolute taxonomies, preferring to drift through stern legislative divisions to challenge the master. As long as there is smoke to challenge smokefree, the latter cannot be absolutely established.

**PART ONE**

# The lay of the smokefree land

# 1

# The difference between tobacco and tomatoes

## Introduction

In what follows, I've tried to draw up a kind of feeling of the smokefree legislation in Australia, what it aims to accomplish, and something of its force. The reader who desires a historical account of its emergence will no doubt be disappointed by my own amorphous and rather affectively rendered offering, but, luckily, it is easily supplemented with one of the numerous more structured historical accounts available.[1]

It is important to note at the outset of this chapter that in this book I make an especial meaning of smokefree. Technically speaking, the particular legislation properly called 'smokefree' describes only those locations and environments that are free from exposure to secondhand tobacco smoke. When I deploy the term 'smokefree', or 'smokefree atmosphere', I mean to refer to something much broader than just the smoking bans enacted by Commonwealth, state, territory and municipal levels of government to deal with smoke in the air in specific places. Within the confines of this book, 'smokefree' means all efforts on the part of the state designed to curtail smoking prevalence, including the designation of increasing amounts and categories of space 'smokefree', point-of-sale presentation rules and packaging laws, as well as anti-smoking campaigns. This use of the term 'smokefree', then, refers to Australia's comprehensive package of *tobacco control measures*, including:

- the world's first tobacco plain packaging legislation, which took full effect from 1 December 2012;

- the new health warnings Competition and Consumer (Tobacco) Information Standard 2011, which commenced on 1 January 2012 and took full effect from 1 December 2012 and which requires health warnings to cover at least 75 per cent of the front of most tobacco packaging, 90 per cent of the back of cigarette packaging and 75 per cent of the back of most other tobacco product packaging;

- record investments in anti-smoking social marketing campaigns;

- the 25 per cent tobacco excise increase which began in April 2010;

- a four-stage increase in excise and excise-equivalent customs duty on tobacco and tobacco-related products: the first 12.5 per cent increase commenced on 1 December 2013, a further 12.5 per cent happened on 1 September 2014 and two more are scheduled for 1 September 2015 and 1 September 2016;

- a reduction in duty-free concessions for tobacco products and

- stronger penalties for tobacco smuggling offences.

These 'smokefree' actions and intentions indicate Australia's dedication to reducing Australians' exposure to tobacco. In Australia, it was not until 1997 that a truly national campaign was launched, and it remains the case that responsibility for developing legislation around tobacco is still largely devolved to the states and territories. While this has at times made for a fairly uneven terrain of tobacco control, in 2008, all state and territory governments in Australia signed the National Healthcare Agreement that has the goal of reducing adult daily smoking prevalence from 14 per cent to 10 per cent in the general population, and halving the adult daily smoking rate, of around 40 per cent, among Aboriginal and Torres Strait Islanders by 2018. Australia became a signatory to the World Health Organization (WHO) FCTC on 5 December 2003, almost immediately after the convention opened for signature. It was among the first forty countries to ratify the FCTC, and so became a full Party on 27 February 2005, the date on which the FCTC came into force. Australia is thus legally bound to perform, in good faith, the full range of obligations set out in the convention.

Beyond this, I mean also to refer to a 'smokefree anthropology', an anthropology, as I described it in the Introduction, just as wedded to the accomplishment of smokefree as is the Australian state. It is with this comprehensive definition of 'smokefree' in mind that I turn to a discussion of 'the smokefree atmosphere'. This atmosphere is tense and heavy, thick with tension – one can feel its force pressing down. This affective atmosphere seems composed of tensions between oppositionary pairs – pro-tobacco interests and notions are, for instance imagined as the polar opposites to anti-tobacco interests and notions. While they are certainly mutually antagonistic, they are, however, only ostensibly oppositionary. However much certain kinds of paradigmatic (pro- or anti-) smoking knowledges, principles and practices are desired to be held apart, the poles of the smokefree atmosphere look remarkably similar.

# On 'atmospheres'

I've chosen to characterize the desire to reduce smoking prevalence in Australia, as it is expressed in the NTS (2012–18) (see Intergovernmental Committee on Drugs (Standing Committee on Tobacco) 2012) and the bundle of legislative and other techniques that have been deployed in its service with the term 'atmosphere': *the smokefree atmosphere*. 'Atmosphere' is a term sufficiently elastic as to capture the prevailing tone and mood of this intention; but I might well have chosen another term – say, 'environment', or 'aerosphere'. I rejected 'environment' very early on, for its inability to indicate the affective qualities that attend 'smokefree', about which I shall say more shortly. I did for a time seriously consider the possibilities presented by 'aerosphere', which has the advantage of capturing the idea that we live (on earth) in an envelope of gases. This is an attractive prospect, because, as I will argue later in the book, 'smokefree' becomes a presence on the basis of its intention to foreground some elemental gases and to banish others that interfere with its (illusory) pure state.

The choice of atmosphere was one I finally made on the basis of the capacity of 'atmosphere' to exert pressure, to push down, to be heavy and 'felt'. This is, of course, a technical, meteorological, definition of atmosphere, but it is metaphorically most ready for application to smokefree – where the pressure exerted, I will argue in this chapter (and indeed throughout this book), is great, heavy and uneven, but never absolute.

Anthropologically speaking, atmospheres are themselves characterized by their capacity to hold within them opposed things. As Rabinow (2007) says, 'atmosphere' conveys a sense of juxtaposition (of word, referent object and/or concept). And Anderson notes, 'The concept of atmosphere is good to think with because it holds a series of opposites – presence and absence, materiality and ideality, definite and indefinite, singularity and generality – in a relation of tension' (2009: 80). Some further remarks Anderson made on atmosphere – in the course of making his own case for the affective atmosphere – will be useful at the outset to orient my discussion about the smokefree atmosphere in particular.

Anderson begins his 'Affective Atmospheres' with Marx's profoundly materialist imaginary of the 'revolutionary atmosphere', made as he marked the fourth anniversary of the Chartist People's Paper with an address to a London audience in April 1856. Marx drew up his 'revolutionary atmosphere' with geographical metaphors:

> The so-called revolutions of 1848 were but poor incidents small fractures and fissures in the dry crust of European society. However, they denounced the abyss. Beneath the apparently solid surface, they betrayed oceans of liquid matter, only needing expansion to rend into fragments continents of hard rock. Noisily and confusedly they proclaimed the emancipation of the Proletarian, i.e. the secret of the 19th century, and of the revolution of that century. The atmosphere in which we live weighs upon every one with a 20,000-pound force, but do you feel it? No more than European society before 1848 felt the revolutionary atmosphere enveloping and pressing it from all sides'. (Marx [1856] 1978: 577)

It is obvious already that my own discussion of the smokefree atmosphere will be much more caught up with the gaseous than it is with the rocky, more with the air than with the hardness of the fissured ground; more with the air's silence than with the loud cracking and crashing of rocks that indicate that revolution has come to pass. The differences in these natural metaphors are great, and they push thinking along different routes. Anderson recognized that Marx utilized a particular epicurean material imagination that permitted him to draw out the contrasts he saw as particularly fitting for describing matters revolutionary – the sturdiness of rock conceals an ocean of liquid matter beneath; its thrashing will soon turn little fissures in great rends in the rock. Such imagery does, certainly, seem apt for describing revolution. Its aptness is due to the contrast it supplies between ocean and rock. As Anderson, observes, whether material, as Marx imagined it, or otherwise imagined, the key to understanding atmospheres – their construction and their force – lies in appreciating the polarities they contain.

This includes an atmosphere's foundation – that it is at once real and not real. Picking up on Marx's turn of phrase, that the people could not feel the force pressing in on them from the atmosphere heavy with the imminence of revolution, Anderson draws out this element of all atmospheres:

> On the one hand, atmospheres are real phenomena. They 'envelop' and thus press on a society 'from all sides' with a certain force. On the other, they are not necessarily sensible phenomena. Marx has to ask if his audience 'feels it'. He assumes not. Nevertheless atmospheres still effect with a certain force. (2009: 77)

The force of the atmosphere, whatever it is, would be affectively registered, according to Anderson. He turns to the concept of affect, regarding it as the site at which the essence of atmosphere makes its home:

> Intensities take on the dynamic, kinetic, qualities of the atmos; 'affects are no longer feelings or affections; they go beyond the strength of those who undergo them' (Deleuze and Guattari [1991] 1994: 164). Since 'affects are becomings' (Deleuze and Guattari [1980] 1987: 256) that are 'experienced in a lived duration that involves the *difference between two states*' (Deleuze 1988: 49). The atmosphere [says Anderson] has long been associated with the uncertain, disordered, shifting and contingent – *that which never quite achieves the stability of form.* (2009: 78, my emphasis)

I will return throughout this book to notions of 'stability of form' and 'the differences between two states' – indeed, these ideas together provide one main analytic foundation for the entire work. For now, though, I want to pick up on another of Anderson's observations about atmospheres, in order to introduce the legislative aspects of Australia's smokefree atmosphere.

## Some thoughts on an uninsurable monkey

Anderson notes that atmospheres often bear down upon or gather up those who are not directly entailed in it, 'albeit in a way that may be only tangentially related to the subject' (Anderson 2003: 78). One way in which the smokefree atmosphere asserts a kind of pervasiveness is in its control of tobacco products and how they appear to people in the public domain. In the early 1970s, some extremely discreet and nondescript gold-coloured text about smoking being a health hazard appeared on cigarette packs, and Australian television audiences witnessed the disappearance of direct cigarette advertisements (in 1975). Since 2012, cigarette advertising has not permitted on packets manufactured expressly to contain cigarettes, a legislative move designed to sever communicative relations between smokers and tobacco companies, and to dissuade potential smokers from being enticed by slick advertising into taking up the practice. But these target audiences are not the only ones that might feel the weight of the smokefree atmosphere: there are much more tangential relations afoot. The force of the smokefree atmosphere might be felt by those who enjoy candy, too – indeed by everyone.

Section 106A of the Tobacco Products Control Act 2006 (Western Australia) prohibits any 'food, toy or other product' looking like a cigarette or cigar. Originally pressed into service to prevent the sale of 'Fags' candy sticks to children,[2] the law states:

> A person must not sell any food, toy or other product that is not a tobacco product but is,
>
> (a) designed to resemble a tobacco product or a package; or
>
> (b) in packaging that is designed to resemble a tobacco product or a package. (State of Western Australia 2006)

Anderson's observation has quite some purchase around this sort of vigorous elimination, of anything that resembles a tobacco product or package (and so communicates the intolerance for tobacco to a wider audience than just smokers or potential smokers with direct contact with packets). However, his words struck me with significantly more force one afternoon as I happened to pass the television set at home and heard a familiar tune playing. It was a Kmart advertisement, set to Shirley Ellis' catchy 'The Clapping Song'.[3] The version utilized in the advertisement replaces the word 'tobacco' with 'tomato'. The original words are as follows:

> 3, 6, 9
> The goose drank wine
> The monkey chewed tobacco on the streetcar line
> The line broke, the monkey got choked
> And they all went to heaven in a little rowboat.

In the Kmart version, 'wine' is changed to 'lime', 'tobacco' becomes 'tomato', 'choked' turns into 'woke', and instead of going to heaven, the monkey and the goose 'go together' in their little row boat.

Perhaps it is not going too far to suggest that the smokefree atmosphere is *so* pervasive that it presses down to ensure that a song penned in the 1950s cannot bring its uncritical inclusion of tobacco into the new smokefree atmosphere. The catchy tune emitting from the television set also disseminates the pervasive politics of smokefree: the smokefree atmosphere is certainly present in the lounge room, present among those who might have no direct relation to its force. Everyone can sing along to it, and those who sang the word 'tobacco' where 'tomato' is now present, like me, might have been prompted to think about why the word had changed. Singing along to the tune with original words, I was brought up sharp by 'tomato', and alerted, right away, to the fact that tobacco is now an unsingable word in advertising. It's a *bad* word. Others, who might be too young to know that the original word was 'tobacco', will never hear the word uttered in relationship to that public-transport-savvy monkey. They will know his predilection for tomatoes, but will never suspect that he used to much prefer tobacco. The atmosphere has changed.

The changes in lyrics promoted well-known marketing blogger Steven Downes to remark on his blog, 'I can only guess that advertiser and agency are trying to avoid any possibility of complaints to the Advertising Standards Board about inappropriate references to alcohol and tobacco consumption and a fatal public transport accident' (see Downes 2014). While Downes may well have meant his remarks in jest, it would certainly be reasonable to think that Kmart *would* attend with the greatest possible care to the standards relating to tobacco advertising, not least because amendments made in 2012 to the original 1992 Tobacco Advertising Prohibition Act dramatically extended existing restrictions on tobacco advertising to the internet, a key advertising site for the company.

Under the *Tobacco Advertising Prohibition Act 1992* Cth. (Australian Government 1992), it is an offence for a corporation to publish or broadcast a tobacco advertisement. The act defines 'advertisement' much more broadly than the everyday meaning of the term; section 9 defines a 'tobacco advertisement' to be any writing, still or moving picture, sign, symbol or other visual image that gives publicity to, or otherwise promotes or is intended to promote, smoking or the purchase or use of tobacco products. An advertiser would do well, indeed, to err on the side of caution, and turn tobacco into tomato.

While, as Downes' remarks suggest, the advertisement as a whole makes a nod to a series of sensitivities pertaining to alcohol and religion, as well as tobacco, tobacco is in a league of its own. Another bit of television might make the point: in 2014, the World Series Cricket championships, which gripped and held the nation for the summer, made sponsorship arrangements with alcohol franchise Beer Wine and Spirits. Arrangements with the purveyors of alcohol remain legal, but the days of the Benson and Hedges World Series Cup are long gone.[4]

Just these few snippets about packs, candy, cricket and tomatoes might indicate that tobacco control is on its way to a hitherto unknown zenith. Certainly, this has produced at least rehearsals of speculation about how far things might go. For instance, the notion that legislation is building to unprecedented levels of intervention was recently depicted in the popular Australian sitcom *Kath and Kim*. In one episode made in the early 2000s, lead character and light-but-regular smoker Kath Day-Knight speculates on how smoking will be treated twenty years in the future. She envisages police raids on the homes of smokers conducted by officers with the power to confiscate tobacco that has become contraband in this version of the future, and to arrest those found with cigarettes. To Kath, this seems the ultimate outcome of a progressive modern approach to smoking denormalization, but in fact such legislation was enacted (and discarded) in the early 1900s in the United States. While it is the case that the anti-tobacco movement was intimately connected with the temperance movement (and so was embedded in a radically different context than the one operational in Australia), it is noteworthy that attempts to tightly control tobacco are not new in the West.

In an article that appeared in the *Smithsonian* periodical in 1989, Tate recounts the events of the morning of 16 June 1909, when radical union leader W. D. 'Big Bill' Haywood was arrested for possessing a cigarette in Ellensburg, Washington, because he was in violation of the state law prohibiting the sale, manufacture and possession of cigarettes. Washington State was not alone; fourteen other states had similar laws at this time, and a further twenty-one were considering them. As Tate notes, after detailing the raft of evils and ailments for which tobacco was then held responsible (including baldness, evil deeds, cancer, acne, constipation, toothache, insanity, unattractiveness, ungentlemanliness, morbid thirst, crime and other social problems) 'in many ways, the antismoking movement of the 1980s is a model of restraint compared with one that began more than a century ago' (1989: 107).

Tate might have been right when she made her remark in the late 1980s about the relative mildness of contemporary tobacco control. However, her model of restraint may well be challenged by proposed legislation under consideration in Australia's southernmost state, Tasmania, which is presently considering banning the sale and supply of cigarettes to anyone born in or after the year 2000, a move that would effectively see (legal) tobacco consumption die with the last smoking generation. If it did, one could imagine plenty of Big Bill Haywood-type arrests. And, in the United States, there have already been legal cases heard and won over thirdhand smoke, in which it has been decided that smoke present as a lingering smell on the clothes, hair and skin is not permissible in the office. So, perhaps Tate's remarks about relative mildness are nearing the end of their life, as smokefree ramps up, and smoking prevalence comes down, across the Western world. After all, as good tobacco scholars, we know we should always question the truth of the word 'mild' any time it is used in conjunction with tobacco.

# Public health interventions and the construction of the smoker

As in other Western countries, smoking in the mid-twentieth century was ubiquitous in Australia. At the end of the Second World War, 75 per cent of men were smokers, along with about 25 per cent of women. According to data drawn from the National Drug Strategy's most recent (2013) household survey, 14.6 per cent of men and around 11.2 per cent of women are smokers (Australian Government Institute of Health and Welfare 2014). The website of the Australian Government Department of Health includes a graph pegging the major public health interventions into smoking to the national daily smoking rate.[5] An excise rise and the Tobacco Advertising Prohibition Act in the early 1990s coincide with rises in the rate, and a plateau precedes the introduction of the National Tobacco Campaign (NTC) in 1997, but the overall picture is one of decline – the rate has roughly halved since 1991.

Aboriginal and Torres Strait Islander smokers have not responded to authoritative health information as smokers in the general population have; according to the Aboriginal and Torres Strait Islander Health Survey, 41 per cent of Indigenous Australians aged fifteen years and over smoke daily (Australian Bureau of Statistics 2013). Indigenous smokers are, however, imagined in just the same rational terms as are applied to smokers in the general population; the only difference is that Indigenous rationality is assumed only to be reachable by very specific cultural means. Thus, as I explain in Chapter 3, Indigenous smokers are the subject of a culturally specific campaign designed to reach the rational person that slumbers beneath the ignorant smoker – all it will take to awaken her is the culturally specific delivery of the right health information.

In public health paradigm, smokers are imagined to be capable of reasoned calculation and able to understand that smoking is harmful and that they should stop to preserve health. But smokers are equally imagined to be vulnerable to the emotional manipulations made by Big Tobacco. The spectre of cancer, for example, was no match for the manipulative marketing pitch made by tobacco companies in the late twentieth century. As Scollo and Winstanley note,

First was the advent of television in the late 1950s, which brought an avalanche of advertisements for cigarettes into the lounge rooms of Australian families, and distracted from concerns about cancer with images of European sophistication, American-style affluence and Australian sunshine and fun that resonated with the optimism and aspirations of a generation wanting to build a new life after two long decades of war and Depression. A new breed of advertising men in the United States, Britain and Australia helped tobacco companies to side-step the health issue with appeals to emotion combined with reassuring, if vague allusions to filters and reductions in 'tar'. (2012: np)

As I will argue in Chapter 3, the smoker is understood – by both public health and tobacco companies – as a doubled character, at once capable of reasoned calculation and the subject of emotional manipulation.

Another construction of smokers is also in evidence, and it is used in *Tobacco in Australia* to explain why not all smokers quit, once they have been presented with the requisite information. Its primary authors Scollo and Winstanley note that during the 1970s, in particular, in Australia, there was a focus on smoking as an *addiction*. There is a strong emphasis on addiction in *Tobacco in Australia*, not only on addiction as a past bedeviller of tobacco control efforts in Australia, but also as a present one. One notion promulgated in this prominent public health publication in particular is that the relapse rate back into smoking after a quit attempt (itself generated by the awakening of the rational agent via tobacco control health information) is wholly due to the addictive properties of nicotine. Addiction looms as a problem difficult to overcome, and one central to the construction of the smoking person – or, rather, the person who dwells alongside, or underneath, the rational person who can be engaged by the right public health messaging.

However, as Bell and Keane (2012) point out, tobacco smoking is actually quite difficult to contain within an addiction framing. Indeed, tobacco smoking has been very strongly discursively separated from addictions generally, because of its incongruence with dominant medical and cultural models of addiction (see also Berridge 1998; Luik 1996). As Robin Room (2003) has argued,

> One of the cultural functions of the concept of addiction is to provide a causal explanation for bad behavior. Addiction is seen as a kind of possession, in which a powerful drug is able to produce behavior that would not otherwise occur. But while smokers may be dependent on a drug to function, their lives generally appear ordinary, orderly, and productive. Because cigarettes do not produce intoxication and remain legal and relatively easy to access, smokers do not fit the stereotype of the out-of-control junkie governed by unmanageable desire, at least until they try to quit. (Bell and Keane 2012: 3; see also Bell and Dennis 2013: 6)

Bell and Keane note that because of the incongruence of smoking as an addiction with the capacity of the smoker to continue unfettered in the business of life, tobacco use has been historically classified as a kind of dependence, a habituation upon which one comes to rely. Indeed, it was only in the 1990s that tobacco became framed by addiction, a move that was

> connected with the development of research on the pharmacology and biology of smoking in the 1980s. … However the collapse of the distinction between dependence and addiction in the tobacco field is also connected with broader shifts in diagnostic instruments and practices, encapsulated in the decision to remove reference to 'addiction' from the revised third edition of the American Psychiatric Association's Diagnostic and Statistical

Manual (DSM-IIIR), published in 1987. Instead, 'dependence' became the preferred catchall label because of concerns about pejorative implications of the former term. (Bell and Keane 2012: 4)

Addiction hasn't been historically part of the dominant framing of tobacco smoking also because of the disciplinary bases that gave rise to smoking as a public health issue, in the latter half of the twentieth century. The public health problem of tobacco smoking had its genesis in disciplines like chest medicine and epidemiology, rather than psychiatry, where other addictions, such as those to alcohol and illicit drugs, have their home. The strong links that emerged, between, 'first, smoking and lung cancer and, later, smoking and heart disease helped establish new standards for causality, and legitimized epidemiology as a scientific discipline' (Bell and Dennis 2013: 5), but they made an inhospitable home for addiction.

Right now, however, it seems to have very significant purchase on how smokers are constructed within public health paradigm, especially in relation to legislative interventions into smoking. I will discuss these at length in Chapter 3.

Another thing that seems to have an extremely tight grip on the production of knowledge in public health is that smokers have stopped smoking as a direct and indisputable result of anti-smoking campaigns. Such a proposition indicates very clearly a reliance on a rational agent, who will respond to health advice as predicted. Throughout, I trouble the reliability of this agent, in and through my disruption of the public health reasons for smoking: ignorance of its harms, and addiction to its nicotine.

I'm certainly not going to propose any half-baked alternative explanations for the drop in prevalence – that isn't the subject of this book. But I do want to set the dogged insistence of public health claims about prevalence against some other terms in which the *appeal* of smoking can be understood, and I do this right at the end of Chapter 7, at the end of the book, when I can be sure that the basis of my alternative theorizing is sufficiently clear.

# The Benson and Hedges World Series Cricket, 1988

Between 1973 and 1976, federal legislation banned direct tobacco advertising on television. This had an unexpected outcome most beneficial to the tobacco companies: it freed up their massive television advertising budget lines for investment in sports sponsorship, since 'accidental or incidental' advertising was still permitted under the new law. Via sports sponsorship, the three major tobacco companies at the time (Philip Morris, Amatil and Rothmans) enjoyed exceptionally cost-effective advertising. By 1980, the three major tobacco companies then operating in Australia were also its three largest sports sponsors. As Scollo and Winstanley note, in a single day's play of a Benson & Hedges-sponsored cricket match televised from Sydney in 1988,

> the Benson & Hedges name received a full 88 minutes of the day's coverage. By comparison, the sponsor of a top rating television program could expect to get about seven minutes of coverage in an hour. ... According to WD & HO Wills, makers of Benson & Hedges, radio and television coverage of the 1992 World Cup of Cricket was beamed to 29 countries. (2012: np)

Such arrangements interleaved smoking even more firmly into the ordinary business of Australian life, as watching the Benson and Hedges World Series Cup was practically a national pastime.

The money freed up from television adverting was also moved more squarely into print media, and became more tailored to recruiting young women smokers, not least because the sports sponsorships were thought to have saturated the male market (see Scollo and Winstanley 2012). Smoking remained well advertised on billboards, and in shop and newsagency window advertising. In the summer of 1986, when the Benson & Hedges World Cup Series cricket played on the TV, high school girls like me sneaked Alpine Lights behind the changerooms at the Tennis Club. We purchased them from fish-and-chip shops whose windows bore posters of pretty girls dressed in white sitting on tropical islands, or skiing in aqua suits down snow-capped mountains. When we were caught smoking, we were in trouble, certainly, but we'd often backchat our parents with observations about who in our own families smoked – so it couldn't be all *that* bad. But, then, it must have been – considering that monkeys are permitted only to consume tomatoes on the street car line these days. The atmosphere has indeed changed.

The battles leading up to the situation in which Kmart felt the need to substitute 'tobacco' for 'tomato' for its monkey were fought in the 1980s around what, exactly, constituted 'accidental' and 'incidental' advertising. Scollo and Winstanley (2012) explain that the dominance of the three biggest tobacco companies gave rise to complaints which were dealt with by the Australian Broadcasting Tribunal. The tribunal was forced to clarify its interpretation of the legislation in 1983 and 1984 in order to decide on whether the complaints regarding breaches of the 'accidental' and 'incidental' clauses were valid – complaints were received about a number of television broadcasts, including the 1982 telecast of the New South Wales Rugby League (NSWRL) Grand Final (sponsored by Winfield), and promotional exposure associated with Benson & Hedges' sponsorship of the Australian Ballet and test cricket. It ruled the complaints to be valid.

A legal challenge immediately ensued; the tobacco companies began proceedings in the Federal Court in 1984. The outcome favoured the tribunal. An appeal was launched by the tobacco companies against the decision – this was dismissed by the Full Bench of the Federal Court in 1985 (Australian Law Reports 1985). The decision included a discussion of the agreement between Rothmans (Winfield) and the NSWRL, which obligated the league to assist Rothmans in the advertising and promoting of its products. This agreement and many others included an 'escape' clause for the tobacco companies from the sponsorships if the type of advertising they sought was restricted or banned by government or other authority. The court agreed that 'the sponsorship arrangement was intended as an advertising opportunity rather than an act of sporting philanthropy'. This was enough for the Non-Smokers' Movement of Australia (NSMA) to allege that a breach of the law had taken place, and that the United Telecasters (Channel 10) was in breach of section 100(5a) of the Broadcasting Act because it televised direct advertising matter. The trial was heard in September 1987 in the District Court in Sydney. The jury reached a guilty verdict, a finding which was almost immediately appealed by United Telecasters (on a number of technicalities). A retrial was ordered, and the decision was quashed. The Department of Public Prosecutions then appealed to the High Court and was successful; in February 1990, more than five years after the telecast in question, the broadcaster Channel 10 was convicted of televising a cigarette advertisement (see Scollo and Winstanley 2012).

At the time that federal legislation banned direct tobacco advertising, Australian states and territories had differing legislation in place pertaining to sports sponsorships. Because the states had differing (or in some cases no) controlling legislation in force, they were vulnerable to tobacco industry threats to move popular events with great revenue earning potential from one state to another, 'the most obvious example of which being the movement of the Motor Cycle Grand Prix from Victoria to New South Wales and back again between 1989 and 1992, instigated by a bitter and protracted dispute over the display of tobacco advertising' (see Scollo and Winstanley 2012: np; Lagan 1991: 7). This is indicative of a broader legislative picture which has its genesis in the different approaches to tobacco control taken by each state.

The beginnings of a comprehensive national approach can be traced to the late 1960s and early 1970s. The director of the Anti-Cancer Council of Victoria, Dr Nigel Gray, pushed hard, and successfully, for anti-smoking messages to be disseminated via television. Twenty-six humorous advertisements were the result. The ads, made on a shoestring and shot in black and white, featured popular English actors Warren Mitchell, Fred Parslowe and Miriam Karlin. In the 1980s, momentum grew. In New South Wales, Victoria, Western Australia and South Australia, government and non-governmental organizations funded statewide tobacco control campaigns, and in Queensland, the Australian Capital

Territory and the Northern Territory, various tobacco control activities were initiated and supported by a host of state-based non-governmental organizations.

The first national campaign on smoking was the National Warning Against smoking campaign that ran between 1972 and 1975, funded at a rate of half a million Australian dollars for each of the campaign years. In a very early nod to smokefree public places legislation that would be introduced decades later, the Commonwealth Department of Health printed cardboard signs that it made freely available to the public requesting smokers not to smoke in the vicinity of the signs.

In 1985, the Ministerial Council on Drug Strategy (MCDS) was formed. A powerful group comprising all Australian state and territory health ministers, Commonwealth ministers for Health and Customs, and the Attorney General, the council allocated AUD $2 million to the 'Smoking – who needs it?' campaign, that was aired on national television, in cinemas and in print advertising from 1990 to 1991. The campaign extended the focus that the states had collectively taken, on young women's smoking, and drew on resources that had previously been strictly for each state's use. The increasingly comprehensive approach seemed to produce results as steady declines were reported in the smoking rate across the 1980s and 1990s. In 1980, the smoking rate for males was 41 per cent; by 1986 it had dropped to 34 per cent, and by 1989, it had dropped further to an even 30 per cent. For women, the rate reduction was not as dramatic. In 1980 the adult smoking rate for women was 30 per cent; by 1986 it had fallen to 28 per cent, and by 1989, it had fallen to 27 per cent. In the 1990s, though, these gains had begun to falter, and the smoking rate levelled off at a stubborn 26 per cent, which led to the development and implementation in 1997 of the NTC. I discuss the effects of this enduring entry into Australian tobacco control in Chapters 3 and 4.

## Smokefree places

Scollo and Winstanley note that it was during the late 1980s that concerns about the health effects of exposure to other people's smoking arose, resulting in rolling restrictions on smoking in hospitality venues and public places, now collectively known as 'smokefree environments':

> Smoking bans have been marked by incremental steps involving advances in scientific evidence and growing public acceptance and political resolve, which have converged to make legislative change possible. (2012: np)

In the fifth chapter, I present an alternative theorizing of the banning of smoking in public places that disputes the notion of progressive knowledge 'advancement' that is exclusively about new scientific information, in favour of an analysis that privileges very old notions of the porous bounds of the body, and its vulnerability to odours borne on the air. This is not as much a blanket disputation of available science as it is a recognition of how non-smokers seem to be responding to the danger presented by exhaled smoke in the outdoor air. Even the briefest of encounters with cigarette smoke often produces coughing, and the shielding of the mouth and nose, as though a single exposure might, as one of the people in my Canberra study put it, 'cause cancer'. Certainly, the science itself does not indicate that cancer is in the air; notions of cancer circulating and being *catching* are related to much, much older ideas about how miasmatic harm circulates, how a bad air emanating from a foul and rotted source, can kill – apparently, in the era of smokefree, in a heartbeat. In a *breath*.

Such reactions are to be expected, given the pace, extent and normalization of smoking bans. Responsibility for creating and maintaining smokefree environments falls mainly under state and territory control, but there are three areas of broad Commonwealth regulation. The Air Navigation Act 1920 (Cth) includes regulations that have prohibited smoking on all domestic flights since 1987 (see Australian Government 1920), In 1996, the Air Navigation Regulations 1947 (Cth) were amended to extend the ban on smoking in aircraft to all international flights operated by Australian airlines (see Australian Government 1996). Smoking on board buses registered under the Interstate Road Transport Act 1985 (Cth) is banned at all times while passengers are on board, pursuant to regulation 51B of the Interstate Road Transport Regulations 1986 (Cth); see (Australian Government 1985, and Australian Government 1986). By the mid-1990s, smokefree policies had extended well beyond airplanes and buses and beyond the public sector. All Commonwealth, state and territory government offices were smokefree, as were many shopping centres, hospitals, schools, childcare facilities and entertainment venues, and bans have continued to apply to more and more outdoor spaces, including transit areas, parks, state forests and national parks, beaches, sports facilities and educational institutions, including some universities.[6] Every Australian state and territory bans smoking in enclosed public places, but the legislation is slightly different in each, as are the definitions of 'enclosed' and what, exactly, constitutes a 'public place'.

## The nuances of public place legislation

In this section, I describe some of the nuances of public place legislation. The reader keen to get to the substantive and ethnographically based chapters may wish to skip over this discussion of the finer points of legislation. But the reader may wish to refer to it after having read Chapter 2, in which the legal distinction between 'public place' and 'public land' is discussed.[7]

In NSW, smoking was banned in enclosed public places from 2007. In NSW, a 'public place' is a place or vehicle that the public, or a section of the public, is entitled to use or that is open to, or is being used by, the public or a section of the public (whether on payment of money, by virtue of membership of a club or other body, or otherwise). An enclosed public place is one in which the total area of the ceiling and wall surfaces of the public place is more than 75 per cent of its total notional ceiling and wall area. In addition to bans over enclosed public places, NSW banned smoking within 10 metres of children's play equipment in outdoor public places, spectator areas at sports grounds or other recreational areas; swimming pool complexes; railway platforms, light rail stops, light rail stations, bus stops, taxi ranks and ferry wharves, and within 4 metres of a pedestrian access point to a public building, from January 2013. A ban on smoking in cars carrying children under the age of sixteen years has been in place since 2009.

In Queensland, smoking is not allowed in any enclosed public places, those being defined as having a ceiling or roof and, except for doors and passageways, completely or substantially enclosed whether permanently or temporarily. In vehicles, 'enclosed' means having a ceiling or roof and, except for doors and exits, completely or substantially enclosed, whether permanently or temporarily. 'Public place' means a place that the public is entitled to use, is open to the public or is used by the public (whether or not on payment of money). In Queensland, smoking is also banned in specific outdoor public places, including beaches, children's play equipment, sport stadiums, within 4 metres of public (i.e. non-residential) building entrances, and at outdoor eating and drinking venues. In 2010 it became illegal to smoke in a car when a child under the age of sixteen is present therein.

In South Australia, smoking bans began in 1999 with indoor dining areas, and progressed to enclosed public areas and shared spaces, all pubs, clubs and casinos. In South Australia, 'public area' or 'public place' means an area or place that the public, or a section of the public, is entitled to use or that is open to, or used by, the public or a section of the public (whether access is unrestricted or subject to payment of money, membership of a body or otherwise). A place or area is 'enclosed' if it is fully enclosed or is at least partially covered by a ceiling and has walls such that the total area of the ceiling and wall surfaces exceeds 70 per cent of the total notional ceiling and wall area. Smoking with children in the car has been prohibited since 31 May 2007. The South Australian Government hopes to ban smoking in all al-fresco dining areas by 2016, and it has banned smoking at covered public transport waiting areas, including bus stops, tram stops, railway stations, taxi ranks and airports, within 10 metres of children's playground equipment, and in public areas or at events declared to be smokefree at the request of a local council or other incorporated entity.

In Tasmania, smoking has been prohibited in 100 per cent of al-fresco dining areas since March 2012. Other outdoor places where smoking is not permitted include sporting and cultural venues and within specified distances of building entrances and ventilation systems. Smoking is also prohibited in a vehicle when someone under eighteen years of age is present. As previously indicated, in 2012, Tasmania began discussing the possibility of eradicating smoking from future generations (those born after 2000), with the Smoke Free Generation initiative. The initiative would make it illegal to ever supply cigarettes to anyone born after the year 2000. In Tasmania, a 'public place' includes a place to which the public ordinarily has access, whether or not by payment or invitation, and an 'enclosed public place' means a place for the use of the public which has a ceiling or roof; and except for doors and passageways, is completely or substantially enclosed by walls or windows.

In Victoria, smoking is illegal in enclosed public places, workplaces, outdoor areas at underage events, and covered areas of public transport stops or stations, but it is permitted in outdoor dining and drinking areas, including rooftops, balconies, verandas, courtyards, marquees and the footpath/street. Since 1 January 2010, it has been illegal to smoke in a vehicle when someone under the age of eighteen is present. In Victoria, 'enclosed' means an area that is, or premises that are, except for doorways, passageways and internal wall openings, completely or substantially enclosed by a solid permanent ceiling or roof and solid permanent walls or windows, whether the ceiling, roof, walls or windows are fixed or movable and open or closed.

In Western Australia, smoking was banned in enclosed public places in 1999, and prohibited in outdoor eating and drinking areas in September 2010. An 'enclosed public place' is a place that has, whether permanently or temporarily, a ceiling or a roof and walls, sides or other vertical coverings so that when the public place's existing closable openings are closed, the public place is completely or substantially enclosed. A 'public place' is a place or vehicle that the public, or a section of the public, is entitled to use or is open to, or is being used by, the public, or a section of the public, whether on payment of money, by virtue of membership of a club or other body, by invitation or otherwise. In Western Australia, it is illegal to smoke in a vehicle when someone under the age of seventeen is present.

In the Australian Capital Territory, The Smoke-Free Public Places Act 2003 prohibits smoking in an enclosed public place (in effect since 2006), in outdoor eating or drinking places, and at underage functions (both in effect since 9 December 2010). Since 1 May 2012, it has been illegal to smoke in a vehicle when a child under the age of sixteen is inside. In the ACT, 'public place' is a place to which the public or a section of the public has access, whether – by payment, membership of a body or otherwise or by entitlement or permission. A 'public place' is enclosed if it is covered and is 75 per cent or more enclosed.

In the Northern Territory, the Tobacco Control Act 2002 banned smoking in enclosed public places (including workplaces) and outdoor venues in 2003, in licensed venues and substantially enclosed areas from 2010, and in outdoor eating and drinking areas in 2011. 'Enclosed public area' means a public area with a ceiling or roof that (except for doorways and passageways) is completely or substantially enclosed by walls, windows, blinds, curtains or other objects, materials or things. 'Enclosed workplace area' means a workplace with a ceiling or roof and that (except for doorways or passageways) which is completely or substantially enclosed by walls, windows, blinds, curtains or other objects, materials or things, but does not include an area of the business that is in or on domestic premises that is not used or intended to be used by members of the public or employees of the business. 'Entrance area' means an area within 2 metres of a door, window or other opening that opens into or onto an enclosed public area or an enclosed workplace area.

The crafting of smokefree legislation over public place has not been restricted to the Commonwealth and state/territory levels. Municipal councils have also been responsible for enacting extensive bans. Herein, definitions of 'public place' are expanded beyond their definitions in state legislation. For instance, in 2004, Sydney's Mosman Municipal Council banned smoking on beaches, in outdoor dining areas, children's playgrounds, council events, playing fields, within 10 metres of all council properties, bushland and foreshore reserves. In March 2007, the ban was extended to every council-controlled public place, including parks, public squares, bus shelters and council car parks. Thus, the only public outdoor places Mosman smokers may light up are on those footpaths that are not located adjacent to council properties, and where state and federal legislation is not contravened, and on public roads.

Municipal councils have, indeed, been at the forefront of implementing legislation in outdoor public place. In 2004, Sydney's Manly Council became the second jurisdiction in the world (after Los Angeles) and the first in Australia to legislate a smoking ban on a public beach. Waverley Council followed suit, implementing a ban on smoking on its beaches including Sydney's famous tourist beach Bondi in December 2004. By 2010, smoking bans on beaches were in put in place across New South Wales councils. Queensland's legislation, introduced in 2005, prohibits smoking between the flags at patrolled beaches, as does Western Australia's, introduced in 2010. Smoking is permitted on Queensland's artificial beaches, but only between sunset and sunrise.

Smoking bans have also been in place over the Great Ocean Road beaches since 2008 under a local law put in place by Victoria's Surf Coast Shire, and on St Kilda, Elwood and Port Melbourne beaches under a ban implemented by Port Phillip Council in 2010. Extensive municipal-level smoking bans are also in place covering children's playgrounds, outdoor sports and recreation facilities. Bans are also operationalized at another regulatory level, that of the public institution.

Some Australian universities are smokefree or are in the process of so doing, including Notre Dame University (since 2002) and Curtin University's West Australian campuses (since 2012). Edith Cowan University, the University of Western Australia and Murdoch University are all smokefree. In NSW, Macquarie University will be smokefree by 2015, and, as I've mentioned, the ANU in the ACT is beginning the process of going smokefree by issuing a survey instrument to determine whether it should be completely smokefree, or retain designated smoking areas on campus. The Australian Catholic University in the ACT has been smokefree since January 2015. Deakin University in Victoria has a 'time since Deakin went smokefree' counter on its site, which, when I looked at it, indicated 341 days, 21 hours, 22 minutes and 39 seconds. South Australia's premiere institution, Adelaide University, has been smokefree since July 2010.

# Legislating the air

Some smokefree legislation attempts to deal specifically with *smoke as a traveller* – a theme I will elaborate in this book. For instance, legislation currently in place in the Australian Capital Territory, New South Wales and Western Australia requires business occupiers to take reasonable steps to prevent cigarette smoke drifting from areas where smoking is permitted into smokefree areas. It is an offence to permit smoke into an enclosed public place from another part of the premises, and an offence if a neighbouring occupier fails to take reasonable steps to prevent smoke from the premises entering an enclosed public place on any other premises. This issue of 'neighbour smoke' has also been problematic in domestic contexts; in 2006, for example, the New South Wales Consumer, Trader and Tenancy Tribunal upheld a case that had been brought by occupants of an apartment against their smoking neighbours. The neighbours were required to stop smoking in their apartment because of the smoke wafting into the neighbouring apartment (see Munro 2007).

Smoke then, can sidle and waft uninvited into those spaces deemed smokefree. Its capacity to do this makes for a very fraught and complex atmosphere, which I now turn to examine.

# 2

# Oppositionary pairings and ruinous smoke

## Introduction

In this chapter, I want to return very specifically to the notion that atmospheres are characterized by the way in which they recognize and articulate the differences between two states. The smokefree atmosphere is replete with oppositionary pairings that are held in particular relation to one another – indeed, they are held firmly apart. My first task in this chapter is to demonstrate that the main forces in this atmosphere – the tobacco industry and the anti-smoking lobby (each containing multiple players – researchers, experts, advocates and agitators, and so on) are not, in fact, as firmly 'apart' from one another as appearances suggest. Underneath the surfaces of the smokefree atmosphere's antagonistic oppositions lie similarly composed notions.

The second sort of work I do in this chapter is concerned with looking closely at how the binary oppositions around time and space that form the foundations of the smokefree atmosphere are never purely established divisions. Crafting binary oppositions that seek to divide smokefree places from places where smoking is permitted, or that attempt to separate a smokefree time from a noxious, smoky precursory period, is also only a surface disunion, as smoke, is a ruinous connector, laying waste to such stern cleavings as are evident in smokefree taxonomy.

## Oppositionary pair: Right and wrong

On 29 September 2014, the Australian Broadcasting Corporation (ABC) aired a special edition of its *Four Corners* programme entitled 'The Seduction of

Smoking'. Run over two evenings, the programme included a segment in which primary-school-age children were invited to respond to industry-branded cigarette packets and to describe how they appeared to them. The children gave responses that indicated that the richly adorned, colourful packets were seductive and alluring, 'pretty', and were, as such, likely to influence them to take up smoking in the future.[1]

Also in 2014, the *Australian* newspaper invoked the ire of well-known Australian anti-tobacco campaigners and professors of public health, Mike Daube and Simon Chapman, when it used tobacco industry-generated reports to claim that plain packaging hadn't worked to reduce smoking prevalence as it was touted and predicted to. They used the 'Perspectives' section of *The Medical Journal of Australia* to give the broadsheet a (it must be said, a richly deserved) dressing down:

> Plain packaging passes the tobacco 'scream test' – the more the industry screams, the more impact we know a measure will have … it is disappointing that a newspaper such as *The Australian* provides support for such approaches [as are taken by the tobacco industry, i.e. in using the industry's own data]. Health campaigners should continue to promote measures that will benefit the community, especially children, even if opposed by powerful commercial interests, and take pride in Australia's capacity to lead the world. (2014: 192)

Such examples indicate that the smokefree atmosphere is present to the extent that its advocates can publicly (and proudly) occupy positions of indubitable rightness.

In the case of the first example, it's easy enough to see how utterly inappropriate it would be to permit a tobacco industry representative to carry out an information-gathering exercise like the one featured on *Four Corners*. And, if such an invitation were put to small children by a tobacco company representative, outrage would indubitably follow. One would be fully justified, if one pointed out, for instance, that subtle cues made in conversation or gesture, or prejudice in the questions, intended or not, might impact the micropolitics of the situation; some might even suspect a more deliberate skewing of the results. But the fact that the questions were put by a man who was introduced by the host, US reporter Peter Taylor, as a dedicated anti-smoking campaigner did not raise so much as an eyebrow. It is perhaps more difficult to situate the staunch anti-smoking advocate in that position, although the questions of bias are equally relevant and exactly the same – except of course for the moral rightness that might be ascribed to the health advocate's position.

In the case of the second example, *The Australian* newspaper stands accused of utilizing biased reports from an industry source – and certainly, Daube and Chapman were right to point out the problems with this. It is quite hard, though, to imagine a similar accusation being levelled at the broadsheet for using data generated by a party with an explicit tobacco control advocacy agenda. For example, I have not yet seen any dressings-down in the press of Wakefield et al.'s 2013 study funded by Quit Victoria, on the effects of plain packaging on adult smokers published in *BMJ Open,* which found that packs reduced the appeal of smoking, and increased smoker's thoughts about quitting. Such reports issue from a genesis at least equally as interested as those from the industry itself. Let me be really clear here – I'm not suggesting that the tobacco industry should be given more access to children in research groups, or to publications in journals, or that it should get more press space in the nation's newspapers. I'm suggesting that we recognize the interested basis of each. I'm interested in stepping outside of both interested spaces.

Tobacco and anti-tobacco are binary oppositions but, like many of these pairings, one dominates the other, asserting, in these cases I've just mentioned, its moral superiority. Subsets of the pair share this trait: the moral rightness or good-ness of the anti-tobacco stance is threaded through its intention to save and protect life, in part by acting to ensure the purity of the air. These trump the morally suspect, perhaps even evil, intentions of the tobacco industry, to enslave smokers into an addiction that will mean death for themselves, and a polluted air for innocent others. The smokefree atmosphere is one constructed of binary oppositions: smokefree places, smokefree time, specific public health knowledge – these are set against their corrupting opposites, held apart to create the illusory sense that they are, truly, contrasting. Certainly, on the surface, they are mutually antagonistic.

This mutual antagonism is evident in *Tobacco in Australia,* which describes an ongoing

> tug-of-war between the forces which promote and facilitate the use of tobacco products and the forces which discourage and inhibit its use; a tug-of-war played out at the individual, household and community levels as well as in the wider culture. ... Continuing progress requires a comprehensive approach to maintain momentum and ensure that government efforts on one front are not undermined by more vigorous efforts and greater investment by tobacco companies on other fronts. (Scollo and Winstanley 2012: np)

## Oppositionary pair: Public health and tobacco companies

One such 'tug-of-war' was recently played out in court, in Australia. In its most recent legislative culmination, in Australia's new plain packaging laws,

Big Tobacco predictably went into battle with the state to retain its last advertising space, the packet. With bipartisan support, the state moved to prohibit tobacco companies from trademarking its packaging. Where previous ministers had been advised that doing so was legally impossible, fresh external-to-government legal advice allowed the federal health minister, at the time, Nicola Roxon, to move forward with the new laws, which were immediately challenged by Big Tobacco on grounds of constitutional invalidity. The challenge mounted by tobacco industry representatives failed and the world now has its very first tobacco plain packaging laws – shortly to be replicated in the UK.

The ruling permitted the State to impose a ban on all brand marks and logos on cigarette packets, to take effect from 1 October 2012, when all tobacco products manufactured or packaged in Australia for the Australian market were required to be in plain packaging. Additionally, since 1 December 2012, all tobacco products sold, offered for sale or otherwise supplied in Australia were required by law to be in plain packaging and be labelled with new and expanded health warnings (Australian Government Department of Health & Ageing 2012). Under the new legislation, which comprises two parts – the Tobacco Plain Packaging Act 2011 and the Tobacco Plain Packaging Regulations 2011 – warnings now cover 75 per cent of the front of the pack (up from the previous 30 per cent) and continued to cover almost 90 per cent of the back of the pack (see Australian Government 2011). All forms of branding were entirely removed: the manufacturer's brand names now appear in small generic font on the bottom of the pack, and the pack itself is uniformly olive brown in colour (Australian Government 2012).

While permitting it to strip the packet of tobacco industry branding, this victory for the state and for public health produced a broader question, about what the state could and should be able to do to regulate the behaviour of individuals. The words 'Nanny State' began to circulate in print and online media. 'One of the most divisive public health policies in recent times, cigarette plain packaging laws were introduced by the former Gillard Government in an attempt to cut down on smoking rates. The [immediately preceding Labour] Rudd government also took aim at smokers with a four-stage hike in the tobacco excise,' wrote news.com.au's Frank Chung in September 2014. The Institute of Public Affairs (IPA) ranked plain packaging laws number 10 in its '10 Worst Nanny State Policies', remarking,

The argument for plain cigarette packaging is one of the most stark examples of how Nanny state regulations treat individuals as childish automatons. … Mandatory plain packaging seems to be predicated on the belief that attractive packaging is enough to convince non-smokers to become smokers, or that for smokers trying to quit, a good-looking logo is just too much to bear. … The National Preventative Health Taskforce's discussion paper on tobacco was titled 'making smoking history'. This is surely a new stage in the public health movement's war against smoking – an open affirmation that the stated goal of the government should not be to reduce risk, or to inform consumers of risks they should be aware of, but to eliminate an otherwise totally legal product.

Well-known public health professor and anti-smoking campaigner Simon Chapman had already made a pre-emptive strike on IPA, making the following remarks in July 2013:

> In Australia, anyone who supports rules and regulations that make products safer or improve public health can expect to come under attack from critics arguing they're restricting freedom and turning the country into a 'nanny state'. These 'nanny state' critics are everywhere and they're superficially persuasive. After all, who wants government to tell them how to live their lives? But scratch the surface and you'll discover nanny state critics are frequently backed by powerful vested interests, like the tobacco industry arguing against plain packaging on cigarettes, or the secretive PR outfit known as the Institute of Public Affairs arguing against the government. (2013: np)

Enemies face off against one another in this atmosphere, from within clearly defined (or at least clearly *ascribed*) positions – one is either against the government, against public health or dedicatedly with it. Attempts to hold the claims of the poles in abeyance and to conduct research *sans* evident commitment to public health goals are subject to classification as 'industry aligned'. A colleague and I were ascribed a position of industry alignment when we issued an invitation to Chapman to come to a discussion forum involving other tobacco researchers on the subject of plain packaging in Australia. He responded to both of us by email, and I cite that communication below with his express permission:

> I can imagine your approaches to plain packaging would be nothing but critical [of the plain packet legislation]. I am spending a huge amount of time with others defending plain packaging against attacks from tobacco industry puppet states like Dominican Republic, Ukraine and Honduras, and vile tobacco funded libertarian right wing think-tanks like the IPA. So you might understand that it's very hard to give any priority to writing defences to criticism from a small corner of academic social science. Of course some smokers feel marginalised, angered and resistant to what tobacco and alcohol control has achieved. So do many gun owners, rev-heads, savage dog owners, anti-vax people, climate change denialists, and people who resent being reminded that tanning can be deadly feel

angered at dominant discourse on their pet issues. It's perfectly legitimate to study and comment on such groups' marginalisation but personally, I'm uninterested in giving any priority to these 'other perspectives'. I'm probably not the first person to say this, but the tobacco industry would be very interested in your work. Maybe you should invite them!

Aligned as Chapman considered us to be to the tobacco pole in and through our work that, he thought, gave voice to the disgruntled smoker, nothing was to be gained from our planned forum. In such a view, since anti-tobacco adherents are already committed to what they want to achieve, it's no use wasting time on discussions that can only ever be face-offs between two warring parties.

Even though Chapman's intention seems to have been to firmly differentiate his own approach from ours, which he saw as playing into the hands of the tobacco industry, his email actually reveals *the substantially shared basis of industry interests and those who opposed them*: the singular pursuit of a particular (minimization or maximization) agenda.

As Mair and Kierans (2007) have already noted, the anti-smoking and pro-smoking polar regions are, actually, topographically pretty similar, in the sense that each side pursues an instrumentalist approach to smoking. Indeed, the only real differentiations that can be validly made between them are in terms of the intentions they each hold (either to banish smoking or else to support its continuation) and their moral or other attachments to those positions. Otherwise, they adopt the same foundational, instrumental approach to smoking. Mair and Kierans describe it this way:

> We have a situation where one group views research as a means to maximize tobacco use, the other to minimize it, with neither side seeking to improve their understanding beyond what they need to pursue their specific goals. As a consequence, instrumentalism, grounded in mutual antagonism, has become a hallmark of orthodox research on both sides. (2007: 104)

Despite the articulation of apparently well-established poles, this is the first way in which two discernible states are *not*, in fact, established.

## Oppositionary pair: A long life or an untimely death

These apparently polar differences between two states are everywhere to be found in the atmosphere of smokefree. Possibly the most obvious temporal example is that pertaining to the future as it is laid out for smokers in the atmosphere of smokefree. Starkly, two possible futures are predicted: either the certainty of a smoking-related death or the promise of an almost immediately healthful life if the smoker quits. Such certainty, either way, is communicated not only by messaging on packs ('Smoking, A leading cause of death'; 'Smoking causes lung cancer … most people who get lung cancer, die from it', and so on, or, 'Quitting smoking results in immediate health benefits; 'Quitting is the best thing you can do for your health and to assure and enhance your chances of living a long and healthy life'), but also in a sort of corporeally generated mathematics that converts practice into duration. As Keane (2002) notes,

> Not only does the purchase and consumption of the drug take up time in the smoker's daily routine, but also the smoker's attachment to its dubious pleasures is steadily subtracting time from the future. The rate of loss has been quite precisely calculated – about 5 ½ minutes of life per cigarette. (119)

The rate of gain has been (even more) precisely calculated:

> The effects of quitting start to set in immediately. Less than 20 minutes after your last cigarette, your heart rate will already start to drop back towards normal levels. After two hours without a cigarette, your heart rate and blood pressure will have decreased to normal levels … 12 hours after quitting smoking, the carbon monoxide in your body decreases to lower levels, and your blood oxygen levels increase to normal … just one full day after quitting smoking, your risk for heart attack will already have begun to drop. While you're not quite out of the woods yet, you're on your way … after 48 hours without a cigarette, your nerve endings will start to regrow … three days after you quit, the nicotine will be completely out of your body … about a month after you quit, your lungs begin to repair … after a year without smoking, your risk of heart disease is lowered by 50% … after 5 to fifteen years of being smokefree your risk of having a stroke is the same as someone who doesn't smoke … your risk of dying from lung cancer will drop to half that of a smoker's … fifteen years of non-smoking will bring your risk of heart disease back to the same level as someone who doesn't smoke … non-smokers, on average, live 14 years longer than smokers. Quit today, and you'll extend your lifespan and live those extra years with a functional cardiovascular system, while being active and feeling great. (Wolfson 2013: np)

These life-and-death calculations are made along parallel lines – they are, essentially, Euclidean flat-space geometry rendered temporal: a future based on definitions, a proof of all theorems from a finite number of axioms or postulates. Having a cigarette? That'll be five and a half minutes off. Not having one for ten years or so? Add fourteen years. The Euclidean metaphor goes further: we could understand these two opposed histories as never-intersecting parallel lines, each running towards a different outcome, depending on what is done now, at the beginning of the line. The metaphor goes further still, if the parallel lines are thought of as (non-Euclidean) hyperbolic parallel lines, which increase the distance between them the farther they run from a common perpendicular.

But these versions of the future, flattened and distanced from one another as they are, running without deviation along a predictable and plot-able course, are often difficult to assert as clearly opposed choices in the life courses of smokers themselves, who might not recognize either future as accomplishable, or desirable, or even fathomable. These lives perhaps follow more anisotropic courses.

Anisotropy is the property of being directionally dependent. It permits analysis of substances or properties that are not uniform in all directions. The exact nature of anisotropy in a material depends on both its composition and the processes through which it has been. This has application in everything from sheet metal fabrication to neuroscience and, I think, analysis of human social life. It seems safe to say that some degree of anisotropy is always present therein, in the sense that we might each understand the future is reasonably directionally dependent on where we have priorly been, and how we are composed. And it is this anisotropic property, found in smokers that have subscribed to neither a future in which smoking cessation is desirable nor one in which smoking continuance is insurance of death, that undoes the surety with which such futures are presented in anti-smoking messaging.

The germ of an anisotropic sense of the smoker is to be found in Diprose's (2008) work on smoking. Following Keane (2002, 2006), Diprose observes that a body subjected to a flattened and determined future such as the one proposed in smokefree's 'either this one of death, or this one, of life' version, will try to emerge from the sense of timelessness that such a certain determination imposes. This body will try to reorient itself to an undetermined future. A nice little demonstration of this was provided to me early on in my fieldwork in Adelaide, when I watched a graphic anti-smoking advertisement with several smokers, in one of those moments when 'the field' stretched out to encompass a gathering in the home of an acquaintance. I'd obtained permission from seven people at the gathering to conduct interviews about their smoking. As we began to talk together, the host's television that had remained on in the background, played one of the graphic anti-smoking advertisements that were still new in the early 2000s, when I was conducting my fieldwork in the South Australian capital. The advertisement was one in which the aorta of a dead smoker, 'age 30', was squeezed onto a hospital tray to produce the sticky build-up within resultant of smoking. Seven pairs of eyes swivelled around to the screen. Stella, a long-time smoker in her 40s, said: 'God, that's gross, isn't it?' Alex, in his 30s, said, 'Yeah. Let's go have a fag.' I questioned both about this reaction as they headed outside to light up. 'Look,' said Stella, 'Everyone knows smoking can kill you and make you sick. The ads have the reverse effect on me; it reminds me that it's probably time for one.' Stella, it seemed to me, did not see her aorta as *that* aorta on the screen, despite the effort made in the advertisement to get smokers to accept that precisely this sort of damage was occurring inside their own bodies, and that just the same future – an early death – awaited them. Alex seemed also to refuse this certain outcome for his own body, as he joined Stella on the veranda for a smoke.

The reaction is one I've come across a great deal as I've chatted with smokers who continue to smoke in the midst of 'information overload' about smoking, as eighteen-year-old Lisa put it when I interviewed her in Canberra in 2012. 'I know all about the dangers of smoking – I'm well educated about it, like everybody else is by now,' she remarked. 'But no one knows how they'll die – I could get hit by a bus tomorrow!'

Not knowing 'how you'll die' is, as Merleau-Pontian phenomenology would propose, good evidence for the idea that a body orients itself towards an open and unpredictable future. Merleau-Ponty (1962) goes so far as to suggest that the property of uncertainty is central to agency – otherwise, life looks as though it might not need a driver at all. Thus, Merleau-Ponty's agent moves forward into a fairly open and undetermined future that has hopes, desires, prospects rosy and sinister on its horizon, rather than pure certainty. And, if it finds itself in a future that is too foreclosed and predicted, as Diprose says, it will try to escape – in the case of the smoker, via the retemporalizing capacity of cigarettes. It does so, I suggest, anisotropically – directionally dependently, variously.

The direction in which a body is oriented depends upon the processes through which it has been. Thirty-nine-year-old Nathan's body had been oriented to quitting, oriented to following that line down towards a long and healthy life. He was doing it, he told me, resultant of a 'bit of a health scare'. I asked Nathan about his attempt in late 2004. I'd met Nathan when he'd been hanging out with Josephine, one of Adelaide's recognizable, hard-core smokers who always smoked in the same spot, outside the accountancy firm where she worked. Josephine dependably appeared near a street planter filled with drooping petunias, where she also stubbed out her cigarettes, before work, at elevenses, at lunch, at afternoon break and at 5 on the dot. She hadn't wanted to be interviewed, but Nathan, who was in the very act of 'borrowing' a cigarette from her as I asked to interview Josephine,

**FIGURE 1** *Image of a clogged artery. Also known as 'The Brie Cheese Scene' in the television advertising version.*

*Source: Australian Government Department of Health Set A Health Warnings – Cigarette Packs http://www.health.gov.au/internet/main/publishing.nsf/Content/tobacco-warn-A.*

(© Commonwealth of Australia)

did. Josephine obliged Nathan's request for a cigarette and, as she did so, she did remark to me that she was often asked for cigarettes – everyone in the near vicinity knew where and when Josephine would be smoking. This, she said, had become an expensive practice for her, and she didn't always oblige especially when she was running low herself. But she did pull out her pack of near-full *Peter Jackson* Dark Blue 50s for Nathan. We left Josephine to her chain smoking and went to sit adjacent to her building to chat. I waited as Nathan lit up the first smoke he'd had, he said, 'for almost a week'. I waited while he inhaled gratefully. 'I've actually quit, you see,' he said, trying to explain why he needed to have Josephine's donated cigarette *now*. 'I don't so much buy that I'm addicted to nicotine,' he said, and continued thoughtfully:

> What I found really hard – the hardest – was that I didn't know what the hell to do with myself. You know when people say they don't know what to do with their hands? Well I didn't know what to do with my whole body. Like after dinner, which is the fag I miss the most next to the early morning one, – well, all of them I missed actually – I don't go outside for that one, because I'm at home. Well, I sat in the chair where my ashtray is, and I just felt wrong. I had nothing to do with my hands. I felt a stranger in my own body. And when I'm taking a break from work. Going outside and just standing there – so not the same. And the house itself; I so miss that smell – it smells like home so much to me – they said on the Quitline that I would start to smell and taste things differently, and I wish to God I didn't. I'll always think smoking smells like home. Mum and Dad both smoked, so I think I even associate it with their house.

Nathan's comments reveal that the unspoken composition of his own body sent this new direction to the healthful future wholly asunder. He hadn't quite realized just how securely cigarettes had inserted themselves into his body, his life. In and through frequent interactions between body and (cigarette) object, the practice of smoking both creates and maintains patterns of body use; our own bodies become ingrained through our interactions with objects including cigarettes. These are part of the 'techniques du corps' (or forms of bodily use) that define how a body is in the world, who it is, where it is, and where it can go (see Mauss [1935] 1979; Jackson 1983). But there is more to it than this; more than bodily use is involved, as smoking infiltrates bodies at the level of the senses.

As Nathan's testimony readily evidences, his unreflected, totally ordinary, processes of smelling, tasting, sitting in his chair, being at home, being himself are all inextricably intertwined with smoking. The thickness of his experience with smoking had not only penetrated his body to give him a bit of a health scare – it had also oriented his hands, his sense of smell, his tastebuds, his sense of what a home was like, how and where he spent his time. Despite his health scare that initially propelled him into seeking a future less portended with hospital visits, Nathan nevertheless returned to his habitual smoking past, for it was this past that allowed him to conceive of his present as liveable and his future as sufficiently uncertain, to the point, at least, that it does not include the absolute certainty of death. As he himself suggested, 'I dunno if I am going to die of lung cancer, but I do know that being without smokes makes me unhappy.' Ironically, from the perspective of smokefree, Nathan used cigarettes to retemporalize his future, to make it just unsure enough to be safe, and just safe enough so he could still feel at home. The smokefree future offered only bleakness; even the prospect of becoming healthier could not entice him to walk into its promise, of fourteen years more life. As I will argue in the next chapter, it's important to attend, anthropologically, to the possibility that smokers draw on ideas and notions that come from oppositionary geneses. Nathan drew on each pole of the smokefree atmosphere when he sat to smoke that cigarette 'borrowed' from Josephine – 'I've quit,' he said, as he lit it up, rejecting the smokefree future on offer, and equally rejecting the one filled with the certainty of death. I will suggest in the next chapter that such inconsistent logics might be worth examining.

None of the things I have said here mean that the set of relations between ideas, experiences and bodily practices are unbreakable. People, after all, quit smoking; some people even manage to do it for good. But quitting might just as easily be filled with the terrifying future of a totally unfamiliar and uninhabited non-smoking embodiment, in which even smelling is horribly unfamiliar. To Nathan, this future looked far more certain and worse than lung cancer, and he turned away from it. This smoking-derived truth is subtended by an intentional arc that opens Nathan's future to a range of potentialities over and above his imminent death from a smoking-related illness. After all, Nathan readily suggested several other ways in which he might die other than from lung cancer: he remarked of his failure to quit, 'Oh well. I'll probably die some other way anyhow. Probably in a car accident – I'm a bit of a boy racer on the road. Always have been.'

The notion of 'the future', as Nathan and Stella's words indicate, might not be thought of as a stark choice between two competing options, of healthful life, or ill health and then death. They may be a good deal more uncertain, bleary and unknown – as, as Merleau-Pontian phenomenology suggests, they must be in order to be apprehended as 'the future' at all; as Merleau-Ponty argued ([1945] 1962), in subjection, such as the reduction of the body to its biological components, the potential embedded in human agency (otherwise known as 'the future') 'goes limp'. The fact that viewers watching these advertisements are not dead or limp goes some way to explaining why many of my own informants, like Stella, refused to accept that their future was indubitably one in which their own lungs wound up on a hospital table, subjected to the interested views of surgeons and coroners, who might make advertisements in which they featured. So goes the anisotropic life of the smoker – and, indeed, most of us.

## Oppositionary pair: The time of smoking and the time free of smoking

The time of 'smokefree' is intended to be increasingly distinguishable from the smoky period preceding it; the period in which smoking was ubiquitous; when 75 per cent of men and 25 per cent of women were in tobacco's thrall, when smoking was omnipresent. This intention to make smoking absent is abundantly clear in both state and Commonwealth legislation. The Western Australia Cancer Council's cornerstone campaign, 'Make Smoking History', for instance, has been running for the last fourteen years, and the Commonwealth Government's Preventative Health Taskforce report, Australia: The Healthiest Country by 2020, produced a technical report optimistically entitled Australia: The Healthiest Country by 2020: Tobacco Control in Australia: *Making Smoking History* (Australian Government Department of Health and Ageing 2009).

Such language indicates the intention to make the presence of smoking into an absence of smoking, and a date for the accomplishment of this time has been proposed. On 7 October 2014, it was reported by news radio station 3AW that the daily smoking rate for twelve to twenty-four-year-olds in New South Wales and Queensland had dropped from 15 per cent to 11 per cent, on the back of the plain packaging legislation introduced two years prior. Professor Mike Daube, the head of the Australian Council on Smoking and Health, used the occasion to verify the impact and success of the plain packaging legislation and also to predict the end of smoking and the beginning of a smokefree Australia, saying he would see the end of smoking 'in his lifetime'. Professor Daube told radio station 3AW 963 Newstalk:

> Older smokers are dying off … and the younger smokers aren't coming up to replace them. I think we're going to see the end of smoking in Australia in my lifetime. (see 3AW Newstalk 2014)

Daube's prediction is one he and his Curtin University team made on a statistical modelling basis in 2005 (see Daube 2005). Seventy years ago, the smoking rate was over 70 per cent; now it's under 15 per cent. Should that trend continue, statistically speaking, there'll be no female smokers in Australia by 2029, and by 2030, there won't be any male ones either. Statistical predictions of these sorts are also attended by more feelingful predictions about the future, insofar as smoking is concerned. A Sydney-based doctor, who sees many smoking patients, remarked to me,

It's now aspirational to *not* smoke. The well-to-do and the well-heeled usually lead social aspiration. They used to be the smokers. We all wanted to look like them; now we don't. It's aspirational to *not* be a smoker. The well-to-do don't smoke; we're hoping over the decades to come that people won't smoke because it's not the 'done thing'. Oh gosh, it was so cool to smoke! And now it's cool to *not* smoke.

These sentiments make clear that a different, aspirational time, is waiting to be ushered in – it will be a time in which the wholesale turnover of class preferences has occurred, in which different categories of 'cool' are operational than before, when smoking was cool, and in which a once ubiquitous smoking presence turns into an absence.

As much as such statements as these vest faith in individuals recognizing and making manifest a class and social competence by quitting smoking or never taking it up, they also quietly reference the underlying prospect of a refusal to be pulled fully into the cool class thrall of not smoking. This refusal may be overt – middle-class tobacco avoidance is, for some, simply not cool. It may also be the case that acquiescence to 'the done thing' is not total: here we may consider secretive or inconstant practices of not-quite-non-smokers who might demonstrate social competence by publicly attending to class expectations, while secretively smoking under the class radar, or else positioning their infrequent smoking as 'social' – something that might well be safely done well within the confines of the middle classes. As Thompson, Pearce and Barnett (2009) note, the overt (class) threat – overtly present in the statement of the medical practitioner quoted above – of being tainted with dirt and disgust – only goes so far. They note in particular that social and secret smoking might be fruitfully conceptualized as 'nomadic identities that … always … [have] the potential to slip into one or other identity more permanently' (2009: 565). Such bodies, who might have a cigarette with a champagne with friends, or might comply with social expectations not to smoke in public and indulge in smoking in private, will always be, in Thompson et al.'s words, 'competent' – including being competent at dodging the compulsions of denormalized, overtly anti-smoking terrains.

Two other elements might also be considered to disrupt the straightforward conversion of smoking presence into smoking absence, and both speak back to assumptions of the pure establishment of a smokefree time. The first of these has to do with the basis upon which statistical predictions of cessation are made: the character and form of the smoker herself. The Curtin University study in which the statistical prediction for the end of smoking was made includes the caveats that anti-smoking programmes must be continued and the tobacco industry prevented from advertising or helping to develop policy (see Daube 2005). However, the study's caveats *do not include* what might happen to that prediction if there is an unexpected stall in smoking cessation, as there was in the mid-1990s.

That stall is understood to have occurred because of a lack of comprehensive campaigning of the harms smoking causes, and was addressed in and through the development of a scare campaign launched by then Federal Health Minister Wooldridge in 2000, and described by him as both 'gruesome' and 'graphic' in its imagery and wording, which I will discuss in detail in Chapter 4. The commitment to what Hill and Carroll (2003) call this 'fear appeal' has been kept up ever since, in that gruesome, graphic national anti-smoking advertising campaign featuring dead aorta, and in 'plain' packaging imagery and wording.

In the seven 'Set A' health warnings on packages, (which run in years ending in an even number) for instance, are included:

- A graphic of peripheral vascular disease, represented in a gangrenous foot just prior to amputation, with the text, 'Smoking damages your blood vessels, which can prevent blood circulation, particularly to your legs or feet. This can result in blood clots, infection, gangrene, even amputation.'

- A graphic of death, represented by a bar chart of other causes of death in Australia, with the text, 'Smoking causes more deaths than murder, illegal drugs, motor vehicle accidents and alcohol combined. Smokers not only live shorter lives, they also live more years with disabling health problems' (see Australian Government Department of Health 2012a).

Set B, which adorns packs in odd numbered years, includes:

- A graphic of foetal harm, represented by a baby on life support, with the text, 'Smoking during pregnancy reduces the flow of blood in the placenta and limits oxygen and nutrients that reach the growing baby. This increases the risk of miscarriage, stillbirth, premature birth, complications during birth, or the baby having a smaller brain and body.'

- Graphic of heart disease, represented by heart bypass operation in progress, with the text, 'Smoking narrows the arteries to your heart, causing them to become blocked. This can cause heart attacks and death. Smoking can double your risk of dying from a heart attack' (see Australian Government Department of Health 2012b).

Images like this will soon be appearing on cigarette packs to make smokers more aware
of the health effects of smoking and to encourage more people to quit.

Every cigarette is doing you damage

**FIGURE 2** *Set A health warnings.*
*Source: Australian Government Department of Health Set A Health Warnings – Cigarette*
*Packs http://www.health.gov.au/internet/main/publishing.nsf/Content/tobacco-warn-A.*
(© Commonwealth of Australia)

As the Australian government's own 2011 research, commissioned to
investigate the case for plain packaging-with-graphic-images, makes clear,
there is a major problem with utilizing 'fear appeal': that the terrifying prospect
of death is effectively neutered by the tyranny of the familiar. *Smokers get
used to health warnings, and so they must be frequently issued with new
and more terrifying ones* (see Parr et al. 2011).[2] As Penny, a twenty-six-year-old

Images like these are now on cigarette packs to make smokers more aware of the health
effects of smoking and to encourage more people to quit.

 Every cigarette is doing you damage

Australian Government

**FIGURE 3** *Set B health warnings.*
*Source: Australian Government Department of Health Set B Health Warnings – Cigarette
Packs. http://www.health.gov.au/internet/main/publishing.nsf/Content/tobacco-warn-B.*
(© Commonwealth of Australia)

hairdresser whom I interviewed in Canberra told me as she took a quick
cigarette break outside her city salon,

These [graphic] cigarette packet labels used to scare the living Christ out
of me. I seriously used to not be able to look at them without wanting to

vomit. Now they're just like, yeah, that's what a packet of cigarettes looks like. You get used to things over time. These don't bother me anymore.

A question is thus raised, about how far warnings will need to go to maintain a status of 'graphic' and fear-inspiring, in an environment in which bypasses-in-progress, dying babies and amputation-ready feet already circulate. What will the mother of all health warnings look like? Of course, we do not yet know what horrors might lie beyond the gangrenous foot or the dying baby, or what new presentation of existing horrors might be made. But perhaps these are not the most important questions. I think a more important one is, *to whom will this warning be addressed?*

Presently, graphic warnings are addressed to the rational agent, whom I will discuss in detail in the next chapter. It is worth noting here, though, that delivering graphic warnings to the smoker who will respond rationally to clear information, by quitting a practice revealed to be very dangerous, invokes a logical chain that *begets* increasingly hard-hitting health warnings. For instance, smoking among pregnant women is not uncommon in Australia; 2012 research by the Australian Institute of Family Studies found 18 per cent of women smoked during pregnancy. The study found that younger mothers were more likely to smoke than older mothers, that almost 37 per cent of mothers under 25 smoked cigarettes during their pregnancy (compared with 10 per cent of mothers aged 30 and over) and that almost 36 per cent of mothers belonging to the lowest socio-economic quartile reported smoking while pregnant, compared to just 4 per cent in the highest-earning category (Australian Institute of Family Studies 2012). Dr Louise Farrell, vice president of the Royal Australian and New Zealand College of Obstetricians and Gynaecologists, describes these results as 'disappointing', remarking, 'We have had a lot of campaigns to get out there very strongly the adverse effects on pregnancy. So it is disappointing that 18% of women still smoke in pregnancy' (see Wells 2011). The underlying logic here is, the stronger the health warning, the clearer the message of harm, the more likely it should be that mothers discontinue smoking while pregnant; hence Dr Farrell's disappointment – the campaigns *should* work.

The example also suggests that stronger health warnings will be addressed to the lowest socio-economic quartile, as we move towards 2030's smokefree horizon. Smokers in this class category have steadfastly refused to become rational agents in response to health warnings, by quitting. In terms of raw numbers, Australia presently has more middle-class smokers than socio-economically marginalized ones – because Australia is an overwhelmingly middle-class country. But smoking is taken up more frequently and quit less frequently outside of this class, and so, relatively speaking, smoking is decreasingly associated with the middle class and increasingly associated with the poor, non-white population. These smokers, who smoke while pregnant, who won't be dissuaded from it even though terrifying warnings 'should' accomplish this, undermine the striven-for, 2030, *temporal* state of smokefree. Daube, who led the Curtin study that predicted the end of smoking in 2030, agrees: 'Of course, there will always be a few smokers just as zero unemployment doesn't really mean zero unemployment' (Daube 2005: np). Just as is the case with unemployment, the people who populate the smoker category in the time of smokefree – after 2030 – will be the non-white poor – as Daube also confirms in his public comments about his study's prediction. These smokers will be the 'not quite zero' of the zero smoking rate.

Even though a case for the absence of smoking is made in statistical terms, and may well come to pass – this state may be difficult to purely establish, and I do not mean simply that it will be hard to establish numerically, at zero. Rather, I'm suggesting that an *abject class* of smokers remains to 'challenge the master' (Kristeva, 1982: 2) – here 'the master' is the middle-class preference for non-smoking. Already, in the realm of space, smokers constitute a source of class contamination, as they sully the air – an increasingly odourless middle-class air – with smoky evidence of their class. They equally contaminate the temporal register, making 'zero smoking' much like 'zero unemployment' – a striven-for time sullied by the contaminating, stubborn continuance of an abject class. The obedient following of the well-heeled into cessation doesn't seem to reflect the statistical profile of smoking in Australia, in which smokers tend to populate the lower registers of the socio-economic order in greater proportions than in the middle classes. It seems that smoking belongs, as a time, to the disenfranchised who stubbornly refuse to relinquish it in favour of a smokefree future, or to submit to medical authority over the truth about smoking, or to inhabit a new identity of 'non-smoker'. They also, it seems, refuse the offer of life, over the certainty of death that comes with smoking continuance. These stayers ruin the clean break with the smoking past that is predicted, by 2030.

Another temporal adulteration menaces the pure establishment of a smokefree future: the presence of thirdhand smoke. The literary theorist Steven Connor (2008) speaks to the temporal disobedience of smoke, noting,

> Smoke is not just matter out of place, invasive, insidious, miscegenating, it is also time out of joint. ... The great innovation of the modern city is not the increase in smoke as such, for we may assume that human settlements have often been smoky, but the institution of the chimney. ... The chimney connects, but in order precisely to keep at a distance, two regimes of space. At one end, there is the hearth. ... At the other end, there is open or centrifugal space, in which precisely, the centre flies out or away. But these two spaces are also different times. The hearth

connotes the here-and-now, the at-hand present. The air is the prospective past, a kind of translucent temporal sink in which our effluents can be not only *à perte de vue*, but also *à perte de mémoire*, lost in and from memory. Smoke is the sign of the reluctant vanishing, of the clinging, malign persistence of the past. (2008: np)

This malign persistence of the past is more than just figurative. Recent speculations about the pollutive qualities of thirdhand smoke permit us to think of smoke in almost heterochronic terms. Bell (2014), for example, observes that we are beginning to see the emergence of 'scientific' reports that describe the sinister capacity of smoke toxicants to hide themselves from view, on surfaces, in the clothes the smoker wears, the scarf, the jacket – these are descriptions of 'thirdhand smoke'. Thirdhand smoke disrupts the integrity of the period called 'smokefree', manifesting in a lurking past that makes claims of a smokefree future dubious. Public health warning signs have begun to appear in the lobbies of hotels in which smoking was once permitted, to warn patrons that smoky residue might 'offgas' in the present time of 'smokefree', ruining its neat distinction from the past. Here, smoke, or at least its lingering legacy, lies in wait in the curtains, the carpets of such places, visibly undetectable, bearing harm a long time in the making. Smoke is temporally uncontainable matter, which apparently has the capacity to preserve itself from the past, lurk in the present and impact future air quality.

## Oppositionary pair: Two spatial states

The temporal distinction between a smoky past and a smokefree future finds thickness and form in spatial terms. One immediate way in which an increasingly smokefree future asserts itself in the present is in the restriction placed on smokers' movements in space. Peripatetic practices undertaken in the new smokefree, when undertaken with cigarette alight, come quickly to constitute particular and immediate sensorial knowledge of the political meanings of space and time, as Isabella, a forty-six-year-old smoker from Canberra, came to realize.

In the ACT, where Isabella lives, robust public place legislation is in place. The initial act dealing with smoke in public places sought to prohibit smoking in enclosed public places that meant smoke could concentrate in the air, in effect, inside a contained area. By 2003, the Smoke-free Areas (Enclosed Public Places) Act was replaced with the Smoke-Free Public Places Act, which has a rather wider reach, since it is not only concerned with keeping smokefree that air circulating inside an enclosed area, and permits smoking to be prohibited outside *enclosed* public place, although not on public land. 'Public land' refers to areas falling outside the legal definition of public place and are not commercially occupied including footpaths, and land adjacent to commercial premises (see ACT Government 2003). Thus, one might, without any fear of breaching the legislation, smoke on a footpath clear of its designated non-smoking zones, on a vacant lot or on other interstitial space.

Isabella, a smoker 'all my adult life', recounted to me the day she was 'yelled at, loudly', by an irate cafe proprietor in the suburb of Acton, close to the ANU. Isabella had just left a cafe on campus where she'd enjoyed a coffee with a friend, and was heading to the centre of town to catch her bus home. She'd lit her cigarette as she left the cafe, but hadn't even thought about how the wind on that blowy day might carry the smoke from her cigarette into the window of another cafe at the edge of the campus, from which an angry head promptly emerged. The chef proceeded to berate Isabella for smoking on the premises of a cafe, even though she was located on public land. Her smoke, however, *was not;* it had preceded her, and had already made it inside the public place of the café.

Isabella's experience clearly indicates that smoking spaces and smokefree spaces are ideally to be kept separate in the era of smokefree, demarcated by law. While the law is clear on paper – the ACT Smoke-Free Public Places Act 2003 prohibits smoking in outdoor eating and drinking areas, in public *places*, and permits it on public *land* – it is very unclear in practice, and extremely difficult to accomplish in this pure legal form that differentiates one kind of place from another. The moving, smoky air refuses to remain sited in place, complicating the legal purity. The ACT government website remarks upon the difficulty, noting,

> A situation may arise in which smokers exhale smoke on public land which then drifts into adjacent public places. If smoke from these areas is drifting into a premises' outdoor eating or drinking area, you may wish to ask the proprietor of the establishment if they could ask smokers to move further away as a courtesy to other customers. However, there is no legal requirement that these smokers move further away. (see ACT Government 2003)

Isabella's experience, highlighting as it does smoke's propensity to move through the air, is actually indicative of the *illusory* purity of the smokefree place and of the impossibility of holding smokefree and smoking spaces apart in the atmosphere of smokefree. Indeed, it is only smoke's capacity to travel that it is at issue here – since Isabella and the outraged chef remained firmly within the two categories recognized by law: the non-smoking public place defended by the chef and the public land upon which Isabella smoked: the spatial state 'smokefree' fails to find stability of form because of the smoky air itself, which *refuses to be stable.* Its instability means there will always be shouting chefs, and the notion of the smokefree place, characterized by the unsullied air within its bounds, will always be illusory.

Smoke wafts into spaces, times, bodies that are supposed to be, in the era of smokefree, increasingly characterized by the absence of smoke. *Smoke itself* has the capacity to cross the bounds that separate one kind of thing from its opposite: the place free of smoke, the time free of smoke. As material, smoke leaks, lurks, sidles, transcends, wreaths silently in and through all manner of proclamations, classifications, categories, taxonomies and the spaces, times and bodies to which they relate – such is its nature. Smoke is a natural disrespecter of such parameters.

# 3

# Reimagining the smoker

## Introduction

In 2007, Mair and Kierans noted the growing alignment between public health goals of reducing smoking prevalence, and social science scholarship on smoking, that I mentioned in the previous chapter. They noted then that this alignment had its genesis in the desire of many researchers to ensure that tobacco companies could not make use of research work, which was often concerned with reporting how smoking figured in the lives of smokers, to promote its own interests. Experiences of the pleasures of smoking, for instance, became problematic to report – what would the industry do with such information? Such concerns have been highly consequential for what counts as research; 'legitimate' tobacco research is now almost always the kind characterized by its commitment to ridding the world of the blight of tobacco (see Bell and Dennis 2013).

Speaking of alcohol and illicit drugs use literature, in which the consequences of alignment with the pole of ostensible rightness have been particularly thoroughly rehearsed, and speaking specifically of anthropological research, Hunt and Barker (2001) argue that it has become impossible for research to issue 'from a mixture of critical developments within particular academic disciplines' in such circumstances. Knowledge is instead constrained within the parameters set by specific policy requirements that are 'often determined by moral, salvation and government entrepreneurs and channelled through the major funding agencies' (2001: 171). Hunt and Barker further note that such conditions dictate how particular fields of expertise are pressed into service. This is highly consequential for anthropology; despite the ostensible 'rightness' of a particular application of the discipline – to, say, attempt to minimize the harms of drug consumption – the cost of this application is borne in the equal minimization of anthropology's capacity to ask critical questions, particularly when it comes to the smoking person and how she is constructed in the smokefree atmosphere.

Tobacco companies and public health experts, each imbue the smoker with key characteristics that in fact, as I will demonstrate, are roughly *the same: each constructs a doubled smoker, the smoker to whom rational appeals can be put, and the mindless consumer who can be manipulated.*

Many tobacco company websites assert that the smoker is a well-informed selector of a product that she knows contains an addictive substance that might cause her ill health. Theirs is a wholly rational consumer, weighing up the costs and benefits of choosing to smoke. But, as the tobacco industry's swift legal challenge to Australia's plain packaging laws made abundantly clear, the industry's smoker is also one who slavishly and subconsciously responds to nuances in cigarette packaging – the shape and size of the letters used in the inviting words, the seductive imagery, the pack colours – all the things that plain packaging legislation took away from the industry, but not before it had mounted a legal challenge to retain its 'bonsai billboard' (see Pottage 2013).

In the industry's imaginary of the smoker are, then, present two versions of the smoker that coincide beautifully with Cochoy's (2002) analysis of the agency of material packaging. Cochoy observes that economists treat the package as a direct representation of those qualities of the product that are apt to engage the calculative intelligence of the rational actor, while sociologists and cultural theorists 'detach signs from products, and identify them as instruments of manipulation' (Pottage 2013: 526).

This doubled consumer revealed by economic and sociological analyses is also strongly present in public health constructions of the smoker. Public health's smoker is the enslaved addict, wholly in the clutches of nicotine. She is also the ignorant consumer who is insufficiently informed about the dangers that tobacco smoking presents – but can be turned into the rational, calculative agent once presented with the correct information.

In both the industry and public health accounts, the rational consumer is privileged. In Australian public health messaging around tobacco, the smoker is much more frequently addressed as someone who can respond to persuasion, who can be reached by health information. The compulsion to smoke, understood as the manifestation of the addictive properties of nicotine, can be overcome by additional pharmacological support. The industry has little choice but to present its smoker as a rational consumer, fully aware of the harms her choice to smoke presents, since it can no longer disguise the harms of the practice, as it once did. A fully informed consumer is the *only* consumer it can validly present.

Academic players, too, invoke both versions of this smoker, establishing either a 'dependent consumer' who is susceptible to begin smoking because she is entailed in dire socio-economic conditions, and susceptible to stay there once she's addicted (as Kohrman and Benson do in their 2011 work) or else a smoker whose smoking accomplishes some purpose – such as entailing her in productive relations of social or material exchange – thus, the rational smoker, smoking with purpose, to array around her a liveable world. Baer, Singer and Susser's smoker, who smokes with the purpose of coping with drudgery and hard graft at work, is just such a purposeful arrayer of the world.

As I've already suggested, anthropologists focusing on smoking have largely aligned themselves with public health's version of the doubled consumer. Perhaps this seems only right and, in the sense that no academic worth her salt would want to actively assist Big Tobacco in peddling its deadly products, it is right. The perils of this kind of alignment are immediately obvious. Less obvious are the dangers of aligning oneself to the 'good' side. For anthropology, these dangers are numerous. In this chapter, I chart some of these perils and offer up an alternative way of approaching 'the smoker'.

## The smoker, doubly constructed

The tobacco industry smoker is largely imagined in the terms of rational, if hedonistic, calculus, making an informed decision to smoke after having weighed up (if this pun can be forgiven) the drawbacks of so doing. Much of this 'drawback' information is now supplied on tobacco company websites – very likely as a consequence of the inability of companies to deny that smoking is harmful to health. This official sort of discourse, which companies have had to accept since the 1990s – when they could no longer deny the health hazards associated with smoking – is typified by an entry on the Philip Morris International (Australia) website (PMIA). This site informs its visitors that 'tobacco products, including cigarettes, are dangerous and addictive. There is overwhelming medical and scientific evidence that smoking causes lung cancer, heart disease, emphysema and other serious diseases' (PMIA nd). It also acknowledges that smoking is addictive, and can be hard to quit. The site also speaks of the pleasure that smoking brings, describing the 'enjoyment' and pleasurable sensations that are to be gained from smoking cigarettes, and particularly from its leading brand, Marlboro. British American Tobacco Australia (BATA) provides a similar characterization on its website, and in responses to the Australian government's regulatory landscape, like this one from 2009:

> While the only way to avoid the risks of smoking is not to smoke, a real world view suggests that a large number of people will continue to choose

to smoke even though they are aware of the risks. ... We accept that public health authorities seeking to reduce the health impact of consuming tobacco products should focus primarily on advising people of the risks. However, BATA also believe that many *informed* adults will still choose to be tobacco consumers. (British America Tobacco (Australia) 2009: 4)

These ideas are underwritten by the notion that the tobacco consumer is the informed rational agent who, eyes wide open, fully appreciates the dangers her enjoyment of cigarettes will bring her, even if she is addicted to them; she goes in knowing cigarettes will be hard to quit, but still makes the informed choice to smoke.

Presumably, the rational informed selector of cigarettes, of whom the tobacco industry speaks on its various company websites, is unswayable by the likes of frivolous package dressings, and still rationally chooses her product, even if it is contained in ugly olive brown packets with pictures of dead organs on them. In fact, tobacco companies have insisted that packaging has nought to do with a decision to smoke. Summing up the industry response after it had lost its High Court challenge, a spokesperson for Imperial Tobacco said, 'Packaging has never been identified as the reason people choose or continue to smoke'. (Pearlman 2012: np)

However, this promulgation belies the enormous ferocity with which tobacco companies fought the Australian government's bid to usher in plain packaging, and the aggressiveness with which it continues to fight it; currently, for instance, Philip Morris is suing the Australian government under an Investor State Dispute Settlement (ISDS) provision in a Hong Kong–Australia investment agreement. This provision, made in a trade agreement between Hong Kong and Australia back in 1993, enables investors to sue the governments who signed up to the agreement, if those governments act in a way that harms investor interests (see Australian Government Attorney-General's Department nd). Nine months prior to beginning legal action, Morris put its Australian-based business into the hands of Hong Kong-based Philip Morris Asia, which enabled it to claim that its trademark and intellectual property had been devalued by the Australian state. This sort of action indicates pretty clearly that the tobacco industry is very much loathe to quit the packets, replete as they were with pretty pictures, alluring colours and appealing graphics. Their attempts to retain this space of communication with the smoker suggest that the industry regards the smoker as a mindless consumer fully manipulable with words, pictures and colours. But tobacco companies are not the only ones who think of the smoking person in this way; public health does, too.

The mindless consumer of tobacco was identified in the government's own research (and in public health research more broadly) in the lead up to plain packaging. The research confirmed the tobacco industry's mindless consumer in its criticisms of packaging enticements, such as colours and appealing graphics, admonishing the industry for enticing smokers in, with appealing colour combinations, then invoked its own mindless consumer. This smoker would respond subconsciously, mindlessly, to a drab olive brown pack printed with a particular sort of font, just as surely as she had responded to the industry's exquisitely embellished one.[1] Indeed, smokers were imagined in just these 'mindless consumer' terms prior to plain packaging, when cigarettes were enclosed behind opaque doors so that smokers could not respond to the subliminal beckoning of an enticing packet. Explaining its point-of-sale legislation, which came into force in 2011, the Northern Territory government issued this public statement:

> Tobacco displays in the retail environment work with other forms of promotion, especially pack design, to raise consumer awareness, promote particular brands to young new, potential and experienced smokers and motivate purchasing. Displays are not only highly visible to smokers, but also to children and those trying to quit. Research shows displays provide a visual cue that can trigger 'impulse purchasing'. (Northern Territory Government nd)[2]

Invoking the mindless consumer who responded to pretty packets, Nicola Roxon, the federal health minister in 2011, declared plain packaging a vital measure in the government's ongoing 'War on smoking'. Plain packaging (which of course, is not at all plain, bearing as it does graphic imagery and text warnings) could be utilized to manipulate how people responded to cigarettes, and thus disrupt the tobacco industry's representation of cigarettes, made in and through appealing packets. As Roxon put it, plain packaging would effectively remove 'the last way for big tobacco to promote its deadly products' (Metherell 2012: np). She gestured to the many studies conducted over the past two decades that 'have backed plain packaging' (Metherell 2012), including the government's own commissioned study (Parr et al. 2011).

The government's study was carried out by Sydney-based consumer and market research firm GfK Blue Moon. The firm was commissioned by the Department of Health and Ageing in 2011 to determine the efficacy of new and expanded health warnings and plain packaging. The report consists of seven separate studies which, taken together, respond to the overarching research goal supplied by the government,: 'to identify one plain packaging design (colour, font type, font size) that would minimize appeal and attractiveness, whilst maximising perceived harm and the noticeability of the graphic health warnings' (Parr et al. 2011: 6). Study Two ('Consumer Perceptions of Plain

Pack Colour') drew on data collected prior to the commissioned period in December 2010 and tested 409 Australian weekly smokers of manufactured cigarettes aged between eighteen and sixty-five for their online responses to eight different colours supplied by the department (including 'caramel brown', 'lime green' and 'dark brown'). The survey utilized Maximum Difference Scaling; respondents were asked to select the pack they thought performed 'best' or 'worst' on the key test dimensions of 'appeal'; 'quality of cigarettes [contained inside a coloured pack]'; 'perceived harm to health', and 'ease of quitting'. On the basis of the findings from Study Two, 'dark brown', consistently considered by respondents as 'harmful to health' and 'harder to quit', was taken into subsequent stages of research, as was 'mustard', for the purpose of comparing the impact of a dark pack colour on graphic health warning noticeability with that of a lighter one. In Study Four ('Consumer Perceptions of Plain Pack Colour with Brand Elements') conducted in January 2011, 455 smokers were asked for their online responses to these two pack colours, on the same key dimensions as well as 'likelihood to smoke'. They were also asked about the impact of brand on perceptions of plain pack colour.

It was only when the GfK Blue Moon research team members noticed that 'dark brown' actually appeared olive when viewed on a computer screen that 'olive green' became a contender for a plain pack colour. It became a strong contender when 'dark brown' was associated more than once with chocolate by respondents, and when 'mustard' was frequently described as 'gold'; the association of both colours with pleasurable and 'rich' objects ruled them out as entirely unappealing colours. Thus, in Study 5 ('Face to Face Consumer Appraisal of Plain Packs with New Health Warnings Using Prototype Packs'), consumers were asked to rank three pack colours: 'mid olive green', 'dark olive green' (closest to the screen colour) and 'dark brown' from best to worst on the key criteria.

Despite 'dark brown' outperforming it in the face-to-face study environment, GfK Blue Moon declared 'dark olive green' the best candidate for plain packaging, since it did not have any positive associations with pleasurable things, like chocolate. The Australian Olive Association was quick to point out that although 'olive green' was not 'chocolate', it nevertheless had appeal, particularly in the form of the fruit after which it was named. Thereafter, the government agreed to refer to the new pack colour in all official public statements as 'olive brown', so as to differentiate it from the fruit, which is classified as either green or black (Wells 2012). Recommendations were also made on font, declaring Lucida Sans easier to read than Arial, and thus more suitable for information written on plain packs. Decisions on size and layout of graphic warnings included enlarging picture messaging on the front of packs so as to deliver a 'stop-and-think' reaction; so doing, according to the research, would 'best convey the seriousness of health risks, and thus [would be] the strongest "dissuader"' (Parr et al. 2011, 171). *Ugly colours, plain-as-day fonts; both could be used to manipulate smokers to regard the packs in a particular way – as unappealing.*

The government's own commissioned study is by no means the only one intent on drawing the smoker in, with colour, Lucida Sans and even with the width and weight of lines and borders. As Roxon said, the government's commissioned study was underpinned by the many existing studies that have examined the impact of packs on smokers (Elliott & Shanahan Research 2009: 5; see also Hammond et al. 2003). These studies have confirmed that the package's exterior colouring and a lack of brand marks enhance the effectiveness of health warnings (see, for example, Goldberg et al. 1999; Hammond et al. 2007; Wakefield, Germain and Durkin 2008). These have also been found to impact perceptions of harmfulness; for instance, some studies have found that smokers perceive certain colours like red and black to be more harmful than others (like silver and purple – see Hammond et al. 2009; Mutti et al. 2011). Also, it has been found to impact the appeal of the product; respondents saw the plainest packs as the least attractive and perceived smokers of such cigarettes as significantly less stylish and sociable, and the cigarettes in such packs were thought to be less satisfying and of lower quality (see Germain, Wakefield and Durkin 2009; Wakefield et al. 2008).

The claims, about the ability of the purpose-designed pack to influence smokers, are made by recourse to research that falls into two main categories. The first takes the form of experimental studies that seek to test how respondents make links between, for instance, graphic warnings, text-based information or colour, and harm, appeal, quality, etc.

These 'looking behaviour' studies abound. Wogalter and Rashid (1998) even go so far as to suggest that a border surrounding a warning affects looking behaviour, a result reported as effective in getting smokers to take warnings seriously in the Australian government's commissioned review of the effectiveness of graphic health warnings, as was using 'danger' colour combinations occurring in nature, such as black, white and red (see Elliott & Shanahan Research 2009).

The second kind of research commonly carried out takes the form of cross-sectional and longitudinal surveys with smokers, in which the impact of plain packaging and warning labels is assessed via participants' awareness of and reactions to the labels (e.g. Hammond et al. 2003, 2007, 2009). This research has consistently found that image-based warnings have a greater impact on smokers than text-based warnings only; that larger warnings are more effective than smaller ones; that plain packaging is less appealing than branded packaging, and is related to judgements about the (reduced or diminished) quality and taste of the product contained within.

Studies in both categories of research tend to conflate the research subject's responses and their smoking behaviour – between, say, noticing graphic warnings more on unbranded packs and quitting. For example, Munafò et al.'s (2011) study, which utilized eye-tracking technology to measure the responses of forty-three Bath-and-Bristol-based smokers to health warnings on branded and unbranded packs, found that respondents looked for significantly longer periods of time at warnings on unbranded packs. The conclusion drawn from this result was that the presence of eye-catching branding prevents smokers from receiving the full impact of health warnings. Despite the failure of their study to establish a link between the amount of time a warning is visually sensed and smoking behaviour, Munafò insisted in an interview with *The Guardian* newspaper that 'the [UK] government should introduce plain packaging of tobacco products and maintain text and visual health labels on packs; there is good independent evidence on the impact of visual warnings on attitudes to smoking and smoking behaviour' (see Tobin 2011). There wasn't; what did exist was the result that people looked at warnings on unbranded packs for longer. What this means is not clear, and certainly not clear to the extent that it constitutes 'evidence' for plain packaging.

There are, in fact, very few studies that move beyond looking at intentions and that focus instead on actual behaviour – one exception is the International Tobacco Control Policy Survey, which found that strong warnings on cigarette packages stimulated cognitive and behavioural reactions that in some cases translated into quit attempts (Borland et al. 2009). However, the researchers involved in that study made no claims whatsoever regarding the effect of the labels on smoking cessation outcomes, which is, of course, a key goal of anti-smoking legislation. As is the case with experimental studies, the relationship between self-reported effectiveness of warnings correlates poorly with actual behaviour change; as Hastings, Stead and Webb (2004) point out, 'effectiveness' is very difficult to judge among subjects who have been placed in an environment in which they are cut off from the ordinary practice of smoking cigarettes.

Effectiveness set entirely aside, we see the presence in such studies of the mindless consumer. In the first sort of research, the smoker is manipulable by recourse to line weight, colour combinations, font size and shape. This smoker responds almost beyond her conscious will – her eyes linger for as long as they will here or there on the packet. Her responses to 'danger colours' are almost primal, beyond her conscious preferences, as she responds to the natural chromatic signals for danger: red, white, black. It seems as though the graphic and textual health information placed on packets is designed to provoke that 'stop and think' reaction – but even this reaction is thought to be best provoked by elements like picture size, colour combinations, line weights and text style. Yet, the words 'stop and think' equally invite the smoker to weigh up information, to engage in calculative decision-making, to respond *rationally*.

# Public health's rational agent

The first NTS (1999–2003) indicated that the calculative, rational agent could be reached, stating that if only smokers were sufficiently educated about the harms of tobacco they might 'make an informed choice about its use' (National Expert Advisory Committee on Tobacco 1999: 10). But an informed choice would be difficult to make in any climate that is hospitable to tobacco. The goal of the strategy was thus 'to improve the health of all Australians by eliminating or reducing their exposure to tobacco in all its forms', to be achieved through six key tactics: 'strengthening community action for tobacco control'; 'promoting cessation of tobacco use'; 'reducing availability and supply of tobacco'; 'reducing tobacco promotion'; 'regulating tobacco'; and 'reducing exposure' to tobacco smoke in the air (Ibid: 2). Other strategies designed to reduce the consumption of tobacco were added to the provision of information about tobacco harms, including the ban on tobacco advertising and the implementation of graphic warnings on cigarette packets.

By the time the second NTS emerged five years later (2004–9), its opening statement read:

> The majority of smokers are not making a free and informed choice to smoke. … It is often said that smoking is a personal lifestyle choice. This ignores the superficial nature of smokers' understanding of health risks. … While consumers are generally aware that tobacco smoking is harmful, many still underestimate the extent of the danger relative to other lifestyle risks. Few smokers are able to accurately estimate their chances of dying in middle age. Most are able to name only a handful of the numerous diseases caused by smoking. Smokers also have little understanding of how tobacco-related illnesses could affect the quality of their lives. Few, for instance, understand that emphysema – one of the most common diseases caused by smoking – is irreversible, life-threatening and incurable. (Ministerial Council on Drug Strategy 2004: 2)

In these examples of expert public health thinking on smoking, the ignorant smoker needs only to be presented with the right information in order to reawaken her underlying propensity to rationalism (as Macnaughton et al. put it, she is 'a person with a stable core and epiphenomenal "behaviours" that can be removed by rational persuasion'). If she cannot be persuaded, she is the addict, the automaton, drawn in to smoking by the manipulations of Big Tobacco, and kept there by her need for nicotine. The addict is treated with pharmacological supports that are currently listed on the Pharmaceutical Benefits Scheme. The ignorant smoker must be educated.

Smoker ignorance is tackled, for example, in the NTS advertising materials, which often distinguish between what *might* happen to people who smoke to deliver a message about what *is* happening to their bodies when they smoke. Hill and Carroll note that the campaign known as 'Every Cigarette Is Doing You Damage', for example, was based on the idea that

> people are more likely to act on the basis of what they experience than what they are told, [thus] the communication challenge for the campaign was to translate the scientific knowledge about smoking into 'felt' experience, rather than induce merely a cognitive appreciation of risk. Acknowledging that people do not think probabilistically or behave 'rationally' in relation to *probabilities*, the core rationale behind the content of the campaign as it was executed was to describe the *certain consequences* of smoking, even if they are less dire than the uncertain ones, such as lung cancer and heart attacks. A slogan 'Every cigarette is doing you damage' to stress the ongoing effects of smoking and to counter the smokers' rationalisation that smoking is like a lottery (you are fine unless your number comes up). (Hill and Carroll 2003: ii9)

The intention, in 1997 and in subsequent campaigns, such as 'Breathless' and 'Symptoms', made under the 'Stop Before the Suffering Starts' campaign launched in 2011, has been to disabuse the smoker's rationalization, that smoking won't kill you unless you are unlucky in the life lottery, with educational materials that ram home the certainty of harm. For example, in the 'Suffering' campaign, the 'certainty' is far greater suffering of smoking-related illness than the relatively minor pain of quitting now. Once thusly confronted, the smoker makes the appropriate rational choice, to quit – as opposed to the false rationalizing that the smoker might be able to do, if she wasn't confronted with some indisputable facts. As Hill and Carroll note, ads in the 'Every Cigarette is Doing You Damage' campaign were designed to deliver a new piece of educational material and were intended to prompt an 'action' response or to reawaken the agent's lurking rationality which would, in turn, prompt the smoker to do as invited on the television screen at the end of each ad: call the Quitline.

The NTS 2011 'More Targeted Approach' was designed to reduce the smoking rate among culturally and linguistically diverse groups, pregnant women, prisoners, people with mental illness and socially disadvantaged groups via specific educational material tailored to each group. One 'selected culturally and linguistically diverse population' targeted in another specialized campaign is Aboriginal and Torres Strait Islander smokers, whose smoking rate is over 40 per cent. Current public health thinking about how to attack the adult daily smoking rate in this population extends the notion of the rational agent, but makes her more culturally specific and relatable to the target group.

The Australian government's flagship health programme, 'Tackling Indigenous Smoking', was tasked in 2012 with delivering the goal set out in the current NTS, 'to halve the Aboriginal and Torres Strait Islander adult daily smoking rate by 2018' (Intergovernmental Committee on Drugs (Standing Committee on Tobacco) 2012: 11). The national coordinator of Tackling Indigenous Smoking Dr Tom Calma, a Kungarakan Aboriginal man, claims a distinct relation between Indigenous people and tobacco, so distinct in fact that mainstream campaigns were not getting through to Indigenous people. He remarked, 'What we need to do is educate people so that they understand the relationship between smoking and poor health and disease and death' (Calma 2011: 29). Where the general population was under informed, or misinformed in thinking of smoking as 'a lifestyle choice' and in not knowing the incidence and consequence of emphysema, Indigenous smokers were completely uninformed, having no understanding of the relationship between smoking and poor health outcomes.

The distinct relationship between Indigenous people and tobacco itself is thought to be based on a number of factors. One is 'cultural' – that is, smoking bush tobacco as part of a traditional lifestyle. Another is colonization and dispossession – that is, smoking became prominent on missions and stations when people were paid in tobacco, the trauma and stress of removal from family for Stolen Generation members, and current trauma from racism, and from high incarceration rates. Another is the reinforcing role that smoking is thought to play in familial and social life, to the extent that people who don't smoke are 'isolated and alienated from the community' (Ivers 2011: 3). Socio-economic inequity is another factor, as is the way in which Indigenous people are considered to prioritize other (more pressing) concerns in their lives over quitting smoking, such as quitting alcohol or illicit drugs. Lesser access to medical services than the general population has is also considered an important factor (Ivers 2011).

These factors together constitute what we might call a 'cultural atmosphere' (which, incidentally, is also to be found enclosing and encompassing indigenous people in Canada and the United States – the interested reader may consult Winter's *Sacred Tobacco, Silent Killer* (2001) as a paradigmatic example). This atmosphere, springing from specific geneses, is thought to be tough to penetrate. Penetrating a thick cultural atmosphere requires culturally specific force.

The Australian government launched a culturally specific and 'hard hitting' advertising campaign urging Indigenous Australians to break the chain and quit smoking' hit the airwaves, newspapers and TV screens in March of 2012 (Calma 2011: 29) as the campaign 'Breaking the Chain'.

Designed to educate indigenous people 'so they understand', one ad featured 'Indigenous Woman' making a testimony to smoking's capacity to negatively impact Indigenous people generally, and the impact of smoking on her family in particular. The script, as it appears on the Australian government's Quitnow website, is as follows:

> Testimonial-style ad from an Aboriginal mother talking about her family's history with smoking disease. The various points she makes are punctuated, where appropriate, with cutaways to old photographs, sick relatives or other memorabilia.
>
> Indigenous woman: I watched Pop die: lung cancer from smoking. Mum had a heart attack: from her smoking.
>
> We see a picture of her family and her voice grows softer with concern for their health.
>
> Indigenous woman: My sis and Uncle Barry have trouble breathing.
>
> She looks sadly over to her sick neighbour's house.
>
> Indigenous woman: Rosy next door had a stroke and the doctor said it was from smokes. I was smoking for years too; but I quit.
>
> We see her own children playing happily in contrast to the illnesses and worry she is experiencing.
>
> Indigenous woman: Cos I don't want our kids growing up thinking disease and dying like that is normal.
>
> She looks directly to camera, strong and determined to change her smoking habits for the good of her community.
>
> Indigenous woman: If I can do it, I reckon we all can.
>
> Break the chain (Australian Government Department of Health Quitnow website (a)).

One Indigenous friend deliberately missing the point humorously remarked to me that 'Indigenous Woman' was 'bloody dangerous – being related to her, or even living next door to her would probably be fatal'.

The underlying theme of this (and advertisements offered in the 'more targeted approach') campaign discussed earlier has been to deliver education about tobacco harms to populations that are 'hard-to-reach' with education campaigns designed for mainstream consumption. Once such audiences are

**FIGURE 4** *'Indigenous Woman'.*
*Source: Australian Government 'Break the Chain' Campaign, http://www.quitnow.gov.au/ internet/quitnow/publishing.nsf/Content/ntc-break-tvc.*
(© Commonwealth of Australia)

reached, the desired outcome is that education will 'lead to further constructive behaviour changes within this audience' (Orima Research 2013: 157) or, in other words, will be equipped to *make a rational decision concerning smoking.*

At once confirmatory of the rational agent and the manipulable consumer, both public health and tobacco industry produce a doubled smoker. Essentially, they imagine the same person – each constructs a smoker within Cochoy's economic imaginary, capable of reasoning to either make an informed decision to smoke or to quit. Each constructs a smoker, also, who is firmly within the sociological domain of imagination. This smoker can be manipulated by public health messaging on the pack – even to the extent that her eyes, lingering on a health warning beyond her self-conscious attention, will deliver the subliminal message that she should quit. This smoker imagined in public health paradigm is at least as manipulable by means of the pack as the smoker who once responded to richly adorned packs distributed by the tobacco industry. Each invokes the same model of the smoker. Thus, neither industry nor public health's imagined 'doubled' consumer permits us new knowledge of the smoker.

## Anthropological reformulation of the smoker?

In the course of alignment with the public health goal of smoking cessation, anthropologists have engaged with and been critical of public health's narrowly defined 'doubled' public health subject, who can only ever be addict or mis-/ uninformed. Macnaughton et al. (2012) argue that the 'emotional and spiritual experiences contribute to the truth of human existence' as much as the explanatory bases offered by public health approaches (455) and they submit that comprehensive qualitative exploration of the smoker's world would reveal what is really needed to fully reveal the smoker: 'a complete picture of smoking meanings' (ibid). Such meanings might be gleaned, for instance, if we were to take seriously, 'descriptions of cigarettes as "companions" or "friends", deep reliance, sensual pleasure' (ibid; see also (see also Carro-Ripalda et al. 2013).

Others, like Kohrman and Benson (2011), two prominent figures in the anthropology of smoking, preceded Macnaughton et al. and Carro-Ripalda et al.'s calls for more ethnographic engagement with their 2011 summons to anthropologists to attend in far greater detail than ever before to 'the subjective experience' of smokers. Specifically, they issued an urgent plea to anthropologists to expand the bases of their present enquiries beyond contextual factors that influence why people smoke in different settings, and the production of gendered and ethnicized smoking patterns. They called for closer examination of those corporate predation and industry-related harm, cultivation of desire and addiction, and governmental management of disease elements, as well as the ethnographically documentable effects of smoking-related illness itself, including the ugly, fraught and sometimes fatal experiences of failing to quit.

Certainly, these calls for better explication of ethnographic context, more coverage of smoking over the life course, and a broader range of reasons that compel people to smoke, beyond addiction and ignorance have produced more analyses of the smoker, but these proffered alternatives for interpreting the smoking person, as I described them in the Introduction to this book, are just as problematic as assuming public health's smoker. There are three reasons for my view.

First, each of the proffered anthropological alternatives is amenable to the public health goal of smoking cessation. Macnaughton et al. make a case for the (complementary) place of the social sciences in the field of tobacco research alongside public health goals, and as Kohrman and Benson recently put it, anthropologists' efforts to find out about smoking must be in the service of furthering a commitment to ending the global tobacco epidemic. Anthropologists must be active in

> confronting tobacco in the years ahead. They must claim a larger role in research, policy debates, and social theory building and better diagram connections between tobacco and scientific production, state formation, the political economy of industry, and the subjective experience of dependent consumers and communities. (2011: 330)

As I suggested in the Introduction, restricting examination to the realms of the instrumental makes for an extremely narrow field of enquiry, permitting only certain kinds of questions, revolving around what causes people to smoke and how they might be stopped, to be asked and answered (Bell and Dennis 2013); this invariably produces only that sort of knowledge that is compatible with dominant paradigms (as well as with dominant patterns of funding, publication, etc.).

Second, whether responding critically to the ways in which public health approaches imagine the smoking agent or calling for the expansion of ethnographic purview, anthropological work generally replicates the view of the rational agent. Smoking behaviour becomes understandable in and through explanatory frames, variously, the public health favoured explanans of ignorance – it is perfectly rational that one who saw no harmful consequence of her behaviour would continue it – or else addiction: it is, of course, rational for the addict to source her drug; unless the agent is, as Macnaughton et al. point out, understood not to be an agent at all, but an automaton, wholly at the mercy of their compulsion (2012: 455). A rational frame might see anthropologists explaining smoking practice by recourse to, potentially, pleasure; maximizing pleasure might also be said to be rational, as indeed might any practice if only one can understand the agent's motivations.

It's worth pausing here to note that although an explanation for smoking by recourse to pleasure is possible, it isn't ever really done in this public health-dominated field. On the rare occasions on which pleasure has been invoked, it's been understood in very specific terms as the fulfilment of cravings – in other words as addiction (see Bell 2013b). In fact, the application of the rational frame dispenses entirely with an understanding of pleasure – the two are incompatible. But from an economic point of view, pleasure is quite important (as opposed to its [addiction] genesis being the most important). Consider 'the happiness quotient', as the US FDA has had to, in its analysis of the costs and benefits of regulations pertaining to graphic warning labels. This is a cost-benefit calculation that calculates how much a loss in pleasure (that smokers suffer when they quit) must be reflected in gains (in fewer deaths and less illnesses). This figure is around 70 per cent – and it has caused much consternation in public health circles, first because it's regarded as too high to properly justify graphic warnings (and this means tobacco companies have grounds to challenge it) (see Chaloupka et al. 2014). Second, the notion of lost happiness is fairly new to public health (or at least the idea that happiness is not necessarily the same as gains in health is new to it).[3] The near-impossibility of invoking 'smoking pleasure' outside of this is testament to the fact that the field is intolerant of any approach outside of 'rational agent awaiting re-awakening', or 'addict'.

Third, anthropologists examining smoking as a specific phenomenon seem to assume that ethnographic engagement is critical to 'deepening' this tightly imagined health subject. Calls to expand the ethnographic basis on which the health subject and her networks are embedded have long been made to counter the claim that people take health risks because they are ignorant of the harms of particular practices (like smoking) or, as Klein puts it, 'Perhaps one cannot simply weigh the advantages of cigarettes against the risks, if it is their very harmfulness that makes them sublime' (185). Williams et al. pointed out in 1995 that risky 'health behavior is very rarely explained by a lack of knowledge' (121). They recommended far deeper and more thoroughgoing examination of the everyday contexts in which smoking occurs, so as we might arrive at the real-life reasons why people smoke. But I don't think 'deeper' ethnography is the antidote to Williams et al.'s lament. I think we need to change how we approach the smoker and to resist the compulsion to translate her world in the narrow terms that avail themselves when the questions are, 'Why is she smoking' (and how can we stop it?).

As I said in the Introduction to this book, anthropological work to date has tended to produce the view that the smoker's world is fully knowable ethnographically in those narrow terms and can be translated for others who dwell externally to that world. One must find, at first, the basis upon which smoking can be explained – dependence, ignorance, as a means for dealing with anger, as a culturally specific coping mechanism – and then elaborate that world in ethnographically fulsome terms for it to become intelligible to externally located others.

This, of course, is not solely a consequence of anthropology's alignment with public health research on tobacco. Anthropology has a very long tradition of translating the otherwise inexplicable lives of others in terms that make those strange others intelligible to external observers, using deep ethnographic means to do so. Anthropologists are very familiar with the idea that groups of 'others' do odd things that are not immediately understandable to external observers; in the case of smoking, smokers do something befuddling and inexplicable to many: they inhale deadly gases that could harm or disfigure them. Other anthropological subjects, like Trobriand Islanders, practise strange magic.

By long-standing tradition, anthropologists are familiar with and even wedded to the notion that ethnographic work can get to the bottom of what seems so strange about inhaling gas or doing magic, and can translate it into the familiar. Consider Malinowski's (1954) insistence that becoming embedded in the everyday contexts of life would yield reliable data about how people live, how they think, how they act. Recognizing in his own data the differences between narrative description and what actually went on, he cautioned that to understand what was *really* going on, the ethnographer 'must relinquish his comfortable position on the veranda'. In a letter to his fiancée, Elsie Masson, Malinowski described his delight at going fishing with his informants and remarked of it: 'This one expedition ... has given me a better idea of Kiriwinian fishing than all the talk I heard about it before. It was also a more fascinating though not necessarily an easier method of working. But, it is *the* method' (in Kuper 2004: 29). And surely it is the method, but it came complete with Malinowski's insistence on how we should understand the Trobriand person – in particular sorts of terms that Malinowski decided would be the basis of his translation: rationality. 'Magic' rituals, derided as the height of irrationality at the time of Malinowski's fieldwork, were revealed under his hand to be highly sensible, a basis that disallowed from that time on the anthropological distinction between the 'primitive' and the 'civilized' person. Trobriand Islanders became intelligible – in Western, civilized terms. Smokers, too, become intelligible, by and large when anthropologists present their inexplicable and puzzling behaviour in rational terms – she smokes because she is addicted, because it permits her social participation, because she is ignorant of its harms, because cigarettes are her friends – they are a sort of social pleasure, that of company, if you will.[4]

There is an internal consistency made, *insisted*, in such analyses as whole worlds are arrayed around the explanans we choose, as we translate only apparently Kafkaesque worlds into the plainly understandable. I recall its seductive invitation well myself.

## Michelle the rational smoker

I last felt it when delivering a paper in 2004 to a panel of doctors and public health experts in Adelaide, South Australia. I reported to the panel the results of my early fieldwork among some young pregnant women smokers and when I concluded and invited the panel's questions, one of its public health members remarked, 'Well, I am both utterly shocked and enlightened! I didn't know that they (smokers) did it (smoked) for that reason (of particular risk avoidance – I'll detail this below). My only question is, how to stop them? Clearly, we need people like you (anthropologists) to get more information on the other aspects of smoking we do not yet know about.'

Trobriand Islanders are rational, smokers are dependent consumers, and, in one of my own early analyses, to which the panel member's remarks, above, were directed, a sixteen-year-old-smoker called Michelle occupies a world characterized by an integrity spun around her decision to avoid risks never imagined in public health warnings. Sixteen and heavily pregnant, Michelle chain-smoked during our hour-long interview. Returning the disapproving looks directed her way by passers-by with equal vigour, Michelle explained that she wanted to reduce the birthweight of her baby; she had learnt from the package warnings 'Smoking reduces the birthweight of your baby' that smoking was an effective way of so doing, and could thus reduce her fear

**FIGURE 5** *Michelle, just as I first encountered her, and her friend Sam, also pregnant, also 16, also smoking.*

of giving birth to a large infant, and so she sought out those packs with this particular health warning on them, and those packs only, to sustain her hope that the health warnings were true and effective.

'I always buy the ones that tell you how your baby can be underweight if you smoke,' she said. 'If I don't get that one, I ask for it. My sister had a whopper – she split from end to end,' Michelle continued, making a ripping motion with her hands, as if she were tearing cloth. 'That's not happening to me – no fuckin' way. If this [she declared, brandishing her packet of *Horizon Blue* smokes] can help – I'll do it.' 'Aren't you worried about the impacts on the baby?' I asked her, unable to keep concern (and perhaps some judgement) out of my voice. 'Kind of – but they told me at [the hospital prenatal] clinic I'd have to quit cold turkey – that isn't gonna happen. Anyway, I know two other girls, smokers both of them, who've had babies over the past couple of months – the tiniest, cutest little baby girls, they had, both of 'em. And their babies are fine.'

In my original analysis of Michelle's remarks about her engagement with the public health information provided to her, I intimated that there was purpose behind maternal smoking – that women like Michelle could dissolve the mystical distance between themselves and the ofetus using tobacco, in order to wrest a bit more control over frightening and uncontrollable elements, like the size of the baby (see Dennis 2006). Later, I developed a more forthright stance – I spoke back directly to the dominant public health framing of smoking practice: that smokers smoke because they are addicted, or because they have not yet been presented with sufficient or culturally appropriate information about the dangers of the practice. I objected to the narrowness of these explanans and suggested that Michelle was compelled by quite other bases to smoke – certainly by quite other ones than addiction, or ignorance, which seemed not to figure in her practice. I argued that a different basis should be at the heart of how we understood Michelle's smoking practice: producing the small baby she wanted and the diminishment of risk of a large one. I argued that some smokers, at least, find potential in the practice of smoking, according to their own designs for rational, outcome-directed action. Michelle weighed up the risks (ripping 'end to end', the pain of birth, the pain of quitting cold turkey) and the benefits (underweight baby) against the evidence she had (two little babies born to friends recently, her own birth to a smoking mother) and made, in the context of her own knowledge, a rational decision perfectly consistent with what I had decided was the foundation of her world – her internally consistent world. I had determined that at its centre was Michelle's hitherto unrecognized capacity to rationally take control of that which was ostensibly uncertain and frightening: the spectre of the enormous ofetus. And I did so by recourse to ethnographic data pressed into the service of my claim that Michelle was a rational risk-avoider; it just took deep ethnography to see her as such (see Dennis 2011).

Later reflection on my interpretation of Michelle's story (see Dennis 2013) reveals that I replicated the very sin I had accused public health analyses of committing. I had simply changed the explanatory basis for Michelle's actions. Instead of being ignorant of the harm caused by smoking, Michelle was aware of it and used it to offset a nastier risk. Essentially, I had arrayed an equally internally consistent world around Michelle, to make her otherwise inexplicable behaviour intelligible to those located outside it. Where public health would have interpreted Michelle as ignorant, and not yet rational, I cast her as already rational, in the context of the accomplishment of her desired goal.

## Michelle, reanalysed

In 2003, Bruce Kapferer urged anthropologists to rethink notions of internal consistency. Arguing that rationality lies right at the explanatory centre of analyses of magic, witchcraft and sorcery, in the sense that witchcraft becomes intelligible in dominant functionalist analyses as a rational mechanism for releasing social tensions and explaining misfortune, or else psychological expressions of desire, or else emergent to control that which is out of one's hands, Kapferer invited anthropologists to step outside of its analytic neatness.

Specifically, Kapferer urged anthropologists to see witchcraft as something more than just a by-product of despair, symptom of social malaise or a frantic stab at trying to reassert control over a world undone by change. He argued instead that the practices of witchcraft were best viewed as sites of invention, as *hybrid forms* to be associated not only with formations of power but also with cosmological fusion and religious innovation.

Following Kapferer's observation, that 'sorcery and magic are hybrid forms par excellence' (2003: 22), I want here to make a parallel case for smoking. As Kapferer notes of witchcraft magic and sorcery, if we dispense with this explanatory mode and introduce one that attends to the structural properties of practices themselves, we begin to see that they work to force together things that are normally held apart (or else they break apart that which is normally whole): as Kapferer notes, these qualities are

> refracted in the monstrous dimensions of sorcery objects, which are frequently an amalgam of different forms, or something in the process of changing shape – a being or object frozen in a transmogrifying instant, in the process of becoming-other, becoming-animal. This process is one that is not yet subordinate to any system of reason or rule. Rather, it is a process at the moment of fusing or crossing different registers of meaning and reasoning. (2003: 22)

By way of making clear my own, current approach to the smoker, let us return to Michelle's case with these ideas, about the pulling together of things that are normally kept apart, just as smoke itself does, in mind. One of the key characteristics of Michelle's practice here is her creativity in forcing things together that are normally kept apart: public health knowledge and smoking practice. Public health information, – smoking can cause a small and underdeveloped baby – was *always* meant to be held apart from smoking practice that causes it. Michelle's is not so much a bounded and internally consistent closed 'system' of knowledge as it is a provisional one, developed in relation to specific events and situations. Michelle extends, adapts, even inverts, existing public health knowledge and its modes of constructing and patterning experience so that they fit her specific pragmatic needs and particularities. In this way, they create new forms of knowledge, dynamic ways of understanding and acting in the world, none of which could be appreciated from the vantage point of internal consistency or from the translatability of rational explication.

# Putting things that are meant to be held apart, together: The internal inconsistency of smoking

Judy, a woman working in my local supermarket just outside of Canberra, told me she had smoked on and off over fifty of her sixty-three years. She believed with great conviction in the iron strength of her father's lungs and her own inheritance of that strength and was therefore immune to the fear campaign she felt the state was running to get her to quit. 'I come from a long line of 'em,' she said, not without pride, as I engaged her in conversation as she worked at the cigarette counter, and then when she took her cigarette break:

> My dad smoked, his dad, and my mum, smokers them all. And, dad was 92 when he died, mum was 87, and my dad's dad had a good innings, too, being close to 90 when he died. Gawd, imagine if it's true what they say, that smoking can take 20 years off what you'd expect to live. How old would that have made my old dad, eh? I make that around 122 years old.

I asked Judy about her responses to the graphics that adorned her packet. 'Well, now,' she said, bringing her glasses down from the top of her head, and peering at the packet. 'This 'un has a pair of lungs on it, see?' 'How does that make you feel, Judy?' I asked her. 'Not scared, if that's what yer after!' she said, with a glint in her eye:

> There are people more disposed to it [lung cancer] than others are – I've got iron lungs, like me old man had. He didn't die of lung cancer, as you might be supposing, and I suppose you are supposing that – well, you'd be wrong! He had a fall, see, down the stairs. He was too old, and his old body broke right up from the impact. Me mum was dead less than a year later – and I don't care what nobody says, she died from a broken heart, yes she did indeed.

According to the WHO, cigarette packets make excellent billboards for harm messaging because they are enfolded into the praxis of the everyday lives of smokers; packs are constantly and mundanely present for smokers 'every time they purchase or consume tobacco products' (2011: 23). Exposure to this billboard and its frightening messages is intended, of course, to appeal to the smoker in a particular way – it is intended to produce the 'stop and think' response, to get the smoker to make the link between the damaged lungs on the packet and the condition of their own lungs, and to reject the grim future indicated by their susceptibility to premature death. In Judy's case, they were supposed to disrupt the good luck of the life lottery, dispensing with the idea that some people were 'more disposed to it than others'. But the frightening information about the relationship between lung cancer and smoking cannot be relied upon to be carried through to smokers 'every time' they encounter it. Like Michelle's, Judy's case seems to indicate that rather than reliably receiving information as it is intended, smokers put public health information together with information of quite other genesis in a provisional process of construction and reconstruction.

Just as intended, Judy draws the information into concert with an introspective look at her own lungs, which she declared to me to be reasonably safe – at least, she was not frightened by the prospect of lung cancer being present in them; she knew them to be resistant, since her father and mother had smoked and had died from quite other causes. This had nothing to do with a lottery; it had everything to do with heredity. The evidence of a lifetime weighed in to Judy's incorporation of the health information she received from her packet. The graphic warnings on packs were always meant to be brought into introspective concert with one's own lungs, but it was certainly never intended to be enfolded into the development of a sense of safety and security in their durable condition. Like Michelle, Judy drew the practice of smoking into concert with the knowledge she already had of it, in an immediate, proximal way, to feel safe enough to continue. The messaging, Judy thought, applied to other people with less fortunate biological inheritances and more susceptibilities. The messaging reassured Judy, as it had reassured Michelle that she might not rip end to end during childbirth.

Perhaps the example par excellence of assumptions of internal consistency is one that highlights cultural consistency. I mentioned earlier the way in which indigenous smoking is addressed in Australia, in programmes that aim to deliver increasingly tailored information about smoking harms. This information is offered up on the grounds that current Indigenous smokers are largely ignorant of its harms, and it is assumed that this is largely because the information with which they are presented is insufficiently culturally specific.

However, when Wood et al. conducted a small study of forty pregnant Indigenous women in Perth, Western Australia in 2008, they found that the women knew plenty about tobacco harms. Theirs represents an initial attempt to consider how pregnant Indigenous women value the health information they have in the social, economic and other circumstances of their lives, rather than to array their worlds around an understanding of an internally consistent Indigenous world, which was culturally sufficient to prevent them from acquiring health information directed at the mainstream population. It also reveals how the women pulled the information on tobacco harms with which they were presented into concert with other kinds of health information they possessed. Wood et al. found that possession of knowledge about the risks smoking poses to maternal and foetal health did not produce a decision to quit; but it was used to make decisions about smoking in context. For instance, some women compared the risk of smoking with other risks they deemed more harmful, such as drinking or illicit drug use, and chose to eliminate those instead of smoking for the well-being of the baby.

Thus, using the knowledge they had about smoking harms in contexts where far greater dangers also circulated, these mothers-to-be had done something good, positive and healthful for their unborn babies. While such actions are often understood to be based on little to no understanding of the dangers of tobacco use relative to other substance use, Wood et al.'s informants did seem to possess all the relevant knowledge. There is, it seems, a difference between having knowledge itself and valuing and deploying that knowledge in any given context, where it might meet up with oppositionary knowledge to form a body of knowledge that works, at that moment, for that person.

It's not always the case that the provisional construction of knowledge about smoking and its harms results in knowledge that is always contradictory to public health aims. Fear of the dangers of smoking might very well produce some most imaginative irruptions – and, given the numbers who have quite, clearly this happens quite often. I'm not interested in effectiveness here – the point I make has to do instead with how we see the smoking person – how we might see, for instance, Karla.

Sixty-five-year-old Karla, who stopped smoking more than two decades ago, is already, for example, mourning the imminent death of her (still living) son Kayden, whom I interviewed in Canberra in 2012. Kayden himself wasn't so worried, but Karla interjected more than once as he offered his views about smoking to me. As he began describing how the government was acting as a Nanny State in its attempts to play up the health implications of smoking, a nigh on hysterical Karla pointed over and over again to the graphic image adorning Kayden's pack; a diseased heart muscle. 'But you'll die, you'll die!' she moaned.

Karla's very alarmed response to her son's smoking may appear to be perfectly obedient to the state's public health agenda – the images are intended, after all, to terrify with the prospect of imminent death. But instead of seeing Karla as someone armed with health information that had hit, exactly, its intended mark, it might be more productive to see it, along with the other examples I have included herein as an elaboration of their own, or as Kapferer has put it, in the terms of

> imaginal fields whose force derives not so much by what it is representative of external to itself, but in the potentialities, generative forces, linkages and redirections that it opens up within itself. ... This is not to be seen as modular or representational of external realities but rather as a reality all its

own, a dynamic space entirely to itself and subject to its own emergent logics [as opposed to the ones we might decide are most compelling from the position of external – anthropological, public health – expert]. The cosmology in which its inner praxis is articulated has no necessary connection to realities external to it and no necessary internal consistency. (2003: 22)

# Come off the veranda

This does not mean that the terrain of smoking is Kafkaesque, and that no one can penetrate its inscrutable, indecipherable thickness. And it certainly doesn't mean we should stop doing ethnography. What is needed is a disruption of the idea that more ethnographic detail equals a reconstituted smoker that departs from the narrowly defined public health subject. No amount of extra ethnography is going to change that – what's needed instead is a suspension of our own surety, about why people smoke, a reorientation of our certainty about single explanans (such as smoking is necessary for risk avoidance if you are a sixteen-year-old girl frightened of giving birth) that yield the outcome 'smoking', that seems to be characterized by much more multiplicity and variegation. What if Michelle was to continue to smoke post-birth of that baby? Would we simply say she is now 'addicted' and have this now array her whole experience of smoking? But it is not simply the case that we need to attend to multiple explanans – it is more that we need to resist the lure of the externally decided explanans itself and the internal consistency of the same. As Kapferer suggests of magic, smoking practice might contain its own 'truth', which is not subject to any kind of falsification that exists independently of it, including falsifications made in public health that insist smoking is bad for you, or anthropology that insists that you smoke because you're a dependent consumer, or because you are after pleasure, or belongingness, or because your socio cultural world makes harm messaging impenetrable. The potency of such a practice as smoking 'lies in its very irreducibility to externalities, which is achieved and effected through its imaginal formation' (22).

Smokers, it seems, like most other people, engage with the imaginative process of recombining elements of systems of knowledge into new combinations that help shape experience and bend it to the needs and particularities of the moment, whether that moment is devoted to making a small baby, or explaining how one inherits the iron lungs of a beloved father that afford protection from cancer, but not broken heartedness. These understandings are not made by or subject to the logics of existing knowledge structures, like public health messaging, but are instead provisional reconstructions of many, and they are organized according to their own internal and incomplete logics. Anthropologists would do well to tend to them thusly.

It's obvious that, among other things, I've really undermined the idea that smokers might be ignorant in the foregoing. I want to pause very briefly here to draw out the important point that something like ignorance could actually be very richly explored by anthropologists. As Flora (2012) has argued, 'ignorance' is not always congruent with 'not knowing'. She argues that ignorance has a substance all of its own, and proposes an internal logic to unknowing. While Flora does not suggest it, this structure might not be complete, and might reach out to other kinds of (un)knowing too. This means that the smoker might be best encountered anthropologically if the disciplinary fetishization of rationality is dropped, so she is not merely assumed to be calculatively responsive to circumstances such that she professes ignorance in order to carry on smoking. A truly anthropologically examined ignorance is very different from accepting public health's ignorant smoker, who lacks knowledge, and must be educated in order to become rational (see also Mair et al. 2012).

The smokefree atmosphere, as I drew it up in Chapter 2, is characterized by the holding apart of things intended and assumed to be one another's opposites – smokefree space versus smoking-permitted space (or, otherwise, public place vs. public land); smoking bodies versus non-smoking bodies; the period of smokefree versus the period that came before it; the public health state (and anthropologists) versus the tobacco companies. But these tensions are tricky to hold taut. They slacken, I have suggested, in the failure of temporal and spatial states, like 'smokefree', to be fully and purely established. The capacity of smoke to waft across time and space and in and through bodies in the pool of public air ensures the failure. Smokers, too, are, like most other people, capable of putting together incompatible knowledge categories that were always intended to be held apart, making a mockery of the sharp distinctions that can be drawn between different kinds of, sometimes even antagonistic kinds of, knowledge (or even 'ignorance').

The apparently polar opposites that make up the smokefree atmosphere are difficult to hold taut also because, as I have argued in this chapter, they tend to operate on similar, instrumentalist bases. The tensions of the smokefree atmosphere, when held taut by anthropologists who see it as their duty to keep at the other pole the deadly tobacco weed and its evil purveyors, permit only a limited view of smoke and smokers, keeping anthropology itself taut and inflexible to thinking about smoking in any terms other than those that continue the good fight. The rest of the book is dedicated to a more flexible approach that I outlined in this chapter, beginning with an inbound breath.

**PART TWO**

# First, second, third and fourth hand smoke

# 4

# Breathing in smoke(free), firsthand

## Introduction

Over the next two chapters, I shift my attention away from an explicit focus on how the smoker herself has been understood in favour of an analysis of the air itself. I look specifically at how the air itself has been explicated by the state in and through the foregrounding and separation of the much more usually intertwined and habitually backgrounded actions, inhalation and exhalation. These automatic and necessarily cyclic respiratory actions have been *decoupled* from one another in smokefree public health campaigns, and have been *foregrounded* in order that the impacts of inhalation on the personal body of the smoker and the effects of exhalation on the body of the public be made evident in state-sponsored public health messages.

In the case of inhalation, the subject of this chapter, notions of the toxicity of smoke-laced air drawn in through the cigarette have been mobilized to usher in an acute, present bodily and respiratory awareness of harm to the smoker. Here, air is explicated in terms of the toxicity it bears into the internal regions of the body when passed through the medium of the cigarette, via inbound breath. Once inside, it causes the smoker's insides to decay.

In respect of exhalation, with which I will deal properly in the next chapter, the harm that is done to (non-smoking) others via exhaled tobacco smoke is conceptualized as *miasmatic* in nature – an operation by which irresponsible smokers, who can be held to account by legislative and socio-moral forces, spread contagious pollution that impacts the entirety of the public body (or all breathers). These exhalations are conceived as bearing with them the decayed internal physical moral and social state of the smoking person (comprising rotted lungs and other parts of the respiratory tract that have direct contact with the air that will be expelled from the smoker's body) such that they might immediately infect other non-smoking persons. Horrified hands are held over vulnerable mouths and noses, frantic waving away of the smoke is undertaken, as non-smokers encounter a whiff of smoke that may be fleeting, but may also be deadly, responding to a miasmatic threat that they may not always be able to see, but can certainly smell. Some take this olfactorily detectable threat so seriously that they understand themselves to be waving away cancer, which can be *caught* in the era of smokefree from exposure to a fleeting encounter with exhaled smoke from a rotted source – the smokers own lungs.

Both personal inhalation and exhalation actions, when rendered through tobacco smoke, rely on particular explications of the air itself. It is quite unusual to attend to the air in this way at an everyday level, since air is necessarily backgrounded in the course of drawing it in and expelling it. But the disattendance that is necessary for us all continuing to be competent breathers and therefore alive is different from forgetting the air in analytic terms, or in other words treating it as a backdrop against which the real action of life occurs. In this chapter, I suggest that bringing the air itself to the fore has become central to the cultivation and mobilization of the smokefree atmosphere. Particular explications of the air itself are central to how its big ideals (i.e. the desire that smoking is made history) and its main goals (i.e. to bring down the Australian smoking prevalence rate) are brought directly to bear on the individual body of the smoker.

Here I am suggesting that it is not simply the case that the state *remarks on or makes clear that* inhaling air via the cigarette presents a health hazard to smokers, and inhaling environmental tobacco smoke is dangerous for non-smokers. As I will make clear in what follows (in my own explication of the state's explication of the air), the air itself is effectively reconstructed, crafted afresh, into something that it wasn't, quite, before its explication: the air is explicated as the harbinger of illness, even death, to smokers and non-smokers.

Newly explicated air is then *mobilized* by the state, acts in its service to bring the smokefree atmosphere to bear on (or, rather, inside) smoking bodies (as well as making its moral shape manifest to non-smokers). Such processes make the air not so much of a backgrounded element as an agent that can be pressed into service by the state to have real and consequential impacts on the bodies it simultaneously sustains. Air gets inside of bodies as breath: taking in the air and releasing it back into the public pool is a necessarily repeated everyday action in which the political, as well as the gaseous, is deposited, especially, as I will point out in this chapter, when one is invited by the state to pause to catch one's breath in the era of smokefree. *Breath bears with it on its* inbound journey not only life-sustaining oxygen or life-threatening toxins (and indeed both at once) but also politics, morals, norms – it brings the atmosphere of smokefree to bear directly on bodies by infiltrating them with a newly explicated air that requires new interpretations on the part of smokers and non-smokers alike. In the era of smokefree, the air is not neutral, or natural. Nor is it a background.

# The theoretical backgroundedness of the air itself

There is an old joke about two fish who meet up in the Pacific. One fish enquires of the other, 'How's the water?' The questioned fish replies, 'What the hell is water?' Just as the water falls beyond the puzzled fish's attention because it's very pervasiveness ensures that it will, scholars have tended to ignore the air. In *The Forgetting of Air in Martin Heidegger,* Luce Irigaray deals directly with what she sees as the particular philosophical folly of forgetting the air. In so doing, she reminds us of some of our assumptions about its characteristics. The book opens with the accusation that Heidegger's metaphysics is one founded upon the value of density or solidity, which she sees as fundamental in his work, in that he begins with 'a solid crust from which to raise a construction' (Irigaray 1999: 2). For Irigaray, Heidegger's is a physics that privileges the solid plane. She remarks that 'whether philosophers distance themselves from it, or whether they modify it, the ground is always there' (ibid). The work that drew this angry retort was Heidegger's essay 'Building Dwelling Thinking', in his *Poetry, Language, Thought*, in which he explicitly links being and the built form. This work contains his observation that the German *bauen*, to build, originally meant 'to dwell':

> *bauen*, … *[is]* our word *bin* in the versions: *ich bin*, I am, *du bist*, you are, the imperative form *bis*, be. What then does *ich bin* mean? The old word *bauen*, to which the *bin* belongs, answers: *ich bin*, *du bist* meaning: I dwell, you dwell. The way in which you are and I am, the manner in which we humans are on the earth, is *Buan*, dwelling. To be a human being means to be on the earth as a mortal. It means to dwell. (Heidegger 1971: 147)

Irigaray immediately takes Heidegger to task on this by posing the question, 'Can man live elsewhere than in air?' She takes a particular view of the air itself, speaking of 'its spreading, nourishing, infinite abundance' (a view that I shall critique in the sixth chapter, on the grounds that it is the case that the air, really, became thought of as 'finite' in the eighteenth century, thanks to an inescapable awareness people had of overwhelming air pollution). Irigaray links this conceptualization of air to dwelling, asking, 'Is there a dwelling more vast, more spacious, or even more generally peaceful than that of air?' Irigaray makes a distinction between the 'open air' and the air that 'lies between things', arguing that Heidegger's philosophy, in its privileging of solidity, is a kind of gathering-in, a petrification or vitrification of the open, fluid, abundant space of the female. She suggests that in setting up his standard, or taking his stand, the male consumes, 'gives his seal'. Thus, Irigaray frames air in terms of the difference between a closed or appropriative use of space in which air is contained, constrained and controlled, and a relation to space that is itself open and relational. On this basis, Irigaray accuses Heidegger of forgetting the air, remarking in her retort that the excess of air is so immediately 'evident' and yet so little 'apparent' that he did not think of it (Irigaray 1999: 8, 40).

Irigaray's counter to Heidegger reveals that when it is thought of, air has tended to be considered as solidity's opposite, and a kind of absence. Marx (1969 [1848]) described the constant change that he saw characterizing a 'bourgeois epoch' as a state in which 'all that is solid melts into air' (475–6), a turn of phrase served, in turn, as a motif for Marshall Berman's diagnosis of 'modernity' as a shared condition in which all grand narratives were subject to sceptical scrutiny:

> I believe communication and dialogue have taken on a new specific weight and urgency in modern times … [and have] become both a desperate need and a primary source of delight. In a world where meanings melt into air, these experiences are among the few solid sources of meaning we can count on. (Berman 1982: 8)

Here, air signifies a loss of grounding, but also indicated is the idea that air is as taken for granted in theory as it is in the habitual continuity of breathing. As Choy (2010) notes, this is 'unfortunate, because thinking more about air, not taking it simply as solidity's opposite, might offer some means of thinking', about, among other things, the 'atmosphere' of smokefree.

Tim Ingold's speculations about the air also reference the way we have tended to think of it as a background against which to act. His insistence that air and other 'non agent' matters cannot be interactant, only the meshwork for interaction, is based on an asymmetry between human or animal partners and the air. This notion is to be found in his 'When ANT meets SPIDER: Social theory for arthropods', which is worth quoting at length here:

> As ANT [Actor Network Theory – the Latourian position Ingold criticizes] and SPIDER [who stands for the proposition Skilled Practice Involves Developmentally Embodied Responsiveness, representing Ingold's own position] are conversing on the forest floor – surrounded by what ANT (the network builder) perceives as an assortment of heterogeneous objects

and what SPIDER (the web weaver) perceives as a tissue of interlaced threads – something else is going on in the air above their heads. A couple of butterflies are dancing. 'Observe', says ANT, 'how in its fluttering, each butterfly responds to the movements of the other. We might even call it a "dance of agency". Clearly, the butterflies are interacting in the air, just as we act-ants interact on the ground in the acrobatics of our collaboration'. 'But have you', asks SPIDER, 'given any thought to the air itself? The butterfly's flight is made possible, thanks to air currents and vortices partly set up by the movement of its wings. ... But what sense would it make to say that the air, in the first case, is a participant in the network, with which the butterflies dance as they do with one another. ... Indeed it would make no sense at all. Air [is not an] object that act[s]. ... [It] is [a] material ... [medium] in which living things are immersed, and are experienced by way of their currents, forces and pressure gradients. True, it is not the butterfly alone that flies but butterfly-in-air. ... But that no more makes the butterfly a fly-air hybrid than it makes the fish a fish-water hybrid. It is simply to recognize that for things to interact they must be immersed in a kind of force-field set up by the currents of the media that surround them. Cut out from these currents – that is, reduced to objects – they would be dead. Having deadened the meshwork by cutting its lines of force, thus breaking it into a thousand pieces, you cannot pretend to bring it back to life by sprinkling a magical dust of "agency" around the fragments. If it is to live, then the butterfly must be returned to the air. (2008: 212)[1]

# Air as agent

But the air might not simply be a meshwork in which butterflies and others act. In his *Terror from the Air* (2009), Peter Sloterdijk does away with the notion of the air as a kind of background condition against which things act, and with the notion that it might be a kind of open or free space. Advanced instead is the idea that the air itself might act, or be made to act. He proposes a conceptualization of air as implicit until it is explicitly revealed as something in particular, a process that is enacted through the marking of air in some way. This, in turn, leads to actions both on the air, including but not limited to regulating it, to legislating it, to protecting it, paying for it, *and* actions in which the air might become agent.

Sloterdijk assigns a date to the point at which this process of explication of air became systematized: the 22nd of April 1915. This was the date when chlorine gas was first used in the First World War. The gas was directed by

German soldiers against French Canadian troops stationed near Ypres. For the first time, the physical bodies of the enemy per se were not the first target of a weapon of war; *the air itself was*. Bodies became the target of an assailant air, a process that Sloterdijk calls 'atomterrorism'. The use of adversarial air has since increased and proliferated; it has been put, for example, to judicial use to effect the death penalty in the United States; and infamously in the use of Zyklon B in Nazi concentration camps. For Sloterdijk, the explication of air has resulted in a shift from its position from backgrounded atmospheric to foregrounded and considered agent; for instance, shifting war from an assault on bodies to an assault on a body's total environment. This is a movement he argues that indicates that 'the real, foundation of modernity is not revolution, but explication [*explizieren*]'. He explains:

> If one wanted to say ... what the 20th century ... contributed ... to the history of civilization, answering with three criteria could suffice ... the praxis of *terrorism*, the conception of *product design*, and concepts of *the environment*. Through the first, interactions between enemies were established on postmilitary foundations; through the second, functionalism was able to reintegrate itself in the world of perception; through the third, the phenomena of life and knowledge were entwined to depths hitherto unknown. Taken together, these three criteria indicate the acceleration of explication of the revealing-inclusion of the background givens underlying manifest operations. (2009: 9)

Let me pause here, just for a moment, to explicate explication.

Explication is as 'thematization' (after Heidegger's use of it in *Being and Time* (1966: 412–15), and speaks to making implicit or latent things 'explicit' or manifest. In his dichotomization of explication and latency, Sloterdijk plays on Heidegger's correlative characterization of truth as *aletheia* (from *alethes*, true, literally: not concealing) and *lethe* (also the root for 'latency', but literally: forgetfulness, oblivion, thus concealment). Hence, for Sloterdijk, explication is 'a re-phenomenalization of the aphenomenal' (32), and it answers 'the [modern] need to perceive the imperceptible' (59).

There are differences in how Sloterdijk and Heidegger each come at this – Heidegger primarily thinks of truth as etymological, as deep explanation akin to reading and in this sense takes 'explication' at its word: *explicit* comes from L. *explicitus*, past participle of *explicare,* 'unfold, unravel, explain', from *ex-* 'out' + *plicare* 'to fold'. Un- or out-folding is a textual metaphor, literally of texts: '*explicitus*' was written at the end of medieval texts, short for *explicitus est liber,* 'the book is unrolled' – or unfolded. Sloterdijk is more *textural,* perhaps, in his 'unfolding', as he intends getting to the characteristic physical structure of reality. Bruno Latour takes a similarly textural, as opposed to a textual, route. Latour's version of explication is *explicitation*:

> History was never about 'modernization' or about 'revolution', but was rather about another phenomenon, … 'explicitation'. As we moved on, through our technologies, through our scientific inquiries, through the extension of our global empires, we rendered more and more explicit the fragility of the life support systems that make our 'spheres of existence' possible. Everything that earlier was merely 'given' becomes 'explicit'. Air, water, land, all of those were present before in the background: now they are explicitated because we slowly come to realize that they might disappear – and we with them. (2010: 75)

Although I will say later that the explication of the air is very different from the explication of the water, and so will mark up some differences between the way explication is understood and applied, the main message is clear in the preceding examples. That message is that as a result of explication, whatever has previously lain in the background, as a mere given or assumed form of, or background to, existence, is brought forcibly into view, its principles unfolded, its possibilities actualized. And Sloterdijk sees the most important and decisive arena of explication as occurring with respect to the atmosphere, since our relation to the air is so necessarily taken for granted in the act of breathing.

While Sloterdijk's position is based on the expansion of a certain and terrifying historical point, it might be more compelling to look at the air's current life, and at its perhaps undetermined future. As Tim Choy (2010) notes of the air in Hong Kong, where his work on a politics of atmosphere (and here I mean to refer to the technical meteorological definition of atmosphere, rather than the affective one I myself am working with) and governance of air is based, contemporary considerations of the explication of the air might include

> doctor's efforts to substantiate the daily mortality risks of poor air quality, the work of asthma activists in mapping ecologies of injustice, efforts to politicize sick building syndrome and multiple chemical sensitivities in the face of scientific uncertainty … – these and others point [not only to the present but also to the] futures for [an] atmospheric politics not [yet] fully determined. (see Choy 2010)[2]

In all of these cases, air might not simply be assumed to be 'there' in the background. Depending on its constitution and the way it might be made to act, it may be life-giving or noxious; and it might be more noxious to the lower classes, who have no choice but to live where the air is the most polluted, than it is to those who can choose to live where the air is better. In either case, an explicit awareness of the air is available – as people choose to move, think themselves fortunate or lament the conditions under which they must breathe.

Choy proposes that an anthropology of the air might proceed on the basis of paying explicit attention to the air, tending to its quality and the social implications it might have for relatedness to or distance from other persons and the political context, in this case, of smokefree.

# Explicating the (firsthand) air for the ignorant agent

Let me pick up on Sloterdijk's point, that our relation to the air is so necessarily taken for granted in the act of breathing. It is here that I will begin to elaborate the entailment of smokers in toxic relations with inbound carcinogen-laden air highlighted by state-run public health campaigns (and here that I also respond to Choy's invitation to make an anthropology attentive to the air as it is brought into the body). This process, of explicating the air by recourse to its toxicity, issues an invitation to the present smoking body – that body made available to the smoker in and through self-reflexive awareness.

Smoke-laced air is explicated in health messaging for *what it really is*: dangerous, poisonous, toxic air that will kill. In its efforts to explicate the noxious quality of inhaled tobacco smoke, the state recognizes the now well-established fact that, although nicotine is the addictive ingredient in tobacco, the harms associated with smoking stem primarily from the carcinogens in inhaled cigarette smoke. These are carefully brought out from the background of the ordinary breathing-in one undertakes as one smokes, to be explicated in and through attention to inbound air that is filled with toxins. This explication is perhaps most evident in the government's 2006 '4000 chemicals' campaign, which makes an explicit invitation to attend to the present inhalation, as against habitual, forgotten, cyclic and ordinary respiration.

A breath drawn in via a cigarette is laced with over 4000 chemicals that are invisibly inhaled, rendering the inhaled air toxic, it explains. '4000 chemicals' begins with a smoker, in this case a young woman, lighting up a cigarette, and ends just as she lets that breath go. As she draws in the smoke, a voice-over informs that the air she takes down into the lungs is 'toxic'; a toxic mix of chemicals that include ammonia, 'the bleach found in toilet cleaner', Benzene, an active ingredient found in paint stripper, and Hydrogen Cyanide, used in rat poison. It is clearly understood in the state's view that such an explication is necessary, as smokers do not adequately understand the danger to which they are exposing themselves as they breathe in with smoke: the young women blithely continues, as graphics pop up, of mouth cancer, a gangrenous foot and an unborn baby.

The blithe continuance, made in ignorance of the damage that the paint stripper/rat poison/toilet cleaner smoke is doing inside her mouth/her blood vessels/uterus, is disrupted by the delivery of new educational information to the smoker about what this smoky air is *really* doing as it is drawn into the body. The campaign designed to deliver this information came into being resultant of a stall in the previously fairly consistently declining smoking prevalence rate. Prevalence fell from around 60 per cent of men and 30 per cent of women in the early 1960s to a stubbornly steady 27 per cent of men and 23 per cent of women in the mid-1990s. Australia's original piecemeal system, in which each state took responsibility for developing its own tobacco control initiatives, had developed into a tobacco control programme that involved Commonwealth and non-governmental organizations. But the unexpected slowdown produced the sense that a new, comprehensive and clearly Commonwealth-directed approach was needed. Just prior to its defeat in 1995, the Labour party earmarked funds for a research effort to reduce smoking in the community and to lift tobacco danger to new prominence on the public health agenda. The incoming Federal Health Minister, Michael Wooldridge, honoured his predecessor's intentions in 1996, committing to increase measures to reduce smoking prevalence in Australia. The first step was pooling the extensive tobacco control knowledge and resources throughout Australia to develop a collaborative national anti-tobacco campaign. The government committed AUD $7 million over two financial years to a cessation-focused NTC. As Hill and Carroll note of it,

> Coordinated by the Australian Department of Health, with advice from an expert advisory committee, the NTC was launched in June 1997. As a mass media led campaign, the NTC is the most intense and longest running anti-tobacco campaign ever seen in Australia. (2003: ii9)

Aired from 1997 on, and designed to target adult smokers aged eighteen to forty, the original media campaign comprised the graphic advertisements known as Artery, Lung, Tumour, Brain (or Stroke), Eye and Tar.

Artery, Lung and Tumour were the first to be released, between June and October 1997. In Artery, a male smoker is shown leaning over the lit gas plate on his stove, lighting his first cigarette of the day. The video script for the advertisement is as follows:

> Unable to find matches, a young man lights his first cigarette of the day from the stove. As he inhales, we follow the swirling smoke past his lips

and down his trachea. Against a dark background we see a section of human aorta on a kidney dish. A doctor's hand picks it up and squeezes along its length. Yellow cheesy 'gunk' comes out like toothpaste. He finishes squeezing and lays the artery down. As our smoker exhales, we reverse back up his throat to see him puff away, *blissfully unaware.* Every cigarette is doing you damage. Voice over: Every cigarette is doing you damage. This is part of an aorta, the main artery from the heart. Smoking makes the artery walls sticky and collect dangerous deposits. This much was found in the aorta of a typical smoker … aged thirty-two. Every cigarette is doing you damage. (see Quitnow 2012)

In Tumour, we join a 'Desperate male smoker at a bus stop', who notes with alarm the imminent arrival of his bus – he's got to quickly finish up his cigarette before it gets to the stop at which he is waiting. We follow his inhaled smoky breath as he takes that last drag. The script is as follows:

A man at a bus stop sees his bus approaching and smokes quickly to finish his cigarette. As he inhales, we follow the smoke down his trachea into his lungs. We settle at a junction in his airway and watch smoke passing through. Cut to cancer growing. The tumour spreads through the airway. We reverse back up the trachea and out to see our smoker still puffing way as his bus arrives. Every cigarette is doing you damage. Voice over: Every cigarette is doing you damage. New research shows how tobacco smoke attacks a vital gene which protects lung cells from cancer. One damaged cell is all it takes to start lung cancer growing. Every cigarette is doing you damage. (see Quitnow 2012)

From November 1997 through until October 1998, 'Brain' entered the advertising mix. An ad about suffering a smoking-induced stroke, Brain was firmly based on the actual pathology documented in a case study of a 38-year-old woman, whose age was underscored in the advertising voice copy to 'emphasize the early onset of disease processes and dispel the myth that you can smoke for many years before the damage occurs' (Hill and Carroll 20013: ii9):

A woman is having a smoke in her back yard. She looks at her children playing inside. As she inhales, we see the smoke travel down her trachea.

Cut to a brain being placed on a surgical table. Gloved hands pick up a surgical knife. We cut away to the surgeon's face during the cut. The cut section is pulled aside and damaged brain tissue oozes from the area of the infraction. We exit as the woman exhales to see her still smoking away.

Every cigarette is doing you damage. Voice over: Every cigarette is doing you damage. Smoking creates blood clots which can cause strokes. Some strokes kill, blind or paralyze. ... Others you don't even know you're having. This is the result of a minor stroke in a smoker ... aged thirty-eight. Every cigarette is doing you damage. (see Quitnow 2012)

In 1999, new campaign materials were introduced in time to coincide with World No Tobacco Day (31 May) 2000. New 'smoker moments' were developed featuring younger smokers, aged seventeen to twenty-four years, to counter ignorance and make the rational smoker, capable of making savvy calculations about harm, to emerge. Research demonstrating a link between smoking and macular degeneration presented an opportunity to 'offer new information and fresh insights on the damage that smoking can do to the body, as well as generating the powerful imagery that had become a key ingredient of the campaign strategy to date' (Hill and Carroll 2003: ii9), resulting in the ad 'Eye'. 'Tar' was also added to the advertising mix.

'Tar' draws on an Australian anti-tobacco television commercial called 'Sponge', originally produced by the New South Wales Department of Health in the 1970s and adapted widely by Australian states and territories during the 1980s. In the 1970s' version, the vision and voice-over describe tar being inhaled through cigarette smoke while a tar-blackened sponge (representing a lung) is wrung out into a cup measure, revealing the amount of tar that settles in the lungs over a year. The more recent 'Tar' commercial abandons the metaphoric concept in favour of graphic reality by pouring a beaker of tar (in the amount a pack-a-day smoker inhales over a year) over an actual lung that has been removed from a deceased body. In 'Tar', we join

> a young girl of around twenty alone in her apartment. She finds a single bent cigarette at the bottom of her handbag, straightens it and lights it up.

> As she inhales we follow the smoke into her mouth and down her trachea. Extreme close up at the smoke passes across a moist airway wall, leaving behind a brown tar stain. Cut to a healthy lung being sliced open. A full beaker of tar is poured onto the cut surface close up as the tar seeps deep into the delicate sponge-like tissue. We reverse up the trachea and out of our smoker's mouth to see her still puffing away on her bent cigarette. Every cigarette is doing you damage. Voice over: every cigarette is doing you damage. Every time you inhale, tobacco smoke condenses in your lungs to form tar. This is a healthy lung. And this is the amount of tar a pack-a-day smoker breathes in every year. Every cigarette is doing you damage. (see Quitnow 2012)

'Eye' describes the process of macular degeneration caused by chemicals from tobacco smoke entering the bloodstream:

> A middle aged man in his car is lighting up a cigarette. As he inhales we follow the smoke into his mouth. We travel down the trachea. Cut to close up eye held open by speculum as we zoom in through pupil interior. The surface of the retina becomes blotchy. Extreme close up as a capillary bursts. Cut to dark 'bruise' spreading across the retina. We reverse up the trachea and out of the mouth to find our driver still puffing away. Every cigarette is doing you damage. Voice over: Every cigarette is doing you damage. Chemicals from tobacco smoke get into your blood stream and can damage the delicate blood vessels inside your eye. We now know that smoking is a major cause of irreversible blindness. Every cigarette is doing you damage. (see Quitnow 2012)

As Gilbert (2008) notes, the techniques used to construct and disseminate anti-smoking messages are replete with power; the medical knowledge, imagery and language dominantly used is not a neutral medium for communicating health information. As Gilbert explains,

> This knowledge, imagery, and language forms part of a broader anti-smoking discourse that legitimates and confirms the 'expert' status of medicine in regard to smoking conduct, and normalizes health conduct according to the medical dichotomy of healthy/non-smoking individuals and unhealthy/smoking individuals. ... These anti-smoking campaigns passively coerce individuals into making 'healthy' choices, by using medical knowledge and a medical conception of what it means to be healthy, as the accepted standard of measuring one's own health. (2008: 99)

The medical knowledge of which Gilbert speaks was supplied to the advertising agency (Brown, Mehuish, and Fishlock) by medical specialists in the cardiovascular, neurology and respiratory fields to craft the graphic ads. These specialists educated the creative development team about the mechanisms and manifestations of tobacco-related disease and assisted the team to translate complex interactions between smoke and organs into lay language.

In recognizing the principles of neo-liberalism at play in the dissemination of health information, Gilbert is concerned with making a *discursive* analysis along Foucauldian lines (as well as with determining whether or not campaigns are effective). I am concerned here with neither; rather I am interested in attending phenomenologically to the *interior life* of the coercion that Gilbert describes. I argue that the air itself is effectively made agent of the state, and works to deliver the smokefree atmosphere direct to the inside of the smoker's body. Just as Gilbert says, it is not the case that the state simply provides neutral information on the content of air with tobacco smoke in it; I add to Gilbert's insight the notion that the state gets inside the body of the smoker, to make 'smokefree' specific, and tailored to the *individual* body of the smoker – in the most intimate of airs – *her own breath*.

# Take a big breath in

In all the commercials produced for the NTS 1997–2005 campaign, the viewer joins the smoker at the specific point at which he or she draws smoke from the cigarette into the mouth – at the 'beginning' of the inhalation phase of respiration. All the commercials in the series share a focus on this inhalation phase, which is taken to begin when breath is drawn in through the cigarette and which ends at the point of exhaling air through the lips. Provided with the camera capacity to follow the smoke down into the lungs or into the bloodstream – a view unavailable to the smoking person – the viewer bears witness to the damage or the potential for damage building in the smoker's internal regions. The lungs, aorta, eye and brain are featured in their turn.

It is *extremely* significant that these advertisements start at the 'beginning' of the inhalation phase, and that smokers are invited to attend to it, and to reflect on it – in a way they would not reflect on respiration in the ordinary course of breathing. As Katz (1999) notes, we do not usually seek to find points in the process of respiration that undermine its ongoing circularity (1999: 340). Also referencing the idea that it falls behind attention, Irigaray (1999) says that breath is a forgotten material meditation in Western metaphysics between ourselves and the world. We might necessarily forget that it connects consciousness to the nervous system, organs to human-produced chemicals, cells to atmosphere. Irigaray's point here is not only that breath is not just breath, but also that it must be forgotten if one is to be and remain a competent breather, and, thus a competent doer of all the things that breathing permits. Of course we forget it: *we must*, in order to be competent breathers.

I'm going to argue in Chapter 6 of this book, after Klein (1993) that smoking permits smokers to *remember* the air outside of themselves, in the sense that it extends their reach beyond the site of the body. In this sense, smoking also entails a kind of *forgetting* of the insides of the body. These anti-smoking advertisements invite smokers to *remember* their insides. This work of remembering is conducted in and through attending closely to inbound breath – this is critical to the explication of the air in the smokefree state.

The marking off of an inbound breath from the broader habitual process of respiration issues an invitation what Langer (1989) following Merleau-Ponty ([1945] 1962) has called the present body. The present body is distinguishable from the habitual body; the latter falls behind one's self-conscious attention in the course of everyday living. Present bodies, on the other hand, invite reflection and allow persons to discover their own activity 'in shaping the world as it is discovered through our perception' (1989: 32). Here, I want to draw specific attention to the activity of breathing in, and to the entrée that provides, to the insides of the body, where breath (momentarily but simultaneously continuously) dwells.

Very often, pain provides access to the present body, as it brings usually disattended interactions between the body and the world into self-conscious (or 'present') attention. If I am walking down the street, for instance, I usually do so unreflexively, simply permitting my feet to interact with the street – to so do is to walk competently. But this disattendance is rudely disrupted if, say, I suddenly stub my toe. The pain means instant self-awareness of my foot and its failure to have performed its unaudienced dance with the pavement. Similarly, specific present attention is drawn to the smoking body in Tar, Eye, Brain and their gruesome companions, in which aspects of the innards of the body normally (and necessarily) just left to get on with things, like breathing, and seeing, are brought into self-reflection via avenues of imminent pain and danger.

James Hagan, whose deep, morose voice well known in Australia, New Zealand and the United Kingdom, provides the catch-cry in the ads, the single line: 'Every cigarette is doing you damage.' This line provides instant orientation to the themes of pain and danger, an orientation that is followed by an on-camera exploration of the insides of the body, where the evidence of pain and danger is to be found.

It's not just that the advertisements (medically, expertly) violently assert that cigarettes will do you damage, as Gilbert tells us. It's more than that. The advertisements issue an invitation to attend to one's own breath as it draws in firsthand smoke. As the smoker reflects on that inbound breath, thick with noxious poisons, she bears smokefree notions down into the lungs, so that expert knowledge of that breath *is in me now*. Indeed, this was the express intention of the campaign; as Hill and Carroll note, the whole idea was that 'the advertisements will work to the extent that the thought, act, or sight of inhaling a cigarette brings to mind the sticky walls of arteries, genetic damage to lung tissue, or the "rotting" that characterizes chronic lung disease' (2003: ii9), or in other words, the effect of the ads would be to usher in a stark distinction between present inhaling body and the habitually respiring body. Where the habitually respiring body draws breath in, 'blissfully unaware', the present body reflects on the rot inside. In a breath, you reflect on it.

Henri, a thirty-five-year-old public servant from Canberra, did not want to reflect on it, but found he couldn't help it.

Henri had no intention of quitting, but was troubled by the fact that he knew what was happening to his lungs as he smoked – 'You can't help but think about what you're breathing in. There's no doubt it's poison. Once you know that, you can't un-know it,' he remarked of the knowledge firmly lodged in his lungs. While Henri continued to smoke, it certainly wasn't in ignorance; he knew. Henri was busy, it seems, putting things together that don't go together – like knowing that the air he breathes in is poisonous, on the one hand, and continuing to draw pleasure from continuing to smoke (poisonous) *John Player Special* cigarettes.

Paul, a fifty-five-year-old chef working in one of Canberra's many restaurants designed to cater for the parliamentary set, knew, too. Paul was old enough to remember a time when smoking was unremarkable, and not really the subject of any public health campaign that made clear its dangers. Now, deep in the time of smokefree, Paul finds the atmosphere pressing down on him, and he felt particularly oppressed by the new knowledge that the atmosphere had made available to him:

> It's awful, actually, knowing what is in the smoke that you breathe in. I think it'd probably be better not to know. I'd rather not know. Sometimes, it bothers me and gets in the way of the relaxing part of having a cigarette. But then again, you could think this way about food, worrying about exactly what is in it. Some people who come in here [to the restaurant] do that, like when people want to know the history of the cow their steak came from, but that can go too far. At some point, it stops being a pleasure and you start being too concerned with food at a level that should probably be left to the scientists and the nutritionists. As a chef, I'm saying: just enjoy! I can ignore the rat poison or whatever when I smoke. Otherwise, what was the actual point?

Paul's remarks perfectly capture the notion that the breath normally ignored as it draws in cigarette smoke is made subject to the state's invitation, to attend to its toxicity and to its capacity to effect pain to unseen internal regions of the body. They also perfectly capture the power that comes with corralling the air itself into this project. Paul not only draws in the air from his cigarette, but the terrible knowledge of its contents. This is a newly explicated air, an air specific to the era of smokefree, and one that Paul can't quite shake away as he tries to disattend breathing in, as he once did, while smoking. Breathing in with smoke is not just breathing in anymore; it's not habitual breathing, it's present breathing, underlaced with the toxin of rat poison that cannot, quite, be forgotten. But neither can this knowledge of danger be fully *remembered* – Paul and Henri still smoke, still remember the outside air, as I'll discuss it in the seventh chapter, still undo themselves from complete containment inside the body, as the ads invite.

As Tim Ingold says, the breath and the air that I am suggesting is laden with the political as much as with the gaseous are inseparable. He argues for a view of the air (the wind, precisely, in his work) that is not so much about the wind being embodied as it is about the body being 'enwinded'. Such a view indicates that body is beholden to the air – the air moves through it, rather than the body containing the air, and that, in relations between the body and the air, *it is the air* that holds the better part of the power. This notion is readily demonstrable in comments that appear in response to thirdhand smoke articles released online, like '"Third hand smoke" is a hazard to baby's health', by Susan Markel (M.D), posted on the Baby Centre website in 2009 (see Baby Centre 2009). One new mother, 'Emily', says: 'I even held my breath when I was pregnant and would walk past someone smoking! LOL I know it is extreme.' The body is beholden to breathe – one can only choose the air it takes in within a short, limits-of-breath-holding window. In this immediate sense, it holds immense power. Theoretically, though, the air is backgrounded and, as Ingold points out, there has been a certain willingness to treat the body as an encompasser of the air. Ingold thinks of it this way:

> At a recent anthropological conference on Wind, Life, Health (Low and Hsu 2008), the issue came up of how the wind is embodied in the constitution of persons affected by it. For my part, I felt uneasy about applying the concept of embodiment in this context. It made breathing seem like a process of coagulation, in which air was somehow sedimented into the body as it solidified. Acknowledging that the living body, as it breathes, is necessarily swept up in the currents of the medium, I suggested that the wind is not so much embodied as the body enwinded. (Ingold 2007: S32)

Ingold also notes:

> David Macauley writes, 'with our heads immersed in the thickness of the atmosphere or our lungs and limbs engaged with the swirling winds, we repeatedly breathe, think and dream in the regions of the air' (2005: 307). But by the same token, inhabiting the open does not yield an experience of embodiment, as though life could be incorporated or wrapped up within a solid bodily matrix. (2007: S31)

The wind, the air, then, can't be wrapped up in the body – and the body cannot be freed of the air's political fluxes. As Choy puts it, some politics can be sensed in the immediacy of the moment of bringing breath into the body.

Smokefree politics is just such a case. As Henri found, bringing breath into the body when that breath was laced with firsthand smoke meant simultaneously bringing in the knowledge of its contents, as explicated by the state – whether he wanted to or not. The state had made an invitation to Henri's 'present body', and, even though he wanted to decline it, Henri found himself accepting it – he couldn't get away from knowing what was in his own inbound breath. Expert medical knowledge had been drawn down into his lungs just as surely as had oxygen, and tobacco smoke.

In the process of being 'enwinded' then, to utilize Ingold's language, the body is equally filled up with the *politics of that wind*, in and through the intimacy of bringing the (smokefree) world in, via inbound breath. In the next chapter, I draw attention to what the consequences of breathing *out* with smoke might be; the state has a just as fulsome an explication of the air, and just as effusive an imaginary of its effects as it does for the inhalation of smoke by smokers.

# 5

# Miasmatic exhalation:
# Breathing out (secondhand)

## Introduction

In this chapter, I shift away from an examination of how firsthand smoke is explicated by the state in favour of an analysis of its explication of secondhand smoke. 'Cigarette smoking produces three different types of tobacco smoke,' explains *Tobacco In Australia*:

> The first is mainstream smoke, the smoke directly inhaled into the smoker's lungs through the burning cigarette. The second is exhaled mainstream smoke the smoke breathed out by the smoker from their lungs. The third is sidestream smoke, the smoke that drifts from the smoldering tip of the cigarette. (Scollo and Winstanley 2012: np)

While the terms 'environmental tobacco smoke (ETS)', and 'tobacco smoke pollution' could both be applied to the emissions of smoke from cigarettes, the term 'secondhand smoke' is the preferred term deployed in *Tobacco in Australia*. Only this term captures the revolting idea that the smoke a bystander breathes in has *been used before* (see Brandt 1998: 168).

Not only has the air been drawn in by another breather, it has been sullied by its circulation around foul and abject material of the smoker's rotted lungs. The term 'secondhand smoke', of course, directs attention to 'the smoke breathed out by the smoker *from their lungs*' (my emphasis), and diminishes the fact that the smoke given off from the burning end of the cigarette itself is much more dangerous to inhale for near-located breathers. Terms that would capture both, like 'environmental tobacco smoke', lack the capacity to stir up disgust. Outrage, maybe, but not disgust. And it is disgust, specifically in response to the idea that smokers emit rotten air, that is central to the state's explication of air containing tobacco smoke.

'Secondhand smoke', is explicated not so much in terms of the toxicity of smokers' exhalations as it is in the *feelingful* terms of disgust. Disgust arises over the idea of inhaling air that has just been circulating around the rotting lungs of a smoker. Of course, we know that that's where smoke has just been, because we've travelled deep down into the smoker's body, in anti-smoking advertisements.

On television, in anti-smoking ads, this smoke is rendered highly visible, but in face-to-face encounters between smokers and bystanders, smoke is more often detected olfactorily. This sensing of smoke, unlike seeing it, infiltrates the body: smelling smoke means smoke is already inside the nose, the trachea, the lungs – and we all know what it does once there. The capacity of smoke to connect bodies through smell is a disturbing one, and it has had some profound consequences – not least for smokers themselves.

The state also explicates the smoky air in less affective and more apparently scientific ways – in formally stated scientific explication of smoke-sullied air. However, this explication, scientific as it appears, is one based on pronouncements, confident assertions and propositions when the science doesn't establish as firmly as is needed the danger of drawing in secondhand smoke – as is the case regarding inhaling it in the outdoor air – thanks to its olfactorily appreciated capacity for crossing bodily boundaries. As Gusfield suggested in 1981, it's hardly ever the case that *objective* conditions are seldom 'so compelling and so clear in their form that they spontaneously generate a "true" consciousness' (1981: 3). The subjective conditions, though, those olfactorily sensed, seem more than sufficient for so doing.

## Explicating the secondhand air

The present NTS (covering the period 2013–18) notes that 'scientific evidence has unequivocally established that exposure to tobacco smoke causes death, disease and disability in the indoors and the outdoors', where it indiscriminately presents risk to any and all users of air. These assertions, that secondhand smoke 'causes a range of serious adverse health effects', and 'tobacco smoke causes death, disease and disability in the indoors and the outdoors' air, in fact make a new explication of the outdoor air. The NTS does so in its insistence that tobacco smoke produces the same poor health outcomes in the outdoors as it does indoors.

In so doing, it stands at odds with scientifically robust explications of the tobacco-laced air – which, in fact, it cites. For instance, while the 2006 US Surgeon-General report confirms that there can be no doubt that secondhand smoke is harmful to people exposed to it in an enclosed indoor environment, it explicitly qualifies the hazard presented by secondhand smoke in the outdoors, noting that it is harmful only when specific conditions are met. Australian scientists, Stafford, Daube and Franklin (2010), themselves strong proponents of smoking bans outdoors, nevertheless note that because there are so many conditions to be met for any harm to result, it is extremely difficult to make sure and certain statements about the harm of ETS in the outdoors:

> In contrast to indoor smoking …, SHS dissipates soon after smoking ceases outdoors. The concentration of outdoor SHS is a product of the density and distribution of smokers, wind direction and speed, and the stability of the atmosphere. High outdoor SHS concentrations are generated by high smoker density, low wind velocities and stable atmospheric conditions. (2010: 100)

Similarly, Klepeis, Ott and Switzer also drew less-than-certain conclusions in their 2007 study measuring outdoor tobacco smoke, noting that 'it is possible for ETS to present a nuisance or hazard *under certain conditions of wind and smoker proximity*' (Klepeis, Ott and Switzer 2007: 522). Such findings only permit these analysts to say that nuisance or hazard is *possible,* not unequivocal. It is *impossible* to state unequivocally that tobacco smoke in the outdoor air is dangerous – it might possibly be dangerous, or, if it definitely is, it is only so, under a number of necessary conditions. The NTS's position is very clear, despite the equivocal tone that the above-cited analysts take: its position is that smoke in the outdoor air *is* dangerous. Period.

It is here that we can appreciate another important feature of explication. Not only does it serve to bring that which is in the background to the fore, it equally performs productive, transformative work. As the philosopher Rudolf Carnap explained, explication is in one sense a process that transforms and replaces concepts taken to be inexact or pre-scientific (like the danger of secondhand smoke in the outdoor air) with new, exact and precise concepts (like its unequivocal danger in the outdoor air) (Carnap 1950; see also Bonolio 2003). This process has been applied to tobacco smoke's impact on the air before. In 1971, for example, the US Surgeon-General's report claimed that tobacco smoke polluted the air for non-smokers, but by 1972 it upgraded its advice, stating that tobacco smoke in the air constituted a health hazard to non-smoking persons. A new explication of the tobacco smoke-laced air emerged: the imprecise and pre-scientific notion that tobacco smoke was a pollutant with the potential to impact health was replaced with scientifically established proof that secondhand tobacco smoke in the air was unequivocally and seriously hazardous to health.

Such certain claims permit the state to 'reorient norms' around what can happen in public space. The current NTS notes in particular that 'public awareness of the risks of ETS has increased and the introduction of smoke free public spaces has become the norm'. *Tobacco In Australia* remarks upon this norm:

> Scientific research is unequivocal about the serious health effects of exposure to SHS. ... As knowledge of the health risks associated with SHS has increased over time, the public has become increasingly concerned about being exposed to SHS and support for smokefree legislation has grown. Prior to the widespread introduction of smokefree policies in public places, many Australians were frequently exposed to tobacco smoke in the course of their everyday lives. A South Australian survey in 2004 for instance reported that most people in that state (74%) were concerned about personal exposures to SHS. [It goes on to note that] 37% of people surveyed were 'exposed to SHS in the street or at outdoor entertainment venues'. (Scollo and Winstanely 2012: np)

Make no mistake: this is where the *circumstance* of which scientists (like Klepeis, Ott and Switzer) speak, like the speed and direction of the breeze, the distance at which people stand from one another and the number of smokers having a cigarette in any given space turns into *stance*. Once issuances are made, explications of the air done and mandated, in authoritative texts like *Tobacco in Australia*, there's nothing *circum-* about the *stance*.

Further to this, the 'stance' becomes resolute *not* by standing on the reliable back of a steadying, confirmatory science – clearly the science is irresolute, equivocal, and most certainly attendant to the 'circum' (as good science tends always to do, given that it is ideally empirically, and not politically, motivated).[1] The resolute and unequivocal *stance*, I think, is endorsed at the level of the sensate. At that level, it acquires the characteristic features and vocabulary of scientific knowledge. Thusly dressed in scientific knowledge, unequivocal claims are possible, because, as Serres (1998) tells us, the classifier 'knowledge' eliminates unstable circumstances 'and levels what stands out as rare. Knowledge stipulates: under the same circumstances ...' (1998: 185: ellipsis in original). Taking Bell's (2011) suggestion that we might be 'legislating abjection' as my cue, I'm going to argue in what follows that the unscientific sense we have of the danger of smoke, that olfactorily possessed knowledge, confirms the equivocal science to yield an unequivocal dangerousness grounded in indisputable bodily experience. The knowledge levels the olfactory and the empirical, combining them. Our bodies know: the nose knows. The olfactory circum- becomes -stance.[2]

# The nose knows danger

One way in which we *subjectively* know the smoky air is dangerous is in and through its capacity to infiltrate bodies. Anti-smoking advertisements present secondhand smoke in just this way. A new advertisement currently airing depicts an Aboriginal woman sitting in the playground, on some play equipment, holding her baby on her lap. She's having a cigarette, and brings it up to her mouth to draw on it. We see the lit cigarette and its trailing smoke pass by the baby's face, and we know, since we see the smoke is trailing into her face, that the baby takes in the smoke as it breathes in. An older woman comes into the playground and admonishes the young mother for 'smoking around that baby again'. An older advertisement depicts a couple smoking in their lounge room as they watch television. We see them draw smoke in, and then see it appear out of the mouths of their children, who are sitting nearby, as the children exhale. In both ads, the smoke thoroughly infiltrates the bodies of the non-smoking children present in the near vicinity. The latter ad makes visually explicit that the smoke has permeated the bodies of the kids.

The notion that smoke connects bodies has to be made explicitly visible on the television; it's actually quite odd to witness the two children in the latter advertisement breathing out the smoke their parents inhaled just prior, because this is not the primary sensory mode in which we appreciate that smoke connects bodies. In face-to-face encounters, its capacity to do so is appreciated primarily *olfactorily*.

As Borthwick (2000) notes, olfaction is a connector of bodies (and of bodies and things) because conjoining is the basis of odour. In order to emit an odour at all – to be sensed olfactorily – an object must break down; this condition is not required to sense an object visually. It is this dissolvability that breaches the boundaries of individual bodies. Le Guérer describes this dissolvability facilitated by smoke as involuntary and intimate; 'The smell that enters the lungs establishes a contact "even more intimate" than the one between taste and the receptor cavities of mouth and throat' [which is largely voluntarily experienced in eating] 1991: 175). Borthwick notes that despite our conception of the clearly defined and demarcated 'individual', when it comes to olfaction, there is caused to be and there remains:

> Part of the other within the subject … olfaction opens the possibility, through the actual embodiment of the other, of another kind of sociality that acknowledges the interconnection with, not the complete separation of, the subject and the other. Further, it begins to shake the ground that holds the subject-other relationship, that is, it shakes the sight-based separation of self and other … if sociality was theorized through smell, how different it could be! Where would the self end and other begin? (132)

Some of these questions, about where the self and other began and ended were raised during my fieldwork, on the basis of smoky communications between bodies. Melissa, a young woman living in Brisbane, and I were talking about smoking. She remembered waiting for a bus in the city when a young man approached her and asked her for a cigarette. She gave him one and inquired of him how he had known that she was a smoker. The young man replied that while he was standing next to her at the bus stop, he had been able to smell the cigarette smoke on her clothes. Louise, an older woman, recalled an experience many years ago when she had gone to a Blue Light disco, in the 1980s.[3] There, she had smoked 'almost an entire packet of *Alpine Lights*' with her friends. Desperate to hide the smell from her father, who was to pick her up from the disco, she went outside and rubbed her hands with the leaves of a fragrant tree that was growing outside the venue. She also borrowed toothpaste from a friend, who had brought along her toothpaste in case she got a love bite; toothpaste, Louise explained, was known to young women to have the capacity to reduce the appearance of the telltale bruise, if it was applied right away. Louise rubbed toothpaste inside her mouth and over her teeth to hide the smell. She planned to explain away the smell on her clothes as the result of other people's smoke. Her father, who picked her up, and who had, according to Louise, 'a nose like a German Shepherd', kissed her cheek and suspected that Louise had been smoking. He sniffed her fingers to confirm this and concluded correctly that fourteen-year-old Louise had indeed been smoking.

Trevor, a gardener, told me that, at work, there was not a special time for 'smoko',[4] and that it was taken when Trevor, the head gardener, felt that it was appropriate. Trevor worked in a garden divided by many retaining walls, and other compartmentalizing devices, which meant that workmates were often not in one another's view. Trevor said that 'when the other fellows smell my smoke, they come over to where I am and that's how smoko happens'.

If sociality were to be theorized through smell, the experiences of Melissa, Louise and Trevor might indeed indicate to us the difficulty of deciding where people begin and end. If the sociality and intercorporeality entailed by smoking were to be theorized through smell, we might draw different kinds of attention to smoke's capacity to dissolve existing social and corporeal connections between persons.

In Trevor's case, smoke dissolved distances between people as the smell of Trevor's smoke wafted to the noses of his workmates, eventually organizing them together in one place and around one activity. In Melissa's case, the smell of cigarettes lingered sufficiently long in her clothes to dissolve a social boundary that otherwise would have remained between her and the young man at the bus stop, who eventually became her boyfriend. Armed with this olfactory knowledge, the man effectively dissolved a knowledge and a social boundary, which led him to dissolve other kinds of boundaries between himself and Melissa later on. Louise experienced a dissolving of the connection that kept her father and herself on good terms; in her father's view, the specific connection that had been dissolved was one of 'trust'. Louise's father then took it upon himself to dissolve some more of Louise's social connections when he grounded her.

While consequential for the parties involved, these are all fairly bland, inoffensive and innocuous dissolutions of boundaries. They indicate that it might be not so bad to conceive of sociality through smell. But when it comes to smoke, the interconnection with, not the complete separation of, the subject and the other is more often than not a most unwelcome interconnection, and always an involuntary embodiment. It is especially unwelcome as secondhand smoke in the era of smokefree. Who wants to be connected, lung to lung, with a smoker, who has rot on her breath? This notion is one that conjures more Douglasian ideas, about disgust – a category that is born in borders and boundaries and margins. Smoke's capacity to cross bodily boundaries and to bear the odiferous traces of its travels with it makes it disgusting – even if the science can't fully establish its dangerousness in the outdoor air. Disgust, based firmly in the knowledge that smoke circulates in and through bodies – and that its odour indicates its capacity to cross bodily bounds – is enough. Jennifer certainly thought so.

# Jennifer, defender of the air

In the summer of 2012, my thirty-five-year-old friend, Jennifer, and I had just finished enjoying a coffee together at an outdoor café near her local beach with her daughters Carrie (6) and Harriet (10) in tow. Jennifer told me she had to get Carrie to the toilet; Carrie was already wiggling, so Jennifer propelled her towards a public toilet block across the way. Two girls in their late teens dressed in bathing suits still wet from swimming and holding lit cigarettes came into visual and olfactory range as we rounded the corner to the women's entrance. Jennifer whipped Carrie and Harriet behind her back and confronted the two girls. 'You can't smoke here!' she said loudly. 'It's a public place. … You're putting my kids in danger! Don't you know how dangerous it is for kids to breathe in tobacco smoke?' The girls, obviously startled, blushed scarlet, blurted out apologies and moved rapidly away, one glancing over her shoulder every few paces at the still angry mother. Carrie, frightened at the suddenly combative tone her mother had used as she berated the smoking teens, started to cry, and Jennifer picked her up. Harriet, though, looked up at her mother and staunchly declared, 'They stink, mummy!' Taking what might have been her daughter's use of the universal schoolyard insult to refer specifically to the smell of the cigarette smoke, Jennifer told Harriet, 'It smells bad and it *is* bad. Smoking makes you sick, *very* sick, so you mustn't ever breathe in cigarette smoke, OK?' Harriet, wide-eyed, replied obediently 'OK'. We proceeded into the toilet block, but it was too late – Carrie had already wet her pants.

I talked with Jennifer later about the incident. 'What *incident*?', she asked, obviously irritated, when I rang her to see if she'd elaborate on what had occurred at the beach. 'It wasn't an *incident*,'

> It wasn't me losing my shit or anything – it was just me having a word to two very silly girls. What, do you blame me? Carrie is only six years old! Her little lungs are innocent! And we were on the *beach*, for fuck's sake, a place where you go to *get* beautiful fresh air. Why should they be allowed to blow poisonous filth into the fresh air? If they want to kill themselves, let them go right ahead – in their own homes. They're not going to contaminate my beach, or my kids![5]

I wasn't surprised by Jennifer's reaction; I'd recorded many such 'incidents' between smokers and non-smokers during my ongoing fieldwork in Canberra. Evident was the notion that exposure to tobacco smoke outdoors might instantaneously cause harm; the rapidity of Jennifer's actions to move her kids behind the shield of her back was the same as that one might undertake to avoid any imminent threat (see Dennis 2014).[6]

Jennifer's condemnation of smokers on the basis of the odour of the smoke they exude becomes even more pronounced in the case of twenty-nine-year-old Misty Parent's experience of waiting for, and then boarding a bus in Canada's capital city, Ottawa, on 11 January 2013. On 18 January 2013, the *Ottawa Sun's* opinion columnist Anthony Furey wrote how Misty had extinguished her cigarette before boarding the bus; municipal by-laws forbid smoking at bus terminals and at street-side bus stops and smokers must be 9 metres from the stop. When Misty boarded, her passage up the steps of the bus pushed the smell on the air towards the driver, who found her smoky smell objectionable. He told her she must move to the farthest back seat where her foul scent would least impact him. In common with many other workplaces and public settings, the City of Ottawa bus service, OC Transpo, has a policy that requires its customers to be 'scent-free', a category that theoretically includes perfumes, as well as those more universally deemed noxious. In common with many other workplaces and public settings, including the scene of the 2011 American Anthropological Association (AAA) conference, OC Transpo has a policy that requires service users to be 'scent-free'. At the 2011 AAA, conference goers were advised in the General Meeting

Information section of the handbook to abide by the 'No Scents Policy' of the conference and to refrain from 'wearing perfumes, colognes or other scent-producing products which may cause discomfort to other guests'.

Such policies indicate an increasing concern with the production and maintenance of an odourless air that is not permitted to express its recent history of circulating in and around and through other (scented/odorous) bodies. An odourless air, as Classen et al. (1994) point out, is not a neutral air by any means. This is *classed* air. Thinking specifically about the class dimensions of smoking which register it as a practice of the poor and the marginalized, and taking up Borthwick's invitation to conceive of sociality through smell, we might say that a particularly middle-class unscentedness, best characterized by the absence of tobacco smoke, increasingly characterizes public participation. This is certainly so on the bus Misty tried to board, and in an increasing array of public places, like the beach, the park, the mall and suchlike. As Classen et al. put it, in public space, the regime is usually one of 'olfactory neutrality' (170), an unscented reflection of the relations between the dominant class, who dominate public space, and outsiders to it, identifiable by their foul odour:

> Olfaction does indeed enter into the construction of relations of power in our [western] society … The centre (the power elite) governs from a position of olfactory neutrality. Formerly power was personal, and therefore imbued with the smell of those who wielded it; now it has become impersonal and abstract, and therefore odourless. While groups in the centre – politicians, businessmen – are characterized by a symbolic lack of scent, those on the periphery are classified as odourless. … The challenge for those in power is how to preserve their inodorateness from the onslaught of odours emanating from these peripheral groups which always seem to be pressing in towards the centre. (1994: 161)

Indicating that Misty's peripherality had indeed pressed too far into the odourless centre, Furey ended his opinion piece in the *Ottawa Sun* with the following: 'This lady's rights as a smoker ended when she got on a bus with a smell *she couldn't keep to herself*' (Furey 2008; my emphasis), a remark that equally underscores the capacity of odour to connect bodies however unwillingly they are drawn into concert.

# Public air

The reactions that Misty and the Australian girls near the toilet block experienced to their odorous emissions demonstrate that the air we inhale is drawn from a public pool. The idea that the air is a shared resource and can never really be 'mine' was demonstrated very effectively in 2008 by magician David Blaine. Blaine broke the world record for breath-holding when he appeared on the Oprah Winfrey show and held his breath for 17 minutes, 4.4 seconds. This provoked suspicious inquiries as to how Blaine had managed to do it. 'Did David Blaine hold his breath for 17 minutes?' asked Brian Dunning, on his website Skepticblog. The University of Pittsburgh's Critical Care Medicine Group also questioned the feat, noting the assistance that Blaine purportedly received from the medical fraternity, including trying liquid ventilation with perflurocarbons. These doubts fit well with historical responses to persons hoarding up the air, which were regarded with lively suspicion.[7]

'Holding back the breath is equivalent to having intercourse with the Soul; drawing it amounts to intercourse with the body,' said the mystic writer Swedenborg, who himself claimed to be able to subsist without breathing for long periods of time. Produced by reversing the ordinary process of vocally marking exhaled air, Connor (2008) notes that ventriloquism was also often viewed with suspicion; its vocalizations were thought to be produced by sucking in the air, marking it a demonic act of speech. These actions arouse suspicion because each work through an insularity achieved by the removal of the breathing body from its ordinary and necessary entailments with the air. If a human body cannot be said to be sustained by an ongoing entailment with the world external, then its life must be sustained by some other-worldly source, in the case of ventriloquism it was thought, by the Devil himself – an indication that the air cannot be 'mine' for long.

The idea that the air contains matter that other bodies have deposited into it is a revolting and unsettling idea, but it is one that goes habitually unrecognized and unregistered, offset as it is by the necessarily habitual nature of breathing. We are only alerted to such uncomfortable notions when odour alerts us to them – but by then it is already too late – the matter deposited by others is already 'in me'; hence the pre-emptive efforts of posting signs on buses alerting the travellers about the demands their fellow breathers make upon the public air pool.

In the case of smoking, revulsion issues not only from the realization that smoky air has been used before by another body that has deposited its matter into the air prior to our own use of it. Revulsion also comes from the realization that air issuing from the lungs of the smoker is *particularly polluted*. The air emitting from a smoker is not just secondhand – it's dirty and dangerous, too. There's rot in it. This is something we surely and certainly know, from anti-smoking advertising. The anti-smoking advertisement 'Lung', for instance, was one of the first three graphic ads to be released under the 1997 NTC alongside 'Tumour' and 'Artery'. In Lung, drawing from that commercial's script, there appears a lone woman having a smoke break outside an office on a wet windy day. She cups her hands to shield her lighter from the wind. As she inhales we follow the smoke through her lips and down her trachea into darkness [voice-over: Every cigarette is doing you damage]. We enter her lungs, travelling through ever smaller spaces and settling on a landscape of delicate lung tissue, like the fine texture of a sponge [voice-over: Lungs are like sponges, with millions of tiny air sacs for transferring oxygen]. As smoke is pulled and pushed through it, we see the membrane being eaten away, creating ugly, black, tar-rimmed chambers [voice-over: Every breath of tobacco smoke, attacks them]. The rotting continues. The lung is turning grey/brown [voice-over: No wonder smokers feel short of breath; their lungs are rotting]. [As she begins to yield that inhalation up, so that it starts to be an exhalation] we reverse back up the trachea and out of our smoker's mouth [voice over and script: Every cigarette is doing you damage. Call the Quitline 131848. (see Quitnow 2012)

Via Lung and its graphic and lingering closeups, we have all entered the smoker's body and borne witness to its decayed state. It is from here that used-smoke issues – not from the innocent lungs of a six-year-old, but from the dark, rotting lungs of a smoker. Jennifer's reactions to the smoke she and her children could smell certainly reference the idea such smoke is revolting, and to be rejected with force. Smoke 'pollutes', it is 'filthy', and even fleeting exposure to it will result in illness, according to Jennifer's explanation for her reaction to it. Her disgusted reactions, and particularly her view that drawing in something stinky could make you sick, call to mind miasmatic conceptions of disease.

## An illness-inducing stench: Cancer is catching

In his *Foul and the Fragrant* (1994), Alain Corbin describes how olfaction in France during the mid-eighteenth century played a critical role in everyday life. At this time, far from being background stage to actor bodies, the air itself acted upon the living body via the pores of the skin through which it could move, and through the more direct route of ingestion. Such action was not only necessary to life but also, depending on its humidity, temperature and which emanations of the earth it contained, air could boost health and vitality. It could equally present grave danger, as it might contain the foul emanations of stagnant water, the stench of dead and decaying matter, and it held in a state of suspension the substances given off by bodies. The contents of the air might cause ills and/or death. This miasmatic conceptualization of ills originally emerged from Greek tragedy and found a hospitable home in medicine where it was considered the root cause of infections borne by putrid, poisonous vapours identifiable primarily by their foul smell.

The emanations of tobacco smoke are presently miasmatically conceptualized in that they are commonly regarded as poisonous vapours capable of bearing illness, no matter how fleeting the exposure. For example, the idea that tobacco smoke wafting on the outdoor air might cause immediate harm is enlivened in the production of a cough from people momentarily exposed to it. Twenty-six-year-old grocery store assistant Rosie, for instance, told me about an encounter she'd had which clearly indicates the ascription to tobacco smoke of contagion (as Bell 2011 describes). One day, a man who, on encountering some of her exhaled smoke as he passed by her in the street turned, coughed and spluttered loudly, and said to her, 'Hey, don't blow that stinking shit on me! I don't want your cancer. It's a contagious disease, spread by selfish idiots like you.' Rosie's encounter with this outraged gentleman strongly suggests that poisonous vapours that contained cancer were located inside Rosie, and were not just a feature of tobacco smoke.

Public health messaging promulgated via television (like 'Lung') and on cigarette packages provides us with detailed information about the toxic air that smokers inhale and its capacity to rot smokers' lungs – here is the dead and decaying matter that is picked up and expelled in an exhalation of already toxic tobacco smoke. The man who coughed upon experiencing Rosie's exhaled smoke may well have felt familiar with the state of her lungs and well acquainted with the black-rimmed condition of their air sacs. He may well have seen, as we all have seen, her lungs turn grey and begin to rot. Picking up on the tag line of the anti-smoking commercials distributed by the NSW government from 2007 on, which set to music some 'memorable scenes' from the existing 1997–2005 campaign, *Everybody Knows* the state of Rosie's insides; they are rotten. And memorable they certainly are, and not just because they are set to the mournful Leonard Cohen tune (*Everybody Knows*). They are memorable for their graphic content. Inside the smoker's body, the aorta is filled with a disgusting off-white paste. It is little wonder that the particular piece of the advertisement depicting the aorta being milked of its 'gunk' was dubbed 'the brie' scene; the oozing, discharging waste is exactly the texture of the thick, creamy, pungent cheese.

The lungs inside the smoker's body, we know from such messaging, are putrid and decomposing, the air sacs upon which their health depends are blackened with a deathly rot. Breath escaping from this rotted flesh goes out into the air to corrupt the state of human relations in the community – Rosie is going to give people cancer, not only from emitting toxic smoke, but in emitting it from the rotted flesh that constitutes her lungs. The scientific evidence for the harms borne by secondhand tobacco smoke may well seem a more compelling explanation for people in the street being so worried about 'catching cancer' from 'selfish idiots' like Rosie. But the fact that the man lambasting Rosie was worried that he'd catch her cancer, and that he thought of it as *contagious*, might say otherwise. As Bell (2011: 49) has argued, we might be legislating abjection – those 'liminial and transitive' qualities of cigarette smoke that permit its movement between bodies – and not just any bodies, but rotting bodies – more than we are legislating for the objectively demonstrable harm that secondhand smoke might do.

As I said at in my opening remarks in the Introduction of this chapter, this seems an effective proposal: the protection of non-smokers from breathing in disgusting 'secondhand' air is a much more readily apprehended foundation for smokefree public place legislation than the objective facts of the harm smoke presents to breathers in the outdoor air. The difference between legislating using abjection and legislating by recourse to objective facts is made clear in the following anecdote. On 13 January 2015, the Queensland Cancer Council welcomed the Queensland government's announcement that it would consider banning outdoor smoking in apartment buildings. The Cancer Council representative, Katie Clift, remarked that this was an excellent proposal, because 'almost one person dies every day from secondhand smoke' (Cancer Council 2015: np). This remark caused one of my dinner companions that evening to wonder aloud whether or not secondhand smoke was actually terminal – or just that it would 'almost' kill you: 'Kills *almost* one?', he said. 'Does that mean he's left alive, but only just, then?' 'Almost one' death is not nearly as terrifying as inhaling bits of rot expelled from someone's lung. Not by a long shot.

Jessica Rowe's reactions were likely much more effective at advancing the Cancer Council's support for the Queensland government's proposal. The former news desk anchor, appearing on a morning breakfast panel called *Studio Ten* with other Australian identities, wrinkled her nose when fellow panellist and former Australian *Women's Weekly* Ita Buttrose said she thought the move was overkill. Buttrose said while she supported most smokefree legislation, the categories 'offensive smell' and 'danger' were being conflated. Rowe interjected, shaking her head and waving away imaginary smoke, telling Buttrose that she wouldn't want her kids breathing in another person's tobacco smoke. 'Yuck,' she declared.

That 'yuck' says it all. It might well be sufficient to banish rot-ridden polluters of the public air from their balconies, and it has already been sufficient to restrict them to public land, that interstitial and nowhere space distinctive from those public places in which pure air is available to the public – like the beach – 'the place you go get fresh air', as Jennifer said. This ushers in some interesting consequences for understandings of who, exactly, constitutes 'the public' and under what circumstances they might do so, as well as revealing the particular capacity of the air to differentiate persons.

# There is difference in the air

Explications of the smoky outdoor air as miasmatically dangerous and dirty require the identification of those responsible for the contamination and to restrict their opportunity to foul the air by restricting their movements in it. *Tobacco in Australia* notes that smoking has been transformed from 'a widely practised and socially acceptable behaviour to one which is increasingly typified as destructive, *dirty*, and anti-social' (see Scollo and Winstanley 2012: np). The classification of smoke as dirty, as Mary Douglas (1966) would tell us, indicates that smoke is matter out of (public) place – as are the smokers who are inextricably intertwined with smoke, whether or not they light up, as Misty found out. It is precisely the pursuit of purification – the classification of smoking and smokers as dirty matter (kept) out of (public) place and the pursuit of its elimination – that has advanced purity's opposite: the result of the drive to eliminate smoking is a dirty, disgusting remainder; a 'zero' of smokers that hang around the edges and are increasingly relegated to the outskirts of the middle-class public.

While public health resources like *Tobacco in Australia* issue the warning that the denormalization of tobacco use, its classification as dirty and antisocial, could have an undesired stigmatizing effect on the socio-economically marginalized, smokefree legislation *has* widened health inequalities by having a far greater impact on the better-off.

The elimination of smoking in public places, as Dovey (1999) argues, means that one is increasingly likely to meet therein a certain kind of person (see also Tan 2013).[8] In the smokefree state in Australia, the 'kind of person' one might meet in public space will not be someone who is smoking. In Australia this smoking person is still, in raw numbers terms, likely to be middle class, but, proportionally, smoking increasingly belongs to the poor, the Indigene, the marginal. These smokers must increasingly populate the nowhere spaces excluded from public place if they elect to smoke in public. And even if the smoker does not light up in public place, she may still be ejected from it: Misty certainly was subject to expulsion from the public space of the city bus. The behaviour 'smoking' and the person 'the smoker' begin to collapse in Misty's case. Thanks to the capacity of thirdhand smoke to stay on the person, she is no longer definable as a smoker only when she smokes – instead, she carries her own permanent atmosphere around with her – regardless of whether she actually lights up.

This indistinction is evident, too, in advice given on the TFA website, which posts regular updates on tobacco control litigation and cases. Remarking on the successful legal argument permitting those with a tobacco smoke sensitivity to be provided with smokefree workplaces, TFA recently entitled its blog, 'those-with-cancer-in-family-history-must-avoid-smokers'.[9] The taxonomic distinction between 'smoking' and 'smokers' has collapsed. As I noted earlier, the executive director of Action on Health and Smoking has pointed to the possibility that those with a family history of cancer may also be entitled to smokefree places – restaurants, workplaces and any places they frequent – and, in the case of thirdhand smoke, 'smokefree places' means places free of smokers, not just smoke. This, indeed, has dramatic transformative effects on the constitution of the public body: on first pass, legislative actions to protect the air and the public which breathes it might appear to be egalitarian, since it is the 'air' being legislated and not persons as such. But the legislation – that which is already in existence and pertains to smoke itself, and that in the wind, that may increasingly apply to 'smokers' – is brought unevenly to bear on the already socio-economically marginalized. Thus, the 'air tells us about difference: in the testimony of pollutants and choking effluvium, an analysis of air reveals who belongs and who does not, who is deserving and who is not' (Adey 2013: 291).

Adey notes how megacities are increasingly productive of secessionary atmospheres, 'often by removal and exclusion, which are not entirely separate from other atmospheric security concerns' (Ibid).[10] It seems the same might be said of a legislative agenda that seeks to regulate the air itself. These agendas harnesses ideas about securing the atmosphere from smoky pollution for the protection of the public, but it simultaneously ushers in a socio-moral code that produces a new norm, beyond 'smoke is harmful'. Smoke is dirty, disgusting, issuing from bodies that do not belong, and must be expelled. Smokefree has marked up hierarchical difference. If we experience different breathing spaces, 'how does this orient our ability to understand others' air spaces, and our ability to share matters of concern?' (O'Loughlin 2010: 4) This, I submit, is a question anthropologists need to put to themselves, as they consider protecting publics from the smoky air. It's a question that needs to be put outside the dominant public health framing. I turn to how it might be phrased, below.

# Colonial anthropology: Eradicating smoke and mosquitoes

While a public health framing would permit us to see that smoking is very much a classed practice, it would not allow us to recognize that the search for purification of the atmosphere in which smoking occurs advances its opposite. This sort of omission is highly likely in a framing in which the most important thing is to clean up smoky atmospheres. But anthropologists haven't really stepped outside this framing. Indeed, the opposite is true: anthropologists have been very active in advancing a key notion in public health, that whole publics require protection from the dangerous waft of toxic killer fumes (see for paradigmatic examples Kohrman and Xiao 2008; Russell and Lewis 2011). Let me say, very clearly here, that the kinds of analyses that advance the public health goal of protecting the public from the dangerousness of smoky air have a valid place, as part of an ideally broad range of disciplinary enquiries into smoking. I am certainly not suggesting that we ditch them. However, as I've already said, those enquiries that are aligned with the eradication of the tobacco scourge are dominant, and they obscure some of the other enquiries that might be made.

The consequences of being deeply implicated in a harm reduction agenda were evident in anthropological activity in colonial times, when the 'scientists of empire', as we might have called them then, like Reed and Gorgas, were involved in the occupation of Cuba during the Spanish–American War. As Alex Nading (2013: 63) notes, these men made mosquito eradication the focus of public health science for the better part of the twentieth century. Their aggressive stance against mosquitoes then, and the generalized disciplinary stance taken against smoking now, fit beautifully into a narrative of Western colonial triumphalism, predicated on the idea that through 'scientific rationality and technical prowess', disciplinary experts could civilize and clean up sullied landscapes (Ibid.). In the cases of both mosquitoes and smoke, priority placed on insulating human bodies from dangerous (tropical or smoky) environments paralleled with the recognition of the inherent porosity of human bodies (the circulation of blood, parasites and dangerous smoke).

This could be quite interesting, anthropologically speaking. For instance, on the porosity of bodies, one might analyse the ways in which the air itself has been pressed into service in the creation of a new smokefree 'atmosphere', as I have above, noting in particular how breathing out with smoke is explicated and legislated so that it can no longer happen in public place. Once backgrounded atmospheric, the air itself, with its capacity to cross bodily bounds and create communities of breathers sharing the same substance, is worthy of foregrounded anthropological attention, especially when the presence of smoke marks up its capacity to connect bodies, and to array them hierarchically, as Adey notes.

We could go further, as I also have in the foregoing: smokefree atmosphere becomes legislatively and practically manifest in rules about where smoking can take place in public. Given that smokers are now concentrated in the lowest socio-economic registers, now that the war on smoking has been largely won among the middle classes in the West, and smoking is now impermissible in most areas designated 'public', smokers are relegated to interstitial spaces of public land – the vacant lot, the kerb, the places to which the socio-economically marginalized are typically relegated. Such a pattern might alert anthropologists to the importance of attending to the category of 'the public', as opposed to dealing with the 'health of the public', as one might if one was wedded to eliminating smoking practice in public space. To return momentarily to mosquitoes, Nading (2013: 63) discusses the findings of Sutter, an environmental historian, who

> recounts a debate between Gorgas's mosquito team and the Quartermaster's Department in the Canal Zone. Gorgas believed that the Quartermaster was preferentially cutting grass in the '(white) married quarters while neglecting other important sanitary cutting in areas that bred and harbored vector mosquitoes' (Sutter 2007: 749). ... For the early mosquito hunters, bent though they were on 'eradicating' the insect scourge, health would arise not just from careful insulation of bodies from insects but also from careful governance of how those bodies moved through space.

Similarly, the health of the population does not arise simply from eradicating smoking, which has largely been done in respect of the middle classes, but depends equally on limiting how smoke can move through space when it emits from those who continue the practice. In the West, that means marginalizing the poor. Anthropologists have certainly recognized the class dimensions of smoking, but analyses have tended strongly towards the political economy variety, in which the tobacco industry appeals to the poor, recruits them into smoking and keeps them there by means of addiction. This kind of attention coincides with the notion that environments conducive to malaria or filled with smoke are presently public health menaces to be dealt by the state with the full support of researchers, as opposed to being opened to all manner of questions, including those that depart from the premise of eradicating the problem. Anthropologists need to recognize smokefree actions on the air as consequential air conditioning.

## Protecting the infinite and pure air

The development of smokefree legislation is, of course, not the first time that the air itself has been explicated by reference to the risks that smoke presents to its otherwise pure state. In 1661, John Evelyn published a pamphlet entitled

*Fumifugium: The Inconveniencie of the Aer and Smoak of London Dissipated.* Written in response to the use of dirty Newcastle coal that had created 'an impure and thick Mist accompanied with a fuligimous and filthy vapour' that dominated the 'otherwise wholesome and excellent Aer', Evelyn attempted to introduce a new understanding of the air, underwritten by evidence of ill health. Evelyn worried that the people

> breathe nothing but which renders them obnoxious to a thousand inconveniences, corrupting the Lungs, and disordering the entire habit of their Bodies; so that Catharrs, Phthisicks, Coughs and Consumptions rage more in this one City than in the whole Earth besides. (Evelyn 1661: 5)

Evelyn warned the principal addressee of his *Fumifugium*, the King, that disordered air would bring about similarly disordered politics:

> The Aer it selfe is many times a potent and great disposer to Rebellion; and that … people … where this Medium is grosse and heavy, are extremely versatile … to change both in Religious and Secular Affaires. (Evelyn 1661: 1)

Evelyn also made proposals to avoid the impending disorder, at first recommending that those to blame – the operators of all the commercial smoke emitting devices, including the furnaces of all the brewers, bakers – be banished to a safely distant location, so as not to pollute the air in which non-emitting persons habitually circulated. Such a course of action, even though it was undertaken in 1661, seems remarkably similar to the splitting up of emitters and non-emitters in evidence in current smokefree place rules across Australia and much of the Western world.

Perhaps unlike current smokefree legislators, however, Evelyn realized that smoke is uncontainable wafting omnitude – or at least it is sufficiently omnitudinal as to connect the spaces within its reach otherwise imagined as separate or distanced (Connor 2008). This realization, borne to him, perhaps, on a stiff breeze that blew commercial smoke across the distance of the whole city, rendered Evelyn's first suggestion unworkable. He quickly proposed a second: the air would be purified by fragrant herbs that could decontaminate polluted air.

While neither of his suggestions was taken up by the King, Evelyn's insights were nevertheless visionary in that he saw that the State and the state of the air might be inextricably intertwined, that there may be opportunity for the state to regulate the air, and that the state would have to be responsible for distinguishing between those who generate smoke and those who do not. Where Evelyn recognized the unhealthy nature of the air, its state was intertwined with and inseparable from a sociopolitical agenda which had as its aim the control of the disordered populace.

Centuries after *Fumifugium*, Tim Choy's (2010) work on knowledge practices in environmental politics in Hong Kong alerts us to the ways in which industrial and automobile pollution foregrounds the air in a manner that makes people think about themselves as uncared for by a state that has failed to secure for them the most basic of resources, breathable air. Again, it is clear that doing things – or not doing things – to the air is often tied up with political agendas, in this case the acceleration of industrial activity and the advancement of capitalism at the expense of those who are left to breathe in its exhaust fumes.

The attempts that Evelyn made to clean the air, and the state of polluted air that Choy describes reference regulation of the air by calling industrial emitters to clean up the air in the name of public health. While the introduction of smokefree might seem continuous with such an agenda, smokefree legislation is brought to bear on individual bodies and holds them directly responsible for the state of the public air. It's why Misty couldn't just hop on the bus, even after she stubbed out her cigarette. It's why Rosie can be held responsible for causing cancer in the street. It's why Jennifer is such a staunch defender of the air, and why it wasn't 'an incident' when she protected the innocent lungs of her daughter from a menace so terrible that it could cause illness in the next breath. Where the science objectively indicates that specific conditions are needed for harm to be caused by smoke in the outdoor air, the foul odour of cigarette smoke, replete with rotting lung, wafting on the breeze is all that's needed to subjectively justify the expulsion of the source. If sociality is to be conceived through smell, then an anthropological attendance to sensorily arrayed relations of power must accompany it. In the next chapter, I expand these themes of the sensory registration of disgust, and its powerful effects – as well as through the sensory register of touch. Neither chapter is intended as a rallying cry to get smoking and smokers reinstated in public place. Each is intended to point out that expelling smokers from public space is just as powerful an act as those that occur between Big Tobacco and its 'dependent consumers' – I'm encouraging anthropologists to attend to them as interesting relations between the person and the state, without encouraging them to defend the right of the smoker to smoke in public place.

# 6

# Abject thirdhand smoke

## Introduction

Expelled tobacco smoke has led us to create smoking zones that appear on our maps as interstitial spaces like the middle of the road. The spatial dimensions are easy enough to see, and even permit insight into how anthropologists have attended to public health interests in space since the colonial era. But state and disciplinary attention to smoke ought also to prompt equally thorough temporal analysis.

I observed in the second chapter that thirdhand smoke has the capacity to cross the barriers erected around an aspirational time of 'smokefree'. The ghosts of cigarettes past emerge to insert themselves into the fibres of the curtains, or the carpet, to harm again, as 'thirdhand' smoke. But the capacity of thirdhand smoke to trouble borders is not confined simply to the temporal. I argue in this chapter that smoke, usually thought of as being dangerous because of its indiscriminate *movement* into any unwilling lungs that cross its path, can, in and through its capacity to infiltrate matter, *become sited*.

Equipped with shape-shifting capacity, thirdhand smoke invisibly infiltrates the solid properties of things (like walls, sofas and hair). It equally utilizes the amorphous properties of the air to be both on the move (in breath, in the air circulating in a room). Once it has been absorbed into the sofa, the sofa becomes a site of dangerous thirdhand smoke emission. In this sense, thirdhand smoke has the capacity to be sited. Researchers can examine such items, and establish their levels of toxicity. Yet, at the same time, thirdhand is equally *unsited* – in the sense that thirdhand smoke contaminates *everything*. We cannot, for instance, simply dispose of the sofa and put an end to thirdhand smoke contamination – it's everywhere else too; in the carpet upon which the sofa sat, in the paint on the walls in the living room where the sofa was, in the air all around it.

I'm giving a goodly press to the sofa because it's the star of a new video released as part of the UCTV 'Prime Cuts' series, which showcases research carried out at the University of California. The clip, which runs for just over two and a half minutes, features an innocuous looking sofa that, having sucked up tobacco smoke, is the source of contaminating emissions (see UCTV 2012). This smoke is passive-aggressive – it will be absorbed, sucked up, by the sofa, but then 'come back off of whatever it is stuck to', says Suzyann Schick in the clip. The presence of this invisible smoke is given away by its smell – a dead giveaway that its absorption by the sofa is incomplete and simultaneously reversible; just as much as the sofa has absorbed it, thirdhand smoke continues to emit into the air *from* the site of the sofa. Penetrative yet outbound, sited and yet not, matter yet air, thirdhand smoke is abjectness par excellence.

And it's not just what you can smell. It's what you can touch too, as Lara Gundel, the other researcher featured in the clip, explains:

> Thirdhand smoke is what you smell when you go into a hotel room where people have been smoking, or what rubs off on your skin if you touch a wall, or if you visit somebody's house and they've been smoking. So that means it's not only there in the air, but it's also coming out of the surfaces. (UCTV 2012)

It's not just smelling thirdhand smoke that's dangerous, then; it's touching it – and one touches it in the form of a sofa, a wall, and in the form of a person. Touching these things is dangerous, as the researchers point out, especially for children who encounter thirdhand smoke from touching familial skin. I pick up on this notion of touch, as well as paying specific attention to smell, in this chapter, to render and analyse thirdhand smoke in two sensory registers.

Thirdhand smoke is also, of course, temporally disobedient. Emitted in the present, yet refusing to be consigned to the past, the 'future presence' of thirdhand smoke has consequences for the accomplishment of a time we might call 'smokefree', but it is especially consequential for smokers themselves because of what their bodies, covered in an invisible but often odiferously evident coating of thirdhand smoke, are thought to do to the bodies of others as they emit thirdhand smoke into the air around them.

As the purported coiner of the term 'thirdhand smoke' Jonathon Winickoff, implies in his public statements about it, thirdhand smoke can be expected to situate smokers as dangerous, in and of themselves. The thirdhand smoke they expel from their hair, onto their skin, into their clothes, sofas, curtains, tabletops, can't be washed off, aired out, or otherwise expunged. And, according to Winickoff, it's even more dangerous to ingest, especially for children, making smokers ticking time bombs whose fuses are lit in the past and constantly, quietly, exploding in the present as they hug your kids, as you sit on their sofas, or as you 'take a whiff of a smoker's hair and feel faint from the pungent smell of cigarette smoke', as *Scientific American* reporter Coco Ballantyne penned in the opening remarks of her interview with Winickoff in 2009. Perhaps, Winickoff foresaw the loathing and fear with which such dangerous people will indubitably be held when thirdhand smoke becomes a well-known public health menace, and perhaps it is why he issues the plea, 'have sympathy for smokers, and help them quit' (in Ballantyne 2009: np), accompanied by his observation that smokers don't know it's harmfulness. Perhaps the phrase, 'Forgive them … for they know not what they do,' is not too dramatic a translation of Winickoff's words. If it is the right sort of translation, it won't last long, for thirdhand smoke confirms the smoker's abjectness, as well as the need to eject her from the non-smoking ranks.

# Thirdhand smoke

Thirdhand smoke describes the particles and gases that remain present on surfaces after a cigarette has been extinguished. It follows 'second' hand smoke, that smoke that permeates an environment and bodies that circulate therein, and 'first' hand smoke, that is actively and intentionally drawn in by the smoker. Technically speaking, thirdhand smoke is environmental tobacco smoke that has oxidized with environmental nitrous acid to produce carcinogens that are not present in either cigarette objects or tobacco smoke, known as tobacco-specific nitrosamines. Thirdhand smoke is the result of a productive process, in which something new is created out of thin air.

Ballantyne (2009) claims that the term 'thirdhand smoke' was initially coined by Wickinoff's research team at the Dana Faber/Harvard Cancer Centre but, as Bell (2014) points out, the trajectory of the concept into public health prominence has been a complex (as a well as a rapid) one, in which claims have been inextricably tied up with the haste of media outlets to make big news of this new menace. Even taking 2009 as the point at which the term first emerged, it is clear that thirdhand smoke is no longer a neologism; a Google search for the term returns over 4 million items, many of which take the form of public health information and warnings. The Mayo Clinic's blog advises that thirdhand smoke

> is generally considered to be residual nicotine and other chemicals left on a variety of indoor surfaces by tobacco smoke. This residue is thought to react with common indoor pollutants to create a toxic mix. This toxic

mix of thirdhand smoke contains cancer causing substances, posing a potential health hazard to nonsmokers who are exposed to it, especially children. Studies show that thirdhand smoke clings to hair, skin, clothes, furniture, drapes, walls, bedding, carpets, dust, vehicles and other surfaces, even long after smoking has stopped. Infants, children and nonsmoking adults may be at risk of tobacco related health problems when they inhale, ingest or touch substances containing thirdhand smoke. Thirdhand smoke is a relatively new concept, and researchers are still studying its possible dangers. Thirdhand smoke residue builds up on surfaces over time and resists normal cleaning. Thirdhand smoke can't be eliminated by airing out rooms, opening windows, using fans or air conditioners, or confining smoke to only certain areas of a home. In contrast, secondhand smoke is the smoke and other airborne products that come from being close to burning tobacco products, such as cigarettes. The only way to protect nonsmokers from thirdhand smoke is to create a smokefree environment, whether that's your private home or vehicle, or in public places, such as hotels and restaurants. (see Mayo Clinic 2014)

The notion that cigarette smoke toxicants could stick to surfaces after the smoke itself dissipated appeared first in 1953, when a research team reported that smoke condensate painted onto mice caused cancer (see Wynder et al. 1953). In 1991, Hein et al.'s study into a then 'unnoticed aspect of involuntary smoking' household dust reported high levels of nicotine contamination in smokers' homes. A study undertaken in 2004 reported in more detail on the levels of contamination and confirmed that it did not occur in homes never exposed to cigarette smoking (Matt et al. 2004). In 2008, vehicles became the subject of enquiry; smokers' vehicles, particularly those of long hauler smoking truck drivers, were found to be saturated with thirdhand contaminant (Matt et al. 2008). In 2011, Matt et al. also reported on how long thirdhand smoke might remain in the home or the car, concluding that it lingered in excess of two months; in the case of the home, even after being vacant for two months and being prepared for new residents, sometimes with new carpeting and paint (see Matt et al. 2011).

Such characterizations of thirdhand smoke illustrate that it is endowed with longevity normally denied to smoke – it is more usually thought of as a fleeting and temporary presence – but also that smoke has the capacity to adhere to things. In its thirdhand form, smoke has shifted from uncontainable wafting omnitude to sticky lodgement. Understood within visual and olfactory frames, smoke is a traveller on the breeze. But in its thirdhand form, smoke is as much a stayer as it is a wanderer, leaving itself staunchly behind, in time and in space, and on the body of the smoker.

# 'Mobile tobacco contamination packages'

The capacity of smoke to stick to the smoker herself has earned her the title 'mobile tobacco contamination packages', a moniker applied by psychologist and thirdhand tobacco researcher Georg Matt. In an article that appeared as 'The Nose Knows: The Invisible Threat of Thirdhand Smoke', Matt told the *Huffington Post*'s Lynn Peeples in 2011:

> I get lots of stories of people with asthma who move into environments that are full of thirdhand smoke and report increased problems, Matt said. This is more than just a nuisance like the smell of dirty socks, added Matt, who called smokers 'mobile tobacco contamination packages'.

Peeples' article itself covered a change in policy governing smoking at the Indiana University Health medical centre:

> Before this week, employees at the Indiana University Health medical centre were free to step off the non-smoking campus and light up a cigarette. Sure, co-workers and patients would probably notice the telltale odor on the smoker's clothes, skin and breath – especially if they happened to share an elevator – but they could do little more than plug their noses in defense. That all changed on Monday, when the medical centre upgraded its policy: Employees are now prohibited from smoking during the workday. Period. The impetus for the new rule is the recently recognized dangers of 'thirdhand smoke', the gases and particles that cling to clothing, hair, furniture, walls and other surfaces long after a cigarette has been stubbed out. (see Peeples 2011: np)

Bell has demonstrated that claims about the dangers of thirdhand smoke currently exist in the conspicuous absence of any evidence of harm – or, perhaps, this absence *is* inconspicuous, in the sense that a lack of evidence of harm has not stopped all manner of immoderate or as Bell describes them, (strikingly intemperate) claims from being made about its harms (see Bell 2014: 158). In harm's absence, Bell proposes that it is instead 'the embodied dimension of thirdhand smoke that has been central to the concept's success' (2014: 165). Noting that the semiotic power of the smell of stale cigarette smoke is frequently referenced in media and public health reports on thirdhand smoke, Bell argues,

> The smell of smoke – like smoke itself – creates a material connection between the smoker and the bystander. ... Moreover, this connection is

entirely involuntary. ... The smell of stale cigarette smoke [which cannot be voided, but once in, stays in, the recipient body – see Le Guerer 1990: 175] is marginal matter in Douglas' sense of the term: in its refusal to respect boundaries, it is dangerous and polluting. In the language of Kristeva (1982), thirdhand smoke is abject: an in-between, ambiguous, composite substance – neither air nor matter – that destroys the boundaries between what is 'me' and what is 'not me'. (2014: 165)

As Bell suggests, thirdhand smoke extends the very same dangers of secondhand smoke through the invasive capacities of smoke, but I think it also differs in two important ways. First, thirdhand smoke coats the smoker in an invisible cloak that stays about her, yet retains the properties of smoke to waft outbound, away from her. Emanating toxic wastes from her insides as she breathes out air that has circulated around her rotted lungs as secondhand smoke *and* emitting noxious poison from her invisible encasement in thirdhand smoke, the smoker, comprehensively, becomes Matt's 'mobile tobacco contamination package'. Inside and out, her abject status is overwhelming. Second, and relatedly, thirdhand smoke not only demands theorizing through smell – it demands it in and through *touch*.

Let us turn firstly to smell and to the relations in which this entails smokers in respect of thirdhand smoke.

# Smell and the thirdhand trickster

This 'comprehensive' smoker is tricky, a trickster, in the sense that she embodies a series of oppositions; her internal regions and invisibly coated, external skin together express the duality of smoke to be at once air and matter, amorphous omnitude and matter. She dwells halfway between oppositionary poles, including those of life and death. She lives; yet her insides are dying – some parts are *already* dead, like the cells of her lungs that have already atrophied and blackened. She assumes the reassuringly solid shape of the person, yet she emanates invisible poisons from her skin and her hair. She might appear to be a good mother, smoking outside and well away from her infant, washing her hands, her face after her cigarette; but even as she returns inside to cradle her baby, she is poisoning it with the invisible matter coating her skin, clothes and hair. My favourite example of the lurking monster beneath the maternal façade is a poster of a baby accompanied by the caption, 'This Baby Now Has Emphysema,' that I saw once floating around the internet – and that I now can't locate. And it is not only her own offspring that her malign presence infects. Almost by magic and certainly invisibly, she reaches out with the odorous power she possesses to disturb and diminish the unborn held supposedly secure inside the wombs of others. As Tobacco.org reported in June of 2009, such acts of olfactory magic bring recriminations:

> Fortunately, says public interest law professor [and *very* interested head of Action on Smoking and Health – ASH] John Banzhaf, the law provides protection against exposure to this substance [thirdhand smoke] previously known simply as 'tobacco smoke residue' which contains highly carcinogenic compounds, heavy metals, hydrogen cyanide (used in chemical weapons) butane (use in lighter fluid) toluene (found in paint thinners) arsenic, lead, and even radioactive Polonium-210 (used to murder a Russian spy). A federal court has held that an employee whose health is adversely affected by tobacco smoke residue has a cause [*sic*] of action under the Americans with Disabilities Act [ADA] against an employer who refused to reduce his exposure in his workplace, and a complaint by Action on Smoking and Health [ASH] recently forced a university to protect a woman and her unborn child whose health was threatened by tobacco smoke residue [thirdhand smoke] on the clothing of an officemate who smoked outdoors. In the latter situation one doctor stated that 'her sensitivity is also to the tobacco smoke residue on the person or clothing of a smoker, not just smoke in the air. Therefore, to protect her health, especially during her pregnancy, she should not be assigned to an office with someone who smokes during the day'. (see Tobacco.org 2009)

Certainly, such odorous characters as this smelly officemate have been accused of creating harm on others before now, on similarly unverifiable bases. Indeed, in the absence of any evidence of those things of which they were accused, their smell proved more than sufficient. As Francesca Matteoni reminds us, bad smells can array an entire, sinister world around its real or imaginary emitters, and are often traced to worlds that cannot be visually apprehended. Matteoni notes for instance that a foul smell connoted 'both demons and the places they frequented' during the renaissance, and that

> bad odour became a peculiarity of the witch as well. In fact it was transmitted to human beings during their copulation with devils, which acquired a corporeal form, snatching the bodies hanged and dead people. Thus the odour of physical mortality distinguished evil spirits. The supernatural stench had already marked the Jews, the unbearable *foetur Judaicus*, which they had allegedly tried to cover by employing Christian blood. Suggesting corruption, decay and therefore a link with supernatural beings, such as demons or the dead, it therefore served to exclude groups or individuals from society, but also to ward off the menace they represented. (2010: 40)

These observations indicate that odour identifies the undesirable other, but thirdhand smoke does much more than simply indicate an undesirable presence. Classen et al. (1994) have emphasized that olfactory perception of 'the other' is deployed as a 'potent metaphor for social decay' lingering in the other – indeed, odour forms the basis of difference that is borne to the established order as a foul smell. This occurs in such a way to indicate not only its power of infiltration, but also its *physical* potential to act in the world. Matteoni notes:

> In fact a strong odour is not only a single body sign of distinction, but it emanates from it, lingering in the air, penetrating into places and things, provoking infection and disruption. Travelling into the air is also linked to blood, according to the existing correspondences between the four humours and natural elements stressed by early modern philosophical and medical theories. In a world [in the 1600s] in which the body had no fixed contours and could be equally healed or damaged by contact with the external environment, where infected air corrupted the blood, and, similarly, a sick body spread disease in its vicinity, smell was either a source of healing or of danger. (2010: 41)

Although Matteoni is not speaking at all here of thirdhand smoke, she might just as well be: the strong odour of thirdhand smoke lingering on the person does not simply identify her as an odorous presence, but warns of the potential lurking within her to provoke infection, or to effect harm, perhaps even to visit it upon the unborn, such is its penetrative, physical force. Odour isn't just a sign, identifying the other who might then become subject to exclusions, dismissals and rejections. Smell is a felt vigour, registered not only at the level of feeling ill at ease about the presence of the other, but actually becoming ill resultant of their odiferous force. Smell is a carnal power, somatically registered, working directly on bodies and borne to them by an air that doesn't respect the presence of bodily boundaries, not even the doubled protected boundary of the womb encased inside the maternal body.

Prior to Pasteur's insights that showed that disease was the consequence of microorganisms, the air itself was endowed with such physical agency. Understood to bring with it a history of its recent wanderings, the air could bear illness on its wings. One could only hope that the air one breathed in had not, just priorly, circulated among the rotted and foul matter, for breathing in such air, which was characterized by its foul smell, resulted in illness. Here, we are permitted the view of the air and its relationship with the body that circulated prior to Pasteur's paradigm-shifting discovery: bodies were subject to an active air, and smell was not just an irritation, but instead illness in waiting. Smell was a physicality, just waiting for deposition into a body by way of the wind where, once deposited, it would grow into the maturity of illness.

It seems there is little difference between these miasmatic conceptions of a smell so powerful that it would translate into physical illness and the phenomenon of thirdhand smoke. A classically miasmatic construction, in which the air is understood to hold in suspension the emanations of the foul, thirdhand smoke is capable of inflicting physical danger and is capable of infecting all breathers by dint of its mode of travel: on the updrafts and downdrafts, the indiscriminate gusts and wafts of the air. And, making it even more dangerous is its sitedness in all of the places where it invisibly settles. As Georg Matt told *Huffington Post* readers, all you can do to keep yourself safe from its lurking menace in a rental car, a hotel room or any other space that may have been at one time inhabited by a smoker, 'If you smell something, keep looking. Be careful and trust your nose.'

Matteoni isn't talking about thirdhand smoke, and I can appreciate that the reader may have formed the view that I'm stretching the point. If that's the case, then consider once again Jemma Wayne's remarks in her 2014 article in the *Huffington Post*, 'Why Smokers Must Be Shamed.' Wayne *is* talking about thirdhand smoke. She agrees that smoking has a certain appeal, but 'what is less appealing is being branded a murderer'. While it's true that Wayne is being intemperate and dramatic here (as is her right in an opinion piece), it does seem to be the case that her remarks about thirdhand smoke's dangerousness resonate with more seriously minded institutional types, as does her insinuation, that thirdhand smoke's capacity to murder is enabled by the smoker's movements among 'us'. Consider, for example, the US-based 'Health Tap', a website that uses doctors to answer the public's submitted questions about health. One query, from 'A Member', is as follows:

> A coworker smokes and I can often smell the third hand smoke at my desk. Should I be worried over this level of exposure?

> A doctor answers: Yes. Very much. Your employer, by allowing this smoke to permeate the work environment is putting your health at very great risk. I would advise you to bring this to their attention immediately. (Health Tap nd)

A murderous menace to all breathers that might be found in any place in which a smoker has been smoking certainly justifies the search for its fouling culprits: miasmatic pollution requires purification, as Gabriel notes[1]:

> Miasma goes well beyond physical or even moral uncleanliness, indicating an affliction that is enduring and cannot be washed away [as is certainly

the case with thirdhand smoke], although certain actions are taken to deal with it. It is a state of rottenness for which individuals may be responsible and are certainly held to be highly contagious. This individual who brings miasma infects everyone he/she touches. … Once unleashed, miasma is capable of afflicting everyone.

## *Everyone*

'Miasma', continues Gabriel,

> brings about a state of moral and spiritual decay, a corruption of all values and human relations of trust, love and community – people suspect their neighbours of being the cause, scapegoating and witch hunts are rife. Thus, a notable feature of miasma … is that the search for purification and expiation frequently helps spread the corruption.

In the case of thirdhand smoke, the language of a witch-hunt is probably not too strong, if there exists smokers who can reach, as if by evil magic, into wombs to contaminate the unborn with their foul stench. And, certainly in the case of thirdhand smoke, we see plainly the corruption of values of trust, love, community, in the very purification techniques that exist to ensure the continuance of the community under such a threat. Michigan's Weyco insurance company, for instance, banned smoking among its employees in 2005, and now engages in ongoing random testing for remnant nicotine among its employees. A fail result means dismissal. No trust here, but plenty of suspicion.

A fail result might also mean a death sentence. On the ABC's most recent episode of its popular show *Save Your Life Tonight*, host Cameron Daddo invited Rene Bittoun, whom he described as an 'antismoking Evangelist' onto the stage to test the carbon monoxide output of hapless sixty-something-year-old, pack-a-day smoking [let's call him] 'Dave'. Hot on the heels of a story about a man present in the audience who had just completed treatment for lung cancer which was 'not his fault', but had come to him instead from being in environments inhabited by smokers, Dave submitted to the test and returned a result of fifteen parts per million (a high reading – a normal output is around four) and was told he was well on his way to thirty, which would 'be fatal'. Dave, offgassing onto the innocent audience members even as he was interviewed, including the man who'd been afflicted with cancer because of people like Dave, was asked if he intended to quit, to which he gave the only answer possible under such circumstances: he nodded fervently. No love here.

Dr Richard Graffis, executive vice president and chief medical officer at Indiana University Health and overseer of its transition to thirdhand smokefree workplace, did not see the need for testing any of his workers as Weyco did. He noted that smokers would in any case be 'self-incriminating' because of the odour that they would exude, if they broke with policy and had a sneaky cigarette during work hours. 'We have no hidden cameras, no Gestapo,' he told the *Huffington Post* (see Peeples 2011). He then indicated that no such *visual* surveillance techniques were needed in any case: 'But if they go outside and smoke, we'll know.' No trust here, only a foul stench to identify the sources of danger.

As Gabriel also notes, miasma issues from the neighbour – *from within*. Matteoni's work is again useful. She notes that during the mid-1600s,

> witchcraft became the greatest heresy because it implied the renunciation of God through a declared allegiance with Satan. But, as Norman Cohn has underlined in his work on the background of the witch-hunt, the main features of this emerging diabolical cult are not to be found far from Christianity itself. Christian literature was haunted by demons and by the dramatized representation of the Devil, which was depicted in animal or disquieting anthropomorphic form and connotated [*sic*] by a heavy smell, in contrast with the spiritual elements exalted by the Christian faith. Yet the devilish monstrosity, that during medieval times had been an attribute of the Jews, was now not only the materialisation of a dangerous otherness. It could be no more marginalized as the evidence of a different ethnic and religious group, but it could, instead, manifest itself in every individual belonging to the community, which became part of the satanic congregation. (2010: 35)

In Australia, the thirdhand menace might be similarly presented to us from within our own familiar territories, activities and circulations. Could the cause of my illness be my office mate? Perhaps it will be the vendor of the next home I'll purchase, who smoked inside and infected the walls which now lie in wait to gently, invisibly and constantly offgas, even through the new paint. Perhaps, as one San Franciscan hotel feared, the source of illness could be the last paying guest allowed to smoke in its bar, its bedrooms, its dining areas. Heading possible litigation off at the pass, it posted a sign in its lobby, declaring to present customers that patrons of the hotel were once permitted to smoke within its walls, and indubitably left invisible deposits on its surfaces. It is almost as if these past guests were still there; current patrons were warned that these invisible people who slept, ate and milled about had infected the place. No one could say who they were, but their legacy lay in wait in the rooms, the carpet, the curtains. Their smoke never checked out of the hotel, which remained haunted by its continued presence. The abject cannot be banished entirely, even under such conditions of radical exclusion as smokefree. It might pop up in the curtains of your new apartment, in the carpet of a rental car, in the last hotel room you stayed in.

The atmosphere of smokefree is new, but it is informed by some very old notions. The Roman poet Lucan wrote that witches' breath poisoned 'air that before was harmless' – this seems perfectly applicable to modern conceptions of thirdhand smoke, especially if we consider an entry on the ASH website, discussing the dangerousness of thirdhand smoke: Smokers' breath can be harmful to health' (see Lucan ([AD 65] 1896).[2] And witches? If the figure of the witch is taken to apply to one who is antagonistic to the social order, then smokers are witches in the era of smokefree. 'Protect Your Family,' screams the ASH website. 'Don't become complacent!', 'Most Nonsmokers ARE Exposed!'.[3]

# Touch: How to deal with witches in the family

Smokers are revealed to be most antagonistic to the social order when they disrupt the familial order – especially where relations with babies and children are involved. A great many websites across the United Kingdom, United States and Australia have begun dispensing advice to new parents, about regulating touch between the baby and family members who smoke. Issuing from within the very breast of the family, the threat of contamination comes from those coated in a sheen of thirdhand matter acquired from smoking. This sheen that covers the smoker seeps from the shirt the smoker wears onto the baby's skin. It comes from the finger offered to the baby to suck, that recently ago held a cigarette. It comes from the hand that stokes the baby's face, the arms in which the baby is held – all these contact points offer up the danger, of nicotine transfer from smoker to baby. While this smoky cloak is at first olfactorily detected, the consequences of recognizing a smelly danger are attended in and through another sensory register – that of touch.

In Australia, the 'What to Expect' website advises that smokers should remove the clothing that they smoked in, wash their hands, face and rinse their mouth before being permitted to touch a baby. This advice is replicated on every website I visited (some thirty in all, across the United States, United Kingdom and Australia). Interestingly, these sites include information about how to manage smokers who react badly to being cut off from establishing haptic relations with the new baby. One poster on the 'What to Expect' site expressed trepidation about giving instructions to her father-in-law about face washing and clothes changing after a cigarette and before holding her new born baby. Another poster quickly responded with, 'Why on earth couldn't you say something?? If some dirty smoker stuck their finger in my babies [sic] mouth, there [sic] life wouldn't be worth living. Isn't standing up for the health and well-being of your baby more important than upsetting your FIL [Father in Law]?' (see What to Expect.com 2012).

It's smell that alerts people to the presence of thirdhand smoke and it's smell that indicates that a bodily boundary has been crossed, whether one wanted it to be, or not, as I pointed out in the preceding chapter. But the fact that thirdhand smoke can shape shift, to become sited on/in/as the sofa, the dry wall or the familial skin, means that relations of thirdhand smoke are haptic as well as odiferous. Where smell entails bodies in relations – willing or not, a politics of untouchability *denies* relations between bodies. The admonition 'do not touch' [my baby] signals a potential danger, but also the purposeful undoing of relations, since families, one might say, are crafted in repeated touches between their members: that is, feeding, stroking, even slapping. Touch itself, of course, is not an innocent sense – as Manning (2007) notes, touch is always, potentially, a sort of violence, whether the toucher reaches out to touch and is stung by the experience, or whether the one who is touched suffers under the ferocious touch of another. The violence lurking, always, in experiences of touch is prefigured in the space of thirdhand smoke, crafting a politics of untouchability that preclude the experience altogether, unless 'FIL' washes, rinses, changes his clothes. Writ large, that is, at the level of the societal 'family', this might mean that we *recognize* the danger of thirdhand smoke by its smell, but *attend* to it in and through the politics of touch. These smokers may in such a regime become *untouchable*, and I deliberately invoke the association with the caste system here. As members of a smoking caste, smokers might have already assumed the status of those who conduct a polluting activity, might already be subjected to societal restrictions, including those pertaining to space. And they might well become people who are not fit to be sensorily encountered through touch even when they are not holding a cigarette – as FIL might find out. FIL is just as dangerous with or without a lit cigarette. Thirdhand smoke has ensured the collapse of smoking and smoker to the extent that even if FIL washes and changes, he'll still be a little bit dirty. It's not hard to imagine the family circumstances in which FIL finds himself writ large, so that smokers – with or without evidentiary cigarette – are untouchable. Obviously, matters temporal come to the fore here. Father in law's past impacts his present; his past smoking envelopes him in a lasting envelope of damage which he wreaks through his guilty touch, pervading and corrupting the future of the child.

The new politics of smokefree, it seems, are of a sensory order, first olfactory, then haptic. And, as I've pointed out throughout, all of these politics are borne through the air – the smell that serves as a harbinger of warning travels upon it; the air bears the mobile smoke deep into the sofa and the skin of the father-in-law, who resultantly become objects of untouchability. But it's not only that we can examine smoke in and through an attention to the air in these ways. It's also the case that an analysis of smoke permits us to speculate upon the air itself – and particularly the matter of its history.

# The air has a history

Thirdhand smoke, like secondhand smoke, is considered to defile and pollute the air, circulating around the things onto which the contaminant has stuck, rendering it unsafe perhaps for years. Thirdhand smoke's refusal to dissipate – even under the cleansing force of a fan or an air conditioner, and even under the pressure of the oppositionary force of water – tells us something about the air itself – or at least how it is conceptualized within the public health frame.

The capacity of the air itself to do the work of dissipation is probably responsible for Luce Irigaray's sense of it as endless, infinite and abundant. But when the air is proved incapable of doing its dissolving work, conceptions of it tend to change. Indeed, the air's inability to vaporize our smoky wastes in the late eighteenth century fundamentally changed the basis upon which it was understood. Air came to be explicated as a finitude when it failed to dissipate the smoke that hung over London in the 1800s. Urban emissions generated from domestic and industrial sources were visually inescapable, so acts were introduced to regulate outputs of smoke from 1821. The air also failed to de-olfactorate emissions, and so the Alkali Acts of the 1870s were introduced to regulate sulphurous and other less visible discharges. As Connor notes, so visibly and olfactorily present were the emanations, the air could hardly be thought of in any other way *but* finite; the air was a container that had edges and limits, and a capacity that was, it seemed, near full.

This thinking was unprecedented and had the effect of imbuing the air with a history. Bearing the evidence of all that which had been put into it, the air revealed its past in its polluted state, and its new inability to bear pollution away from the source of its emission, and into the past. As Connor points out, the capacity of the air to seemingly take pollution away is not just a spatial capacity; it's a temporal one, too. That which we did to the air yesterday does not remain in it today, having been borne away someplace in its infinity and to sometime in the past. The new incapacity of the air to do both in the 1800s revealed its spatial contours (as pollution stayed 'here') as well as its temporal edges (the pollution is still 'here today'). As Serres (1998) reminds us, the air has always been thought of as ahistorical. Cyclic, certainly, but never with its own linear history. Thirdhand smoke reveals this history – a history of what has been done to the air, evidence that the air cannot erase, and which stays sited in place (here) and time (now).

At the same time that we are reminded of this foul history of the air and the air's temporal and spatial edges, the clean air that is to be protected from (second and) thirdhand smoke is thought of in infinite terms – this is clean air, fresh air, the air that all breathers deserve to inhale. It is this air that must be protected; 'People deserve clean air, especially when they are in the hospital,' Matt told the *Huffington Post*, as though the air itself was free from anything that might sully its purity, and would remain so as long as it did not become contaminated with smoke (see Peeples 2011). Coco Ballantyne's 2009 contribution to *Scientific American* on thirdhand smoke drew an angry retort from Michael McFadden, author of *Dissecting Antismoker's Brains*, on the grounds that the air is already profoundly unclean. In response to claims made in the Ballantyne's article that suggested thirdhand smoke was particularly dangerous because it took simultaneously particulate and gaseous forms, McFadden wrote,

> People outgas all the time, getting rid of relatively massive amounts of bodily poisons such as formaldehyde (use to preserve corpses), benzene (used in lighter fluid), acetone (nail polish remover) and many other such things. It's part of normal bodily function. Do you worry about such things? Do you run out of a room when someone else walks in and starts breathing that stuff all over you? Of course not, because there hasn't been a multi-billion dollar fear campaign blasted at you over media for the last 30 years about such nonsense. (see Ballantyne 2009)

Besides being a nice demonstration of the polarity of the smokefree atmosphere, and besides being an even nicer demonstration of how similar the two poles are – note the similar language McFadden uses to describe the 'outgassing' that people do 'all the time' is the same as that which anti-tobacco advocates use to advise of thirdhand poisons – and despite the fact that this type of defence of smokers' rights is EXACTLY the sort of thing I'm writing AGAINST, McFadden's remark is very much *about the air*. That's the part of it I want to attend to. Specifically, it is centrally concerned with the conditions under which the air is marked up, foregrounded, made dangerous, as opposed to when it is backgrounded and unregarded – as it *must* for ordinarily outgassing people to circulate among one another – for a society made of bodies to exist at all. Secondhand smoke-contaminated air is marked up sufficiently for Western Australia's Curtin University's campus to be called a 'Clean Air Campus' on the basis of secondhand smoke's absence – despite its proximity to a major road. The contaminants from vehicular emissions is another air we largely have to ignore in late capitalism, for life to continue in the way we're used to; it's only when it's unliveable that such pollution is the subject of any real outcry. The Nonsmokers' Movement of Australia entitled its submission to the Tasmania Government's proposal to make Tasmania generationally smokefree, 'Everybody has the Right to Breathe Clean Air', and the Australian anti-tobacco website OxyGen notes that 'each time you smoke a cigarette, chemicals are released into the atmosphere, polluting the [hitherto unsullied] air'. 'The public has the right to clean air,' asserts the Australian NTS, which seeks to secure the air from threats made to it in the form of second and thirdhand smoke.

In all the foregoing examples, 'clean air' is best regarded as air that has had its pollutants backgrounded, rather than wholly absented. It is air that has managed to consign waste emissions, for instance, to backgrounds such as the past, banishing it from our present, and 'other spaces', banishing it from our presence. Such air is an infinite air: that is, such conceptions of the air as 'clean' rely wholly on an idealization of the air, a notion based on the thesis of infinitude indicated by the state of the air as 'clean', ahistorical and unhinged from place. Another oppositionary pair of smokefree is here revealed: of finite/infinite, as Irigaray's infinite air is compared against an air thickened with its own history and containment within polluted place. Of course, the pure and infinite air is unobtainable imaginary, just as surely as the notion that the outdoor air is thick with cancer is an inflated imaginary. 'Clean air', 'smokefree' air, cannot be established while so ever the air has a history. The presence of thirdhand smoke in the air ensures it has a history.

## The second law of thermodynamics

As a way of restating my claims in this chapter, I submit the following short passage, crafted around a couple of complaints made by ordinary people. To orient the reader to it, I offer this: our air may not be clean, and we can probably live with that. Probably most people realize that there are emissions a-plenty in this 'clean' air – from cars, chemicals in the ordinary furnishings of life, planes, industrial production. The thing that we really can't put up with is when the air is *dirty, and by dirty I don't mean objectively polluted*. The air is dirty, I think, to an upsetting degree, when it marks up its capacity to slip over the boundaries of bodies and bear matter between them. This is Mary Douglas's explanation of 'dirt' – as matter out of place – bodies blurring and moving out of their assignation as solidities – an assignation undone by the stench of smoke.

> Do you know what irritates me? When people think rainwater is completely new, and that the water that they get from the tap is somehow different and less pure. That's crap of course – there's no new water. It's *all* been here before. It's *all* used. Dickheads.

These remarks belong to Polly, a former colleague of mine. She made them as part of her ongoing complaint about the protests occurring in her town over the city council's plans to convert waste water to drinking water. Polly couldn't understand what the fuss was about, and was firmly of the view that the people of the town should just 'get over the idea of drinking their own toilet water – it's all in their heads'. The shocked and unwilling populace did not get over it, and the plans to recycle water in that drought-stricken city did not move forward. This water was objectively clean – it had to be, in order to be offered up at all. But when the mayor of the town drank a glass of the treated water on television to show how clean it was, people began to regard her with a certain disgust. 'She drank poo water!' exclaimed a work colleague as we drank our coffee together the next morning. 'She did not!' exclaimed an outraged Polly. Of course, Polly is right: the water had no traces of poo. But it *did* contain the traces of others who had used it before, even if they would never show up in a lab test. And we all knew it. That's what made the water undrinkable: the presence in it of others and their matter.

At the other end of the country, a decade later, Rita Rhodes wrote her local paper, the *Advocate*. Her letter was published in the 'To The Point' section of the newspaper:

> It has become so tiresome for me to read the same sentiments regarding second-hand cigarette smoke in open spaces. Time and time again, I read in your letters to the editor about the difficulties experienced by some people while passing a bus depot in our city. Do the authors ever contemplate other toxins they may encounter while living their daily lives? Vehicle exhaust fumes, every-day household cleaning products, as a couple of examples. May I suggest a hermetically sealed bubble to enable existence on our planet? (*The Advocate* 2014: np)

Rita's mention of the hermetically sealed bubble rather makes Polly's point – that, as the second law of thermodynamics clearly tells us, there isn't any new water, or air, in earth's closed system. But it also makes the point that we do not wish to be reminded of their prior use by bodies before us – and particularly when those bodies are particularly polluting. No one is willing to drink water marked by a fecal otherness. No one wants to breathe air marked by cancerous, rotten otherness.

It might be more upsetting for us when the air is marked 'dirty'. As Polly and Rita would likely acknowledge, water and air are different kinds of things – as Connor puts it, 'Water occupies space, air *is* space.' Or, as Irigaray might say it, air is not a being or thing. Being not bordered or bounded, the air has thus served as an endless receptacle for waste. We're used to it doing this work. Water, with its edges, its shores, its finiteness, cannot be thought of in quite the same way – polluted water can be relegated to the space of undrinkability; less choice is available in the case of the air. But that has not stopped policy from trying to encapsulate it in smokefree spaces.

Ironically, given this legislative effortfulness, it's only when air is profoundly polluted that it is regarded as encapsulable-in-space, since it is only ever at this point that we're given to seeing air as edged, or finite. Despite Irigaray's outraged insistence to Heidegger, that the air itself is characterized by its infinitude, its abundance, we have had an appreciation of the air itself as *finite* since the 1800s. This appreciation is one that comes with the realization that air's capacity to carry waste away not only from where we are, but also from our *present*, is a limited capacity.

The atmosphere of smokefree seeks to protect a pure, abundant air that is entirely free of waste, sulliable only by the foul expulsions of tobacco smoke, secondhand or thirdhand. But the fight to jettison them can never be truly won; first, because the air can never be the pure infinity that provides the imaginary basis for smokefree, and second, because thirdhand smoke stays – as waste – as so refuses to be consigned to the past.

# 7

# Fourthhand smoke: Going to Flavor Country

## Introduction

In Chapters 4 and 5, I attended to the explication of firsthand smoke and secondhand smoke, respectively. I dedicated attention to the ways in which the state directs interpretation of inhaling and exhaling smoking bodies, in Gilbert's (2008) terms, how the state coerces the smoker in and through powerful medical narratives, and in my own terms, how the state utilizes the intimacy of our involvement with breath to deliver the smokefree paradigm deep into bodies – smoking and non-smoking. In the sixth chapter, I examined how miasmatic conceptions of harm are central to the explication of air and matter containing thirdhand smoke, and how new witches are born of its odorous presence, and punished in and through expulsion, including from haptic relations, even familial ones. These chapters have each been concerned with the effects of explication on smokers as they circulate in the smokefree atmosphere. But what of smokers themselves? What do they do with the air itself? In this chapter, I turn my attention to an analysis of how smokers themselves might contemplate and regard their own breaths, and to what ends their own smoky inhalations and exhalations might be put. I'm calling these smoking breaths *fourthhand* smoke. This naming is meant to indicate that smoky breaths have potential beyond what is indicated for them in explications of firsthand, secondhand, and thirdhand smoke. All these breaths move beyond the confines of the body that state explication of firsthand smoke makes clear; they move right past the secondhand smoke that the smoker expels into the lungs of other breathers and the thirdhand residue that marks them as witches, on their way to the destination 'Flavor Country'. Fourthhand smoke is the smoke that causes the smoker to remember the air outside of herself. In this chapter I continue to attend to the sensory to make my claims – and I rely in what follows on touch and vision, that together elaborate the notion of outbound travel from the body site.

# Explicating the air in cigarette advertising

Of course it is not the case that the public health state has a monopoly on explicating the air. The smoky air has also been pressed into service as the agent of tobacco companies to great effect in claims that are made about smoking pleasure and where smoky air can take the smoker. Almost all cigarette advertising bears the smoker away from the confines of her body, even – or perhaps especially – as she breathes in with cigarette smoke.

As I suggested in Chapter 4, the one main aim of the public health state's messaging is to *constrain* the smoking person to the site of her own body, so that she *must* attend to the damage occurring inside of it. This attendance to the present body begins with a breath in, but in cigarette company advertising, even when inhaling, it's the capacity of cigarette smoke to take the smoker away from her own body site that counts. It is this capacity of smoke to travel on the air that permits escape from the site of a body that may not be, in the era of smokefree, a particularly pleasant place in which to be constrained, filled as it is with dying organs. As Leclerc (1979) says, one might smoke to 'remind oneself of air, throat and lungs', but *not* to dwell upon them, as one might if one attended obediently to anti-smoking advertising, but instead to 'smoke so that it [smoke] passes through me … to smoke in order to try, to try again an exit from this receptacle-self, garbage–can and tabernacle. … To smoke in order to pass beyond. And to breathe even beyond breathing' (123).

# Come on, come to Flavor Country

In his *Smoking is Sublime* (1993), Klein reminds us that Leclerc smokes,

> so as not to forget her throat and lungs and air, to be traversed by something that circulates between inside and out. The puff of the cigarette is air that reminds her of air, a breath beyond breathing that recalls the fact that we live not only within ourselves but outside ourselves, in and of the air we breathe. Cigarette smoking allows us to effectuate an exit from our … selves … to experience ourselves as a part of what we are not, outside our familiar interiority. (178)

The interiority of which Klein speaks is, I have suggested, a profoundly unpleasant place to dwell, filled as it is in the era of smokefree with rot, clots, aorta filled to bursting point with brie-cheese gunk. Escaping it in the context of smokefree may well be extremely appealing; but escaping the site of the body is a core and ordinary tendency of the body, as contemporary philosopher Serres observes:

> The body goes out from the body in all senses. … The body never persists in the same plane or content but plunges and lives in a perpetual exchange, turbulence, whirlwind, circumstance. The body exceeds the body, the I surpasses the I, identity delivers itself from belonging at every instant, I sense therefore I pass, chameleon, in a variegated multiplicity. (1998: 408–09)

As Jack Katz (1999) points out, smoke offers a most ready demonstration of the capacity of the body to exceed its sitedness – in and through its necessary utilization of the air. Katz advances a notion of out-boundedness from the body site in his observation that marking the more usually invisible exhalation phase of respiration with smoke accounts for a great deal of the appeal of smoking. In Katz's formulation, smoke visibly moves beyond the physical sitedness of bodies, and this visible move outbound through breath effectively extends one's own *personal* reach in the world (1999: 340).

This notion of extension from the site of the body is very often referenced in cigarette advertising, to the extent that escaping or going to someplace beyond the place where the body dwells is very much a major theme. Indeed, an absolutely extraordinary proportion of advertisements for cigarettes have picked up and extended the metaphor of escaping someplace other and better than the location of the physical body via smoke.

Before the restrictions on cigarette advertising and then packets applied, invitations to a range of enticing destinations were everywhere on offer. I used to be able to, in some cigarette-speak, *come to* where the flavour is, to *Marlboro* Country. It's rugged there; there are streams to be crossed and cattle to be wrangled. It's a masculine country, too – craggy, challenging, hard. I used to be able to go to the 'whole new world' (of rugged coastline) of Camel. And, don't forget, 'Players go places'. I could once take the 'Road to Flavor' with Raleigh, and, if I were a man, I could go to 'Where a man belongs' with Camel. I could 'come up' the waterfalls of Kool. To smoke a Lark was to go up in a hot air balloon, according to its recurrent advertising imagery. I could go back 'Down Home', with Winston. It is also used to be possible for me to 'escape' the crowd, with *Old Gold*. Even the polar regions were fully accessible: *Arctic* lights could take me there. I could accept an offer to visit the 'Country Fresh' alpine regions with *Salem*. In Australia, I could go on *Holiday*, linger at *Longbeach*, and I certainly used to enjoy taking in the crisp terrain offered by way of *Alpine*.

I had originally planned to insert some pictures into this chapter, from the days when package design was all-important. These images were extremely appealing; people still buy them today, on internet sites that sell vintage posters. However, it's hard to get permission from the copyright owners to do so, since tobacco companies are not inclined to do anything that facilitates the placement/appearance of cigarettes or cigarette advertising in books (or indeed any other media). I have found this to be the case even though they're not paying for placement, and even though the images depict packets from decades ago. I think we should regard this development as part of the emergence of the smokefree atmosphere that I've been attending to throughout. Without visual aids to help me, I'm going to attempt an analysis of some packet text.

Travel (to a particular, and particularly desirable destination) is an utterly overriding trope in cigarette packaging prior to plain packaging, but it's not limited to graphics. On an old packet of *Peter Stuyvesant* Lights I have fondly retained from before the time at which plain packaging was introduced into Australia is to be found the following message:

> Mild choice tobacco plus the Modern Filter make Peter Stuyvesant the International Passport to Smoking Pleasure![1]

Leaving aside the Modern Filter, I want to draw out a connection between 'smoking pleasure' and 'passport' to add another, sensory, element to the notion that smoke travels and takes the smoker, in a sense (or, more accurately, the specific senses of taste, smell and vision) with it.

In traditional philosophy,[2] the bearer of the look is assumed not to move and 'sits down to look, through a window at the blossoming tree: a statue posed on affirmations and theses' (405). Serres argues against such an assumption, and insists instead that receptivity, in the Kantian sense, does not characterize viewing, which is not as much about passively looking and seeing (or otherwise receiving) visible objects as it is about 'visiting' with them. The term 'visit' and the verb 'to visit' mean at first 'seeing'; 'they add to it the idea of itinerary – the one who visits *goes* to see' (334). Such a notion of vision might be likened to the activity of the senses proposed by Abram in *The Spell of the Sensuous*, in which he proposes the senses as responses to invitations issued from beyond the body, and in which he understands vision in particular to be 'on the move' (see also Connor 1999: 6). This suggests that the sensing body goes to visit or temporarily dwell in what is seen. The fact that what is seen in this case, smoke, is also on the move – up, up and away to Flavor Country – makes a certain sensory logic of passports, itineraries, escape to tropical islands and the easy journey to Down Home, where a man belongs. Smoky breath goes places beyond us and cigarette companies were shrewd to imagine for us several appealing destinations.

When cigarette companies issued us invitations to those destinations, we might have analysed them by beginning with the notion that, as Katz says, the visibility of smoke reveals to us the kind of outbound travel that our smoky breaths might undertake that our (only ontologically) sited bodies cannot. We might have then proceeded to the idea that we can have the destinations of our international travel, requiring a passport, imagined for us by Peter Stuyvesant, or we can simply take a quick in-between-work breakout in Flavor Country.[3]

We might also have entertained the notion that taste, along with vision, was also important to this sort of travel in (at least) two ways: 'small t taste', and 'Capital T taste'.

## Small t taste

Serres refers to the Last Supper (among other banquets) in the 'Tables' section of *Les Cinq Sens*, which deals with taste and smell. Two bodies, or, rather, two sides of one body, emerge from the banquet. On the one hand is the body of the Assumption, 'the body raised up in language', which, as the result of linguistic petrification, is reduced to the condition of statue, and is no longer able to taste and smell. Set against this linguistic body is the body consumed at the Last Supper. This body circulates in the forms of bread and wine, and is never fixed or held still, but is, as Connor notes 'a mobile transubstantiation'. In Serres' formulation, this latter body is one imagined in sensory range of taste, rather than vision or hearing, which registers the linguistic body. Serres uses the example to suggest that taste belongs in a different sensory category from vision: that which is seen need not be dissolved to be seen. But that which is tasted *must* interact with the body and be dissolved by it in order to be tasted at all. This is a description of 'small t taste': a sensory project that is all about the dissolution of boundaries. As Borthwick puts it, 'A metaphysics premised in sight's subject-object split cannot include the object's dissolvability' (2000: 133), whereas in the case of taste (and smell), object dissolvability is entirely necessary to our tasting (and our olfactory) projects.

In the case of smoking, vision and taste combine in a sensual knot that enables us to entertain the notion of visiting places like Flavor Country. In the

first instance, inbound breath takes the smoke down into the lungs, and it may
be viewed as it emerges outbound for Flavor Country. But taste also plays a
role. The smoke that goes in is not the same as the smoke that comes out;
tasting smoke makes the smoky air part of us, and *makes us part of the smoky
air, so that it is my breath going to Flavor Country*. 'Flavor' works in association
with 'Country' because it allows the immediacy of experience (small 't' taste)
to become intertwined and connected with an outbound breath, that is part of
me because I have held it inside my body and worked upon it with my taste
sense, essentially dissolving it into myself. To see is to visit, and to taste is to
have become part of. Now, part of the smoke I see, I make personal journeys
outbound to Flavor Country. Even now that I am personally implicated through
taste in the smoke I expel out to Flavor Country, however, my body remains in
its familiar ontological place as I watch the smoke I have worked upon travel
to its destination.

## Capital T taste

A sense of tastefulness (or Big T taste) determines whether this destination is
one I travel to first class, via *Benson and Hedges*, or economy with (on) *Holiday*.
The use of destinations like Holiday beaches or Alpine mountain as a key part
of smoking advertising once referenced an aesthetic of taste, an aesthetic
that allowed smokers to judge smoking pleasure through a visual metaphoric.
Different destinations for different classes enabled distinctions between
brands to appear in geographic, vacationing-opportunity terms. There were
certainly elements of this sort of taste, (that Borthwick calls 'Capital T Taste'
(ref)) involved in the purchasing of Dunhill or Benson and Hedges cigarettes
at the high end of the cigarette market, as opposed to Holiday or Long Beach,
some of the cheapest brands available in Australia. Buying Winfield Blues (or
'Winnie Blues', as they were affectionately known among those of us without
much disposable income) in my hometown in socio-economically depressed
North West Tasmania was a different thing entirely from contemplating buying
Dunhill or Benson and Hedges cigarettes, at the higher end of the market.
Some destinations were always more expensive than others; some smokers
were restricted to the cheapest and most touristy beaches, like Long Beach,
and would never have been able to afford to go on the skiing holiday on offer
in glitzy, glamorous St Moritz.

Visual invitations to such desirable vacation destinations – to come down
home, to come up to the mountains, to come to the beach or to visit Marlboro
Country, escape the everyday, or be in the sorts of places that Players are,
are no longer made in Australia. Packs (along with other, earlier cigarette

advertising to which packs stand in syntagmatic relation) are long gone. Olive brown wrapping, unadorned by any industry markers, has taken its place. But Capital T taste yet permits travel to class destinations. In other words, even a plain pack – or even no pack at all – permits class distinctions to be operationalized by smokers. This suggests that the pack is not quite the reliably constant presence that it is assumed to be, in public health view. It also suggests that packs are manipulable in and through the (class) means of the smoker.

## Olive Brown is *Not* classy

In 2011, the University of Bordeaux's Frederic Brochet, who was at the time engaged in obtaining his PhD in oenology, became interested, essentially, in how small t taste relates to Big T taste. He devised a mischievous experiment in which he invited fifty-seven well-regarded wine experts to sample two glasses each of red and white wine. The wines were, in fact, all the same brand of white wine, but two had been tinted with red food colouring. On sampling the 'reds', the wine experts deployed the (class) language of their craft, remarking upon the 'jamminess' of one, the 'crushed red fruit' evident in the other. None of their number declared the red to be, in fact, a white, and none, apparently, had a palette sufficiently discerning as to pick out 'cochineal' as a defining flavour. The wine had made its invitation in class terms, in Big T taste terms, and the experts responded to it by registering the wine's (T) astefulness at the level of (t)aste.

Brochet carried out a second test, equally mischievous, in which he selected an unremarkable but drinkable Bourdeaux, and served it in two very different looking bottles. The first was a delightful fancy *grand-cru*, the other an ordinary *vin-du-table*. Brochet set the same group of wine experts the task of ranking the wines. The grand cru was, 'agreeable', 'woody', 'complex', 'balanced', 'rounded'. The vin du table performed rather poorly; the experts described it as 'weak', 'short', 'light', 'flat' and 'faulty'. Only twelve of the experts declared it 'drinkable'; the rest weren't inclined to imbibe at all. Again, the experts responded in exactly the same class terms that had been used to invite them: they knew class when they saw it, and they came to the party.

In Brochet's tricky experiments, a sensory knot tied the visible (bottles, colours of wines) to the tasty. The conjoining of the two permitted circulation around the realm of the Tasteful; a route with which the experts were familiar. Cigarette packs are entirely devoid of such markers – so smokers have to make their own travel plans to classy (or less classy) destinations. Marley and Olivia certainly did.

Marley, twenty-five, presently 'of no fixed address' as she was 'between partners', was staying with relatives as she worked out a plan. A heavy smoker and a light dresser, Marley complained loudly about the shoddy treatment she'd encountered at her local supermarket, Woolworths, colloquially, 'Woolies', just before plain packaging came was introduced. 'God, people shit me!', she exclaimed:

> I was in line at Woolies, and there were two girls behind me, who work at [real estate agent] L.J. Hooker … [Marley remembered that the week before, one of them 'got cheeky with me' when she asked Marley about how much money she made a week, 'with a look' that implied Marley did not make enough to rent any property on the agency's books]. I turned around to go once I had my smokes [Holiday 50s] and one of them, the tall one with the long blonde hair, whispered to the other one, but I still heard, 'Hey look, cheap smokes for a cheap ho.' I would've taken them on, right, but I was on my own, so I just called them dumb sluts, and they didn't say anything back. Gutless.

While Marley's Holidays marked her out as cheap, Olivia, a forty-five-year-old, middle-class self-described 'lifer' smoker who works in administration at one of the Canberra's three universities, was talking with me about the arrival of the new plain 'olive brown' packs. Having seen them on the news, Olivia declared 'utterly repellent – so ugly! It's the colour of a garbage bag, a bin liner! Anyway, it won't affect me. In fact, as soon as they put those absolutely ghastly and revolting pack images on, I went for a *case*.'

> 'Isn't it gorgeous?' she asked as she held aloft a gold shimmering case, 1920s style, for my inspection. 'What am I, a bum?!' she continued. 'I'm doing this with style, no matter what the Health Minister thinks,' she insisted, laughing. 'Some people like smoking, but I refuse to be categorized with teenage boys and bums and those people who buy their fags by the carton – no, no. I'll emboss my own, thank you, if the government has decided I can't buy them in a packet appropriate to my image!' As Winstanley notes, the government indeed decided not to supply packs that might appeal to anyone's image, electing instead to enfold packages into the environment of denormalization by 'disfiguring' 'once-elegant tobacco packets'. (Winstanley 2012)

The change from packs that might have been 'elegant' and thus appropriate to Olivia's image to ones that are indistinguishable for one another makes it possible that Marley might welcome the class anonymity of uniform 'olive brown'. It won't be her cigarette brand that marks her down as a 'cheap 'ho'.[4] It's equally possible that Olivia might do everything in her power to reinstate the class dimensions of smoking once available to her from her pack, just so those who see her know she's no bum, no teenage boy, no Marley, who crudely buys her cheap Holidays in bulk. For Marley, this may be a blessing – it will certainly make it harder for swanky real estate types to judge her class position by her packet, at the very least. In the wake of the erasure of classed brand insignia, Olivia will be doing her best to remind observers that while she may be in the minority in her middle-class smoking, she'll retain its markers of deportment and material as she sits to smoke – with poise, elegance and an expensive-looking case.

Olivia's refusal to engage with her pack might tell us something of the danger of assuming the rational agent who will respond to pack warnings as predicted, and about the pitfalls of assuming that the cigarette pack itself will remain present with the smoker to deliver its messages. While the WHO assumes that packages are always present, 'every time' the smoker 'purchase[s] or consume[s] tobacco products' (WHO 2011: 23). Olivia's intention to operationalize her class position by decanting her cigarettes to a case indicates the possibility of absenting the pack altogether, so she is not subjected to encountering it every time. Hers may not be an isolated ethnographic curiosity, given the number of websites that offer smokers the opportunity to purchase cases. One such site, www.elighter.com, states:

> The government is now passing laws that will require cigarette companies to display unpleasant pictures of lungs. Because of this, people have started using cigarette cases instead of the old-fashioned pack. Smoking is not good for health and we encourage everyone to quit smoking. But if you have to smoke then why not use a cigarette case to carry your cigarettes in style?

So, it seems, Olivia can still travel to classy destinations after all. Even though they are not on the pack to beckon her, a bejewelled case is a first-class substitute.

I have suggested that old, industry-branded packets once called out to smokers in their imagery of mountains and beaches, and that such calls echo what the practice of smoking already does: it bears the person outbound from the body site to pleasant, fulfilling places far away: taste and vision combine in a synaesthetic knot and together respond to the invitation made on packs. The removal of that invitation on plain packs does not, it turns out, preclude the possibility of travel – it's just that you might have to imagine the destination for yourself. But it's not all bejewelled 1920s destinations. The smoker might well find herself travelling to a destination nobody wants to go to: the rotted insides of your own lungs.

# All flights to Flavor Country have been grounded

Plain packaging, of course, is a complete misnomer. Where there were once snow-capped mountains, rugged coastlines and glorious tropical beaches, there is now a greatly enlarged graphic image of one kind or another – indeed, there are fourteen currently in circulation, organized into Set A, and Set B, which I described earlier. You will recall that one package image depicts a gangrenous foot, photographed just prior to surgery to remove it. Another shows a diseased heart muscle, post extraction from the dead smoker's body. Another image is of a length of aorta, gunk spilling from its cut end. An eye held open by specula adorns another pack. A cancerous tongue lolls on the front of another, its outgrowth so large that it no longer fits in the mouth. Could it be that the taste of cigarettes in plain packages is related to these unappealing destinations?

Immediately after the three-month transitional period for plain packaging in Australia, the ABC reported that 'studies are showing that smokers appear to find the taste of plain packaged cigarettes to be worse than branded cigarettes' (see Wynne 2012: np). One long-term study that began prior to plain packaging legislation and concluded two years after the legislation had been implemented also reported that smokers regarded all cigarettes as tasting 'the same': 'After plain packs hit the shelves they [smokers] were saying that they'd noticed a deterioration in both the taste and quality of their cigarettes,' noted Ashleigh Guillaumier who served as a research assistant on the study conducted by the University of Newcastle (see ABC 2014: np).

In a comment that clearly marks the smoker as a mindless consumer, responding to the manipulations made via packet design, Simon Chapman told the ABC that he wasn't surprised by such reports:

We know from internal tobacco industry documents that were made available about 10 years ago after legal action in the US that the companies knew there is nothing between the brands and that the differentiation is all in the coloured boxes. … From a public health perspective we couldn't care less whether smokers are moving from one brand to another, but if people are quitting, which was the whole intent of the [plain packaging] legislation, then that is a fantastic result. (see Wynne 2012: np)

I am not as interested in the effectiveness of plain packets (or not) as I am with how the invitations they issue (or not) to smokers are understood and where they might take them.

# The bitter taste of a gangrenous foot

Kevin, a thirty-three-year-old Canberra man and on-again-off-again smoker who works in IT, described these tastes as 'bitter' and 'harsh' as he chatted with me about the effects of plain packaging in early 2014:

> When they brought in plain packaging I wasn't smoking, and when they first started talking about plain packaging, I thought 'that will NEVER work. People will never fall for that. But most of my friends were smoking at the time. The first thing they did was to go out and try to source packets that were not clad in olive green. One friend even photocopied his old packet [with branding still on it] and made, like, a hundred labels out of it on his printer, and stuck those over the top of the green ones. I was amazed that he did that. It's not like it would change the taste, especially as he could appreciate that they were the same no matter what label was stuck on them – he was doing it himself! But a lot of my other friends, girls and blokes, did say that the taste had changed and that the cigarettes were bitterer or harsher tasting than before. They didn't all smoke the same brand, either.

Prior to plain packaging, the packet did for tobacco companies the work of supporting what breathing out with smoke does – it rammed home the possibility of extending beyond the site of the smoking body. If the notion of travel is as central to the appeal of cigarettes as I am suggesting, then the *only* place that smokers might understand themselves headed for is the interior; postcards of that destination adorn the packs and they certainly issue an invite. Prospective visitors, however, may be uninclined to attend such places. This invitation, as I argued in the fourth chapter, is the invitation to the present body; one attends by drawing an otherwise unreflexive breath into self-conscious attention, on the back of images, whether moving on television or still on the pack, are breathtakingly graphic, and are intended to be. If the prospect of leaving for a beautiful, rugged or otherwise appealing destination can induce feelings of, in cigarette-speak, 'escape', then it certainly stands to reason that being invited into the rotting lungs invokes the opposite, a very bad taste in the mouth. The suggestion I have made above, that people travel with smoke, and that certain destinations are shrewdly imagined for them, goes just as much for the tobacco companies as it does for the public health state: it's only the destinations that are different. And, certainly, smokers RSVP to the state's invitation made on packs that used to beckon smokers to the mountains, and that now beckon them inside themselves.

I did not encounter a single informant who did not respond to the invitation proffered by the state on plain packets. This does not mean that all responded in the affirmative and agreed to come inside the rotted lungs – indeed, many refused – but they all responded. Some participants observed the packet, did not like what they saw and covered it with images they preferred – the equivalent of responding with a response in the negative. Some, like Haydn, kept the pack they considered least worrying and decanted their cigarettes into it so as not to have to be confronted by more troubling ones. For Haydn, the heart muscle was confronting as it made him think of his own heart – largely because there is a strong history of heart disease in his family. This, perhaps, is the equivalent of receiving the invite, knowing what attendance might exact from you, and sending an RSVP in the negative. Haydn decanted his cigarettes into a packet with a different destination on it – a postcard from a place he reckoned he'd never visit: 'the one with the baby on it'. It was safe enough to keep a postcard from that only imaginary destination in his pocket; he knew he'd never go to Baby. Heart disease was an undesirable destination, but he knew he might one day be forced to go there. He rejected the invitation, with all of the force available to him: he refused to even look at it. But rejecting the pack does not mean that Haydn enjoyed full control over how the packs appeared to him because, in order to refuse it, he first had to encounter it.

This sort of engagement with the packet, in my view, is more important to recognize than whether or not pack warnings are effective. Whether or not the messages 'work', there is some sort of communicative relation afoot, once between smoker and cigarette company, and now between smoker and state, that is acknowledged, and negotiated. Examination of this communicative relationship, examination of how the materiality of the pack is involved in relations, between the state and the person, and between the person and smoking, are examinations that can only occur outside of attendance to the power of the packet to shape smoker responses.

Some who received the state's invitation to travel to decaying destinations presumably accepted them, and quit – although, the circumstances of my methodology for accessing smokers – by their public act of smoking – precluded meeting any of these, who, perhaps, agreed to the invitation issued by the state to go down into their lungs, hearts, eyes, aorta along with their inbound toxic breaths, examine the damage and quit. Whether they made an RSVP in the positive or negative, all received the invitation. *But it is possible, even when the invitation to attend to the innards of the body is accepted in the acknowledgement of the fearsome, graphic pack, that smokers will not be trapped within the toxic corporeal container.*

# Smoking to remember the air

The intention of the state is to have smokers attend to their breaths as they smoke, so as to remember what those smoky breaths are doing to the insides. But smoking draws interior regions into concert with the air 'out there' so that even a strict attendance to respiration might remind us of the air outside the body and of our capacity to act in and with it.

In other words, attending to the interiority of the body, or to its usually backgrounded acts, like breathing, may not always and uniformly result in constriction, powerlessness and the feeling of being trapped inside a corporeal jail, or as Lundin puts it, the feeling of being 'torn from a context' (1999: 15). Tearing people from a habitual context, of breathing unreflexively with smoke, is, of course, how the state presents the smoking body back to smokers – in and through the constricting lens of damage to its interior components. It is, profoundly, held deliberately apart from the context in which people smoke.

Despite recognizing the propensity of the expert biomedical gaze to compartmentalize and contain, Lundin (1999) also points out that the opportunity to look inside the body is *not* the exclusive purview of the medical expert. Indeed, the views that experts offer are made available to the expert. Lundin argues that seeing these regions of the body allows her informants, who are organ transplant patients, to grasp and make less alien those regions, to make them 'more their own'. In her ethnographic work, Lundin tracks how patients take those organs or islets or other biological material and imagine it in certain terms that accomplish something for them in the world. As Lundin sees it, these patients gain agency and control by paying attention to that which, as social scientists, we often reject as a source of agency: the biological body.

Available to Lundin's patients is a kind of bioethical agency that is enacted in the taking of responsibility for one's own biological capital. As Rosi Braidotti (2007) has suggested, this sort of agency has the capacity to force the abandonment of the naturalist paradigm (that would reduce life to the biologically determined). This is because embedded in this notion of agency is the idea that one will have a high degree of lucidity about one's own biological existence, which might have been priorly unknown.

It is difficult to think of the smoker as gaining any agency at all from knowing the condition of the heart, lungs and brain, that are expertly presented in anti-smoking advertising as failing, but smokers in my study often *did* take account of their bodies and their breath – in quite different ways than are imagined for them in anti-smoking discourse. These imaginaries are enriched by the biotechnology of cigarettes themselves. Biotechnologies are political because they are mobilized within the confines of regimes – that is, an anti-smoking regime, a tobacco company regime, 'and so participate in the reproduction of normalized, productive, compliant subjectivities that are compatible with a neoliberal political economy. … But disciplinary power that renders bodies docile … does not exhaust or even best characterise, the political dimension of biotechnologies' (Diprose 2008: 145). Here, Diprose means to suggest that biotechnologies, including cigarettes and the public health or other discourse that surrounds them, can be brought into the service of interested agents, whatever else the biotechnology is meant to accomplish at the level of the cells – a pleasurable sensation, satisfaction, in one regime, imminent death in another.

As Lundin (1999: 8) has noted, one prominent feature of biotechnology is its capacity to get us to consider 'the boundary between focusing on the alien as a risk or as a potential'. Cigarettes are situated as one biotechnology that offers to consumers both risk and potential, although from the public health point of view, we can only see 'risk'. As Merleau-Ponty ([1945] 1962) noted, potentiality is never wholly suppressed by the threat of risk. And potentiality is never really free of risk. Some smokers, at least, find potential in the risky practice of smoking. As Klein says, 'It is not enough to know that cigarettes are bad for your health in order to decide not to smoke.' He also notes:

> The moment of taking a cigarette allows one to open a parenthesis in the time of or ordinary experience, a space and a time of heightened attention that give rise to a feeling of transcendence, evoked through the ritual of fire, smoke, cinder, connecting hand, lungs, breath, and mouth. It procures a little rush of infinity that alters perspectives, however slightly, and permits, albeit briefly, an ecstatic standing outside oneself (1993: 16).

## Come breathe on me, honey

Megan used her smoking to alter perspectives on what her smoky breath could do *for* her, rather than do *to* her. She used her smoking to craft a body of extension, rather than one constrained within damaged biological borders, but she used her breath, her body, her own internal biological capacities, to do it. Megan certainly was interested in tracing her smoke as it slipped into and out from her, but not in the way the state intended, as she sat at the bar to seek out casual sex with strangers.

During the course of my ethnographic encounter with her, I established that Megan used the physicality of cigarettes, in particular their length, to extend her own reach in the world. Megan effectively utilized the dissolving boundary between cigarette object and her own hand when she spoke of her attempts to 'look sexy and elegant' as she smoked. Megan said: 'I always smoke long cigarettes, Super Kings, and lately, I have been considering using a cigarette holder' … she looked disapprovingly at her hands. 'My hands are really pudgy, and my fingers are short and squat,' she complained. 'When I hold a cigarette, like this', she said, holding up her 'smoking fingers', my whole arm looks longer, and I feel more elegant. It's like wearing false eyelashes, for that illusion of length'. 'What do you do with your other hand?' I asked. 'Champagne flute', she replied instantly. 'Longstemmed'.

The holding of cigarette object in the short fingers of the pudgy hand effectively extended these shortcomings into the longer reach of Megan, as the cigarette became part of fingers, the fingers part of cigarette. Megan had her longer hand. In that ethnographic encounter, Megan also talked about what she did with the smoke that she expelled if she happened to be flirting with someone while she smoked with lengthy elegance:

'If I'm interested', she said, 'I like to blow my smoke up around the side of his face, like a caress.' She stroked the side of my face in an upward motion,

**FIGURE 6** *A caricature of Megan in action.*

to show me what she meant. She indicated with her fingers that the smoke trailed up beyond the face and whispered away. I asked her if it worked. 'They get the message,' she replied. 'How about if you want them to leave you alone?' I asked, intrigued. 'Then I blow it straight in their face, into their eyes,' she said, grinning maliciously. 'It's like giving someone a smelly slap in the face, without getting charged with assault.' 'Does anyone do it to you?', I asked 'Yep. You can tell, if a man lets the smoke just slide out of his mouth, as opposed to blowing it out while he's perving on you or flirting with you, you can be pretty sure he wants to slide something else into you as well.'[5]

In her involvement of cigarettes in her flirtatious practice, Megan capitalizes on their potential to disrupt compliance (including to particular standards of sexual conduct, to state regimes of preferred breathing, without smoke). She also rejects a future in which her body moves ever closer to the mortician's table, and reorients it to a future where unpredictability is paramount. In her procurement of sexual pleasure via carefully dispatched cigarette smoke coming from deep inside of her, Megan equally procured an altered perspective. This was a perspective she got by attending to her own internal process of breathing, and directing it outside of herself – and towards others encompassing them in a sociality born of attention to the breath. Megan also obtained body-altering perspective – elongated and elegant hands – in and through her smoking, as she stood, ecstatically, outside herself – outside her own pudgy hands, outside her own habitual breathing – to make herself anew, and making new relations, using the cigarette object and the respiratory means of her own body. Smoking permitted her to do it – both its capacity to mark her breath and have it do sexual work, and in its physical capacity as the cigarette, to elongate her hand. Megan remembered the air outside of her and used her smoke to craft relations, make connections, ask questions: Will I have sex tonight? With whom? Those questions, for her, are *always* up in the air.

# The rational agent and the travel agent

Those tiny rushes of infinity that Klein talks about become available to us in moments of bodily extension, when we escape ourselves. What if we were to theorize smoking in and through these rushes of infinity, these escapes to places beyond us, like Flavor Country? I've done precisely this in the foregoing. Let us think a moment more about Megan, who is doing in her flirtatious bar work exactly what Serres (1998) regards as utterly foundational to the body's existence – she's enacting its compulsion for ontic dispersion beyond the physical limits of the body. As bodies, asserts Serres, we are bound to do this, and he and Katz (1999) remind us that some things appeal to us precisely because they highlight corporeal extension. For Serres, it's the human fascination with the trampoline that best highlights the body's compulsion to get out of itself. For Katz, it's the dramatic visual demonstration that smoke makes of the air leaving the body. For Megan, it's the capacity of smoke that came from the inside of her to touch a man – so that he will touch the inside of her, later. Megan leaves herself, yet stays in her own body site.

Other things besides cigarettes do this. Think of all the things we have today that permit us to transform spatial and temporal perception, to play with location and presence, to take the body out of itself while permitting it simultaneously to stay, that Megan didn't have in 2004, when I interviewed her in that smoky bar in Adelaide. Sophisticated mobile communication devices are the readiest and most dramatic demonstrations available to us of travel outbound from the site of the body, entailing us as they do in travel to places that needn't be imagined, even as we stay sited in our body-place. In terms of their capacity to effect travel, cigarettes and mobile technologies could well be regarded as part of the same order or register of appeal. They send us outbound. They remember to us the world and bear it in to our bodies, just as they send our bodies out to the world. One of these areas has attracted analysis underpinned by an exciting phenomenology of movement, of the relations of things with bodies, of the reworking of spaces and times, of categories of 'here' and there' (see, for example, Richardson 2005 – in whose work we might, tellingly, substitute 'mobile device' with 'cigarette' and still come out with a very satisfactory analysis). Analyses like that are lost to smoking and to smokefree, which does at least as much mucking about with these categories. What would an analysis of cigarette smoking look like, if it were to be theorized through an attendance to travel? This is the critical point: it would look rich, full, unconstrained, unpolarized. It would look *productive.* I think we'd find the richness of analysis we see pertaining to mobile technology, which has attended to relations between bodies and things, the appeal of travelling from the site of the body.

# Conclusion

**W**hat a curious thing to do, to mark one's breath with a visible cloud as it emerges from deep within. What a curious practice, to breathe in a pleasurable, friendly poison that renders the lungs subject to rot, makes the eye's blood vessels liable to burst, and makes thick, toxic, brie cheese clog the aorta. What a peculiar continuance smoking is, when lighting up could make a person so subject to abuse, when it makes her a rotted miasmatic source of infection to others, when it excludes her from public places, perhaps even from holding a baby, or from working in an office with somebody else. How curious that it also endows her with the means to escape the confines of her own body.

How can such a thing be understood? How can the era of 'smokefree' be understood? How can they coexist?

I have suggested that we begin by dispensing with interested frames that would align disciplinary enquiry with certain kinds of outcomes, however praiseworthy they might be. This is not to say that anthropological work that is interested in helping to bring about a cessation goal should be stopped forthwith. It is only to suggest that there is room, and a good deal of it, to open smoking up to a different sort of anthropological enquiry that would also see us looking into this fascinating new era called 'smokefree'.

Such a broadening out of disciplinary enquiry as I am advocating means that at least some of us need to disattend to public health goals and reattend to some important anthropological ideas and their consequences. One of these is agency. I have pointed out herein that most anthropological analyses of smoking itself have taken a particular view of the smoking person – indeed, they have fully embraced the notion of the rational person and have proceeded to do the translation work so typical of anthropological accounts of the lives of (strange, inexplicable) others on that basis. Find the rational basis for this odd practice and a life becomes understandable, translatable – and, of course, its direction becomes changeable.

I've proposed something else, something that seems to me capable of doing a different sort of work, more revealing of bases and foundations and assumptions than it is concerned with translation. In essence, I've proposed that we look first at the context in which smokers are entailed – the smokefree context – and lay bare its binary oppositions. Revealed, they indicate, among other things, the intention of differentiation, the intention to hold things firmly apart: smokefree knowledge, such as 'smoking will produce a low-birthweight infant' was always meant to be strictly held apart from smoking while pregnant. Yet, Michelle had no problem putting such opposed knowledges together. Michelle, who wanted a small baby, took this knowledge from a public health source, and this knowledge from her mother, her sister, her friends, and produced a world that arranged itself in provisional ways. It seemed to have no internal consistency – and now that Michelle has had her baby, maybe that particular world doesn't even exist anymore. My own initial compulsion was to translate it into terms that would see Michelle drawn as an already-rational character who didn't need to be made rational in and through quitting smoking. This was propelled by an anthropological history in the making since Malinowski's rendering of the Trobriander as a rational magician whose world could be easily intelligible if only you began with the right terms and with a skilled translator.

*I'm not a translator.*

I don't know why Michelle acted as she did, and to me, why she did and what we might do to stop her from so doing once again are questions that are of little interest, in terms of advancing disciplinary understanding of the practice. But I do know how smoking and smokefree coexist. What is interesting, and what might add something to our knowledge, is that Michelle forced things together that are normally kept carefully, orchestratedly, apart. So did Judy. Her lungs were fine, made of iron they were, and so resistant to the tobacco peril. But as she pointed out, no one's heart is that invulnerable. Heartbreak will get you every time.

Smokefree places are intended, and legislatively so, to be held apart from places in which smoking is still permitted. But Isabella couldn't quite contain her smoky expulsions to the legislative parameters made for it. A smokefree time, too, might be impossible to hold strictly apart from the smoky time that precedes it. Also held apart in the smokefree atmosphere are two notions of the air: the infinitude of the pure and unsullied air, and the contained, polluted air that troubles and threatens it.

These polarities and their smudgings and blurrings duly revealed, the air comes into the foreground. As enlivener of smoke, the air is explicated in very particular ways: as infinity, as finitude, as toxic agent of the state, as the tobacco company's smoky traveller. Air is not the backdrop against which the real action occurs – it *is* the action. It's the air's capacity to tell us about difference, in its historical testimony of pollutants and choking effluvium, that is instrumental in determining who can be in public place, and under what circumstances. It's the air itself that bears a smoker up and away, to Flavor Country, or to the much less desirable location of the rotted lung. Travel to the latter destination is something one might avoid – perhaps by covering up the olive brown pack with its gruesome graphics in order to prevent the bitter taste of such places from interfering with the experience of smoking what, ostensibly, is still a *Marlboro* cigarette. It is air itself, as inbound breath, that bears the big politics of smokefree down into the lungs along with life-giving gases. Big politics are made intimate in the capacity of a breath to draw in the world, the atmosphere.

But as I have also pointed out, particularly in and through analysis of an interview with Megan the flirtatious bar smoker, intimate air can be and is utilized by the smoker herself, to accomplish her own things, to do work in the world. Thus, a self-reflexive attention to the breath, as smokers are invited to make by the public health state in its anti-smoking campaign advertisements, may not result in obedient attendance to the lungs. Intimate attendance to one's insides might go elsewhere, and even entail others. For Megan, it usually led to the bedroom. To get there, Megan used her own biological capacities to extend herself, through the air, through her breath, to effect social relations with others. She went outside herself by recourse to her own interior.

Despite the fact that people like Megan could refuse the invitation of the state to attend to her own breath in a particular way, the smokefree atmosphere is still tense and heavy; it's fair to say that an atmospheric pressure pushes down on smokers, however entailed they remain in smoking, however much they ignore the messaging, however much they decant cigarettes into fetching, purpose-designed cases, however much they use smoke to flirt and craft sexual relations. This is a serious atmosphere, a consequential one, in which even notions of 'the public' are tweaked. This is an atmosphere in which the sources of odorous contamination are sought out and held responsible for the fates of the unborn. This is a profoundly powerful atmosphere and it is made so in and through the intimacy of breathing in and out with smoke(free). Anthropologists must attend to this power just as readily as they attend to the power-laden relations within which smokers and Big Tobacco are entailed, for they are just as interesting, and just as consequential, and just as worthy of disciplinary attention.

This investigation I've made of the smokefree atmosphere, then, has smoke-like, escaped its intended confines to say perhaps more about the air itself, as it slips into bodies, slips out of them, becomes agent for state and agent for *Marlboro*, as it emerges from the background to the foreground, to be explicated in the service of powerful interested parties – tobacco companies, the public health state, and even those who just want to improve their chances of hooking up at the bar. We can access these potentials of the air in certain sensory modes, as I've pointed out throughout. They can't be accessed in and through the current frame, which looks with purpose – that is, searches instrumentally.

Moreover, the astute reader will certainly have appreciated the way in which explications of the air in certain sensory registers – predominantly smell in the smokefree space – are firmly connected to an increasing human control over the air. Now, after having bent the air to our will, having made it come into our service in our travels, our communications, our wars, and not least making it bear our waste away from our present and our presence, the air can never again be in the background. It must always be watched, monitored, surveilled.

In watching it, monitoring it and surveilling 'it', we also equally monitor those who would pollute it, and in and though their pollutive actions, harm other persons. Smoke is the mark of the polluting emitter, but it is also the jet stream to Flavor Country. And, while so ever it is both, the war on smoking will continue. Anthropologists might consider studying the war, rather than only taking up a place in the battle.

# Notes

## Orienting notes

**1** From 6 December 2004, smoking was banned in all enclosed public places in South Australia. Restrictions in enclosed licensed hospitality premises were phased in from 2004, and a total ban applied on smoking in all enclosed areas of pubs and clubs from 1 November 2007.

**2** The astute reader will have already noticed, even this early into things, that there are more female presences in the form of interviewees included – this is not deliberate; indeed, I did not formally attempt to strike a gender balance – whomever was inclined to speak with me, spoke with me when I made my approaches in the street, or in the other contexts that I've described in this opening orientation to the book. But this empirical imbalance will not be the thing that will make many readers worry will be just how minimally I've attended to the gendered and sexed dimensions of tobacco use in the latter parts of this book. Gender is, frustratingly, present and absent throughout this book. In fact, I've deliberately disattended gender, in order to avoid the very sort of translational work I am so critical of, throughout this book – which I shall discuss in detail shortly, but here I will briefly state here as my concern with not attempting to render smoking legible via the identification of particular translational terms – gendered terms included. That said, this decision means that my phenomenological analysis replicates all those problems that Weiss (1999) originally identified with Merleau-Pontian phenomenology when it first became popular among social scientists – namely, that he assumed a sort of foundational body that was white and male. The bodies I identify herein, largely, aren't. Many of them issue from beyond the middle classes, the white majority, and most are female. I've attempted to reveal, as much as I can without delving into the translational, the lived gendered dimensions of bodies who appear to smoke in peculiarly gendered and sexed ways herein.

## Introduction

**1** As I complete the manuscript for this book, Tasmania's maximum security prison, Risdon, was entering its first week of smokefree. Cigarettes were banned at the institution on 1 February 2015. The smoking rate in Tasmania is 22 per cent, and the prison population's rate is 89 per cent.

**2**  I mean this in proportional, not raw number terms – there are still many more middle-class smokers in Australia because it is a predominantly middle-class country.

**3**  (https://web.standford.edu/dept/anthropology/cgi-bin/web?q+node/95).

**4**  Bell observes: 'Demanding that all researchers take an explicitly anti-tobacco stance because of the nefarious uses to which their work *may* otherwise be put by the tobacco industry amounts to a gag order' (2013a: 6).

**5**  At one level, the infiltration of public health goals into the discipline has been manifest in the ways that anthropologists all too readily engage the lives of smokers in whom they are interested, most often as dependent consumers. But anthropologists who have questioned the veracity of such characterizations of the smoker have also tended to produce narrow terms in which to characterize smokers' lives. This has involved translating the strange activity of smoking into terms that make smoking intelligible to others.

**6**  It is worth noting that Chapman's combatant in the debate, Jeff Collin, argued against the proposal on the grounds that it wasn't the smoker who required attention, but instead the real vector of the epidemic – the tobacco industry. As a public health advocate himself, Collin does not dispute the public health incentive to deal with the epidemic, only the focus of its intention.

**7**  This is a response that, I think, is bundled, straightforwardly, as actions to assure health but which, as I shall demonstrate in this book, also accomplishes other work, such as the relegation of smokers to certain kinds of polluting categories – and this has consequences of its own.

**8**  For full details of the case, refer GASP website: http://www.njgasp.org/emerging-trends-issues/thirdhand-smoke-concerns

**9**  Full details of this case are available on the Tobacco Free Arizona website, at https://tobaccofreeaz.wordpress.com/2010/03/17/those-with-cancer-in-family-history-must-avoid-smokers/#more-1797.

**10**  Full details of this case are available at http://ash.org/4dangers.html. See also http://archive.tobacco.org/news/276822.html, which also carried the story.

# Chapter 1

**1**  While very obviously committed to making smoking history, and somewhat whiggish in tone, the *Tobacco in Australia: Facts and Issues* resource produced by the Cancer Council, provides an overview of the legislation in historical terms. This is available in one form in the document as a timeline. The comprehensive online resource is available at http:///www/tobaccoinaustralia.org.

**2**  The law was again utilized in June of 2014 in the Western Australian Supreme Court ruling that banned e-cigarettes on the grounds that although they do not contain nicotine, they nevertheless breached the law in their resemblance to combustible tobacco cigarettes.

**3** *The Clapping Song* was written by Lincoln Chase and was originally recorded by Shirley Ellis in 1965. However, readers may be more familiar with the Belle Stars' 1982 version, which charted at 11 in the United Kingdom (but not at all in the United States). The next year, Pia Zadora recorded her version of the song that charted at number 36 in the United States.

**4** On a side note, a lawyer colleague of mine did suggest to me that Kmart could have left the monkey chewing tobacco in its ad and, if troubled by the Advertising Standards Board, could have offered the defence that the monkey does in fact die in the song – so, it's really not supporting the consumption of tobacco – indeed, it makes the opposite point, that death is the result. I don't know if my response to her suggestion means I should go into advertising law: I pointed out that the monkey didn't die from a tobacco-related illness, but instead was killed in a horrible street car accident, so that defence wouldn't work.

**5** Visit the Australian Government Department of Health website at http://www.health.gov.au/internet/main/publishing.nsf/Content/tobacco-kff#footnotes.

**6** By 2001, smokefree public places legislation had been enacted in New South Wales, Victoria, the Australian Capital Territory, Western Australia and South Australia (public dining areas only). The ACT government was the first to ban smoking in restaurants, in 1994. It caught on; within a decade, all states and territories had adopted smokefree indoor dining legislation.

**7** The interested reader may consult the state and territory legislation I cite in this section by visiting http://www.tobaccoinaustralia.org.au/table-15-7-1-implementation-dates-aus on the *Tobacco in Australia* website. Interestingly, the insurer Allianz also includes this and more up-to-date information (i.e. post 2012) under its Life Insurance tab, as 'an area of public policy that's dynamic, controversial and quick to be implemented' (see http://www.allianz.com/life-insurance/nsw-bans-building-entrance-smoking.

# Chapter 2

**1** These kinds of information-gathering exercises follow studies that confirm the impact of graphic health warning messaging and unappealing pack colour and design on reduction and cessation (Elliott & Shanahan Research 2009: 5; see also Hammond et al. 2003). I discuss the assertions made in these sorts of studies in a fulsome way in Chapter 6, along with packaging more generally.

**2** This is a variation on a priorly rehearsed argument, promulgated in the 2004–9 NTS, which insists that the issuing of increasingly hard-hitting health harm information ensures that smokers receive and fully appreciate accurate messaging in an environment where smoking is already known to be harmful. In this environment, their knowledge about smoking harm rapidly deteriorates into a superficial understanding of the health risks associated with smoking.

# Chapter 3

**1**  For examples see (Hammond et al. 2009 and Mutti et al. 2011).

**2**  Scollo and Winstanley (2012) note in *Tobacco in Australia* that 'point-of-sale advertising has always been important to the manufacturer, providing the last chance to persuade a customer to choose a particular brand. The increase in price competition between the companies in recent years means that the smoker is more likely than ever to select a brand at the counter. It has also placed cigarette advertising among soft drinks, sweets and chewing gum and is likely to have had some impact on the juvenile shopper' (2012: np).

**3**  The *New York Times* ran a story on this happiness quotient and what its effects might be, in August 2014, entitled, 'In New Calculus On Smoking, It's Health Gained vs Pleasure Lost' (see Tavernise 2014).

**4**  Although I take what might be called a traditional anthropological approach to smoking and smokefree, rather than an applied or aligned one, I do not regard smokers in Kafkaesque terms – in other words as agents pursuing a practice so odd that only the highly trained anthropologist can make sense of it.

# Chapter 4

**1**  Actor Network Theory is the Latourian position which Ingold criticizes. Ingold debunks *networks* and introduces *meshworks* instead.

**2**  Equally, it includes the atmospheric politics of environmental tobacco smoke, a politics that is rather more elaborated and whose future seems in large measure to be determined, at least in the sense that we have something called 'smokefree' that is legislatively enforced.

# Chapter 5

**1**  I know this is likely to be a highly contested sentence – hence my use of 'ideally' therein.

**2**  Bell has priorly recognized this line of argument in her submission, that present legislative frames designed to change norms act on the political, and not necessarily on the objectively demonstrably harmful, aspects of smoke in the outdoor air (see Bell 2011).

**3**  A regular weekend night disco held for the underage (under 18) crowd in Australia during the 1980s.

**4**  'Smoko' is Australian (and New Zealand) slang for a short cigarette break taken during work. The general consensus seems to be that the term was first used among sheep shearers in the late 1800s, and so it has obvious close associations with (gendered) working class (see McDonald 1992).

Currently, the term is widely used to describe any short break – such as a coffee break at the office.

5  As will become particularly clear in Chapter 6 of this book, 'innocent children' with unsullied lungs are a recurrent theme in claims about the capacity of smoke as a harbinger of death. Jennifer's kids were central to her claims of legitimacy about telling off the smoking girls: Jennifer didn't 'lose her shit' in her own mind, because 'innocent children' were the victims of the smoke she encountered.

6  Note the shielding, maternal work that Jennifer does to protect the clean bodies of her young children in response to the leaching smoke of dirty teenaged bodies. I wondered whether Jennifer's reaction would have been even more heightened had those belching, polluting bodies been male, as it seems possible to me that the expelled smoke of a male might be somehow distinguishable from 'female' smoke – a point I elaborate in note # 45, when I speculate on Megan's smoky expulsions in the bar.

7  http://www.skepticblog.org/author/dunning/.

8  For a comprehensive investigation of the politics of exclusion ushered in with smokefree legislation (in Singapore), see Tan (2013), who goes much deeper into this than I can here, as he focuses exclusively on the spatial dimensions.

9  https://tobaccofreeaz.wordpress.com/2010/03/17/those-with-cancer-in-family-history-must-avoid-smokers.

10  It's not just a legalistically produced environment we are talking about here, one pressed down upon us by law makers. As Sloterdijk ([1998] 2011) says in 'Bubbles', the first volume of his *Spheres,* humans are always located in bubbles that protect them from the outside – they are climatologically tuned spaces or spheres that allow immunity – and people adjust these spherological environs. We are, I am suggesting, witnessing the adjustment in what I am calling 'the atmosphere'.

# Chapter 6

1  While speaking of business structures and how they can be understood within a miasmatic frame, Gabriel also notes in this piece that 'contemporary variants of miasma can be found in concerns over toxic fumes and secondary inhalation of tobacco smoke' (2008: 3).

2  See ASH website, http://ash.org/4dangers.html.

3  http://ash.org/4dangers.html.

# Chapter 7

1  Peter Stuyvesant Lights Package Advertising.

2  That is, Idealism, Realism, Neotheism.

**3** It is not that the case that the explication of air made by tobacco companies refers to air that is exclusively outbound; although it is the case that I am invited to 'come to Flavor country', or 'Down Home', smoke travels in more ways than just the visibly traceable way that Katz notices. Places are also borne to me on the inbound wind. The movement of smoke-laced air into the body equally references travel, as the smoker takes in the taste of places far flung – the crisp flavour of regions alpine, the taste of Flavor Country, as one takes in the air present 'right here', but which may be imagined to have come from elsewhere – a technique presently also used to great effect by Air Wick and other air freshener brands. Take its Rare Scents Collection, for instance, which is: 'inspired by the purest and rarest scents in nature. Transform your home with the delicate notes of silky Vanilla paired with subtle woody tones from the lush rainforests of Madagascar or feel exhilarated by fresh, crisp bursts of Snowy Mountain berries. With the Air Wick Rare Scents Collection, you can escape to the world's most amazing destinations in the luxury of your own home.' Such luxurious scents come from elsewhere, beyond the odorous kitchen or bathroom, and permit the householder to draw in the mountain or the woods, on the strength of an inbound breath. Air from the mountains and the rugged terrain of Marlboro Country or Down Home can be drawn in by the smoker in and through the synaesthetic knot that unites taste and place. Just as a wine aficionado can taste the qualities of the soil that nourished the grapes that were its source, a smoker, with a little more abstraction of the notion of 'place', can take in imaginary terrains, in which tobacco itself was never grown, like the fresh mountain air that characterizes the taste of Alpine cigarettes. These are places far from the body as it smokes on, say, the interstitial public land of the footpath to which it is legally constrained. But the international passport to smoking pleasure provides a passport out of such constraining lands and into other destinations more appealing.

**4** Note here how instrumental smoke and smoking are to Marley's classification as a cheap 'ho. In a phenomenological vein, we might note that a particularly cheap, perhaps dirty, smoke reveals her porousness. Olivia's engagement with a classier smoke reflects her middle-class sensibilities, including those to which her body is firmly held, in the taking in and letting go of smoke: she won't open her body up to just any matter; hers are rather more policed permeations.

**5** To continue the musing I began in note 33, note here how Megan's use of smoke trails, lingers, whispers softly up the side of her intended partner's face, inviting him to respond. Note how the man's 'response' smoke will indicate to her 'whether or not he wants to slide something else' into her as well. Even in smoky form, it seems that her smoke is indicative, invitational, while his is rather more active – already, penetratively, sliding into her. These emissions, it seems to me, are deeply sexed, deeply gendered.

# References

3AW Newstalk (2014), 'The Death of Smoking is Nigh', Broadcast 7 October 2014. Available online: http://www.3aw.com.au/radio/the-death-of-smoking-is-nigh-20141006-3jhey.html (Accessed 19 October 2014).

AAA Program (2011), 'Conference Handbook: Traces, Tidemarks and Legacies: 110th Annual Meeting Montreal QC., Canada November 16-20', *American Anthropological Association.*

Abram, D. (1996), *The Spell of the Sensuous: Perception and Language in a More-Than-Human World*, New York: Vintage Books.

ACT Government (2003), *Smokefree Public Places Act.* Available online: http://www.legislation.act.gov.au/a/2003-51/li.asp (Accessed 10 July 2014).

Action on Smoking and Health (ASH) website (nd), Available online: http://ash.org/4dangers.html (Accessed 5 January 2015).

Adey, P. (2013), Air/Atmospheres of the Megacity, *Theory, Culture & Society* 30 (7/8): 291–308.

Air Navigation Act 1920 Cth. (1920), Available online: http://www.comlaw.gov.au/Details/C2011C00273 (Accessed 30 June 2014).

Air Navigation Regulations (Amendment) 1996 Cth., reg 4 (1996), Available online: http://www5.austlii.edu.au (Accessed 2 July 2014).

Air Navigation Regulations 1947 Cth., reg 25 (1947), Available online: http://www.comlaw.gov.au/Details/F2009C01019 (Accessed 4 July 2014).

Allianz Insurance (nd), Allianz Insurance website. Available online: http://www.allianz.com.au/life-insurance/nsw-bans-building-entrance-smoking (Accessed 30 September 2014).

Anderson, B. (2009), 'Affective Atmospheres', *Emotion, Space and Society* 2: 77–81.

Australian Broadcasting Corporation (2014), 'The Seduction of Smoking' Broadcast 29 September 2014. Available online: http://www.abc.net.au/4corners/stories/2014/09/29/4094654.htm (Accessed 2 October 2014).

Australian Bureau of Statistics (2013), *Australian Aboriginal and Torres Strait Islander Health Survey*, Canberra: Australian Bureau of Statistics. Available online: http://www.abs.gov.au/ausstats/abs@.nsf/mf/4727.0.55.001 (Accessed 21 December 2014).

Australian Government (1992), Tobacco Advertising Prohibition Act 1992. Canberra: Commonwealth of Australia. Available online: http://www.comlaw.gov.au/Details/C2010C00100 (Accessed 10 January 2015).

Australian Government (2011), *Tobacco Plain Packaging Act* 2011. Canberra: Commonwealth of Australia. Available online: http://www.comlaw.gov.au/Details/C2011A00148 (Accessed 25 September 2014).

Australian Government (2012), *Australian National Tobacco Strategy 2012-2018,* Canberra: Commonwealth of Australia. Available online: http://national

drugstrategy.gov.au/internet/drugstrategy/publishing.nfs/Content/nts-12-18-callsubs (Accessed 12 October 2014).

Australian Government Attorney-General's Department (nd), Tobacco Plain Packaging, Investor State Arbitration. Available online: http://www.ag.gov.au/tobaccoplainpackaging (Accessed 3 February 2015).

Australian Government Australian Institute of Health and Welfare (2013), *Tobacco Smoking National Drug Strategy Household Survey.* Canberra: Commonwealth of Australia. Available online: www.aihw.gov.au/alcohol-and-other-drugs/ndshs/ (Accessed 15 December 2014).

Australian Government Department of Health (2012a), Set A Health Warnings – Cigarette Packs. Available online: http://www.health.gov.au/internet/main/publishing.nsf/Content/tobacco-warn-A (Accessed 6 December 2014).

Australian Government Department of Health (2012b), Set B Health Warnings – Cigarette Packs. Available online http://www.health.gov.au/internet/main/publishing.nsf/Content/tobacco-warn-B (Accessed 6 December 2014).

Australian Government Department of Health and Ageing (2009), 'Australia: The Healthiest Country by 2020. Tobacco Control in Australia: Making Smoking History: Technical Report 2'. Canberra: Commonwealth of Australia. Available online: http://www.health.gov.au/internet/preventativehealth/publishing.nsf/Content/tech-tobacco (Accessed 1 September 2014).

Australian Government Department of Health website (nd). Available online: http://www.health.gov.au/internet/main/publishing.nsf.

Australian Government Quitnow website a (nd), 'Break the Chain' Campaign, Available online: http://www.quitnow.gov.au/internet/quitnow/publishing.nsf/Content/ntc-break-tvc (Accessed 1 July 2014).

Australian Institute of Family Studies (2012), *The Longitudinal Study of Australian Children Annual Statistical Report 2011*, Canberra: Commonwealth of Australia.

Australian Law Reports (1985), *Rothmans of Pall Mall (Australia) Ltd v Australian Broadcasting Tribunal; Benson and Hedges Co Pty Ltd v Australian Broadcasting Tribunal.* ALR 1985: 58: 675.

Baby Centre (2009), Baby Centre website. Available online: http://blogs.babycentre.com/mom_stories/third-hand-smoke-is-a-hazard-to-babys-health/ (Accessed 12 February 2015).

Baer, H., M. Singer, and I. Susser (2003), *Medical Anthropology and the World System*, Westport: Praeger.

Ballantyne, C. (2009), 'What is Third-Hand Smoke? Is it Hazardous? Researchers Warn Cigarette Dangers May Be Even More Far-Reaching', *Scientific American Online* 6 January 2009. Available online: http://www.scientificamerican.com/article/what-is-third-hand-smoke (Accessed 13 January 2015).

Bell, K. (2011), 'Legislating Abjection? Secondhand Smoke, Tobacco Control Policy and the Public's Health', *Critical Public Health* 21 (1): 49–62.

Bell, K. (2013a), 'Whither Tobacco Studies?', *Sociology Compass* 7 (1): 34–44.

Bell, K. (2013b), 'Tobacco Control, Harm Reduction and the Problem of Pleasure', *Drugs and Alcohol Today* 13 (2): 111–18.

Bell, K. (2014), 'Science, Policy and the Rise of "Thirdhand Smoke as a Public Health Issue", *Health, Risk and Society* 16 (2): 154–70.

Bell, K. and H. Keane (2012), 'Nicotine control: E-cigarettes, Smoking and Addiction', *International Journal of Drug Policy* 23: 242–47.

Bell, K. and S. Dennis (2013), 'Editor's Introduction: Towards a Critical Anthropology of Smoking: Exploring the Consequences of Tobacco Control', *Contemporary Drug Problems* 40 (1): 3–20.

Bell, K., L. McCullough, A. Salmon and J. Bell (2010), '"Every Space is Claimed": Smokers' Experiences of Tobacco Denormalisation', *Sociology of Health and Illness* (32) 6: 1–16.

Berman, M. (1982), *All That Is Solid Melts into Air: The Experience of Modernity*, Harmondsworth: Penguin.

Berridge, V. (1998), 'Science and Policy: The Case of Post War British Smoking Policy', in S. Lock, L. Reynolds and E. Tansey (eds), *Ashes to Ashes: The History of Smoking and Health*, 143–62, Amsterdam: Rodopi.

Black, P. (1984), 'The Anthropology of Tobacco Use: Tobian Data and Theoretical Issues', *Journal of Anthropological Research* 40 (4): 475–503.

Bonolio, G. (2003), 'Kant's Explication and Carnap's Explication: The Redde Rationem', *International Philosophical Quarterly* 43 (3): 289–98.

Borland, R., H. Yong, N. Wilson, G. Fong, D. Hammond and K. Cummings (2009), 'How Reactions to Cigarette Packet Health Warnings Influence Quitting: Findings from the ITCT Four-Country survey', *Addiction* 104: 669–75.

Borthwick, F. (2000), 'Olfaction and Taste: Invasive Odours and Disappearing Objects', *The Australian Journal of Anthropology* 11 (3): 127–40.

Brady, M. (2001), 'Historical and Cultural Roots of Tobacco Use Among Aboriginal and Torres Strait Islander People', *Australian and New Zealand Journal of Public Health* 26 (2): 120–24.

Brady, M. and J. Long (2003), 'Mutual exploitation? Aboriginal Australian Encounters with Europeans, Southeast Asians, and Tobacco', in W. Jankowiak and D. Bradburd (eds), *Drugs, Labor and Colonial Expansion*, 31–58, Tuscon: The University of Arizona Press.

Braidotti, R. (2007), Bio-power and Necro-politics: Reflections on an Ethics of Sustainability, Springerin (7). Available online: http://www.springerin.at/dyn/heft_text.php?textid=1928&lang=en (Accessed 12 September 2014).

Brandt, A. (1998), 'Blow Some My Way: Passive Smoking, Risk and American Culture', *Daedalus* 199: 115–76.

British America Tobacco (Australia) (2009), *BATA and the Australian Regulatory Landscape: Response to the Preventative Health Taskforce Technical Report 2, 'Tobacco Control in Australia: Making Smoking History' January 2009* British America Tobacco Australia.

Calma, T. (2011), 'Tackling Indigenous Smoking', in J. Tinworth (ed.), *Of Substance: The National Magazine on Alcohol, Tobacco and Other Drugs* 9 (2): 28–9.

Cancer Council (2015), 'Property Law Review Clears Air for Smokefree spaces', Posted 13 January 2015. Available online: http://www.cancerqld.org.au/page/news/property_law_review_clears_the_air_for_smoke_free_spaces (Accessed 30 January 2015).

Carnap, R. (1950), *Logical Foundations of Probability*, Illinois: University of Chicago Press.

Carro-Ripalda, S., A. Russell, S. Lewis and S. Heckler (2013), 'The Making and Changing of Smoking Persons in Public Health Policy and Practice: Ethnography of a World-First Illicit Tobacco Program', *Contemporary Drug Problems* 40 (1): 21–46.

Chaloupka, F., K. Warner, D. Acemoglu, J. Gruber, F. Laux, W. Max, J. Newhouse, T. Schelling and J. Sindelar (2014), 'An Evaluation of the FDA's Analysis of the Costs and Benefits of the Graphic Warning Label Regulation', *Tobacco Control Online*. Available online: http://tobacconomics.org/wp-content/uploads/2015/01/Chaloupka_TC_FDA-Analysis_12-30-14.pdf (Accessed 15 February 2015).

Chapman, S. (2012), 'The Case for a Smoker's License', *PLoS Med* 9 (11): e1001342.

Chapman, S. (2013), 'One Hundred And Fifty Ways The Nanny State Is Good For Us', *The Conversation*. Available online: http://theconversation.com/one-hundred-and-fifty-ways-the-nanny-state-is-good-for-us-15587 published 2 July 2013 (Accessed 12 January 2015).

Chapman, S. and B. Freeman (2008), 'Markers of the Denormalisation of Smoking and the Tobacco Industry', *Tobacco Control* 17 (1): 25–31.

Choy, T. (2010), 'Air's Substantiations', Paper presented at the Berkeley Environmental Politics Colloquium, 5 February 2011. Available online: http://gobetrotter.berlekely.edu/bewp/colloquium/papers/ChoyAirEp.pdf (Accessed 15 November 2014).

Chung, F. (2014), 'Plain Packaging, Bicycle Helmet Laws, Nightclub Lockouts: Has The Nanny State Gone Too Far?' Available online: http://www.news.com.au/finance/economy/plain-packaging-bicycle-helmet-laws-nightclub-lockouts-has-the-nanny-state-gone-too-far/story-e6frflo9-1227046385962 (Accessed 30 September 2014).

Classen, C., D. Howes and A. Synnott (1994), *Aroma: The Cultural History of Smell*, London: Routledge.

Cochoy, F. (2002), *Une Sociologie Du Packaging ou L'âne de Buridan Face au Marché (Sociology Packaging or Burdian's Ass to the Market)* Paris: Presses Universitaires de France.

Connor, S. (1999), 'Michel Serres' Five Senses', Paper given at the Michel Serres Conference, Birbeck College, 10 May 1999. Available online: http://www.bbk.ac.uk/eh/eng/skc/5senses.htm.

Connor, S. (2008), 'Unholy Smoke', Paper presented at the London Art Workers Guild Evening of Talks Accompanying the Exhibition: Smoke, 13 November 2008. Pump House Gallery, Battersea, curated by Implicapshere, London.

Connor, S. (2011), 'Review of Peter Sloterdijk, Terror From the Air', *Critical Quarterly* 53 (2): 107–12.

Corbin, A. (1994), *Foul and the Fragrant*, London: Picador.

Daube, M. (2005), 'Australian Smokers – An Endangered Species', *Journal of the Australian Medical Association Western Australia* 45 (7): 13–13.

Daube, M. and S. Chapman (2014), 'The Australian's Dissembling Campaign on Tobacco Plain Packaging', *Medical Journal of Australia* 201 (4): 191–92.

Deleuze, G. ([1970] 1988), *Spinoza: Practical Philosophy*, trans. R. Hurley, San Francisco: City Lights Books.

Deleuze, G. and F. Guattari ([1980] 1987), *A Thousand Plateaus*, trans. B. Massumi, London: Continuum.

Deleuze, G. and F. Guattari ([1991] 1994), *What is Philosophy?*, trans. H. Tomlinson and G. Burchill, London: Verso.

Dennis, S. (2006), 'Four milligrams of Phenomenology: An Anthrophenomenological Analysis of Smoking Cigarettes', *Popular Culture Review* 17 (1): 41–57.

Dennis, S. (2011), 'Smoking Causes Creative Responses: On State Antismoking Policy and Resilient Habits', *Critical Public Health* 21 (1): 25–35.

Dennis, S. (2013), 'Golden Chocolate Olive Tobacco Packaging Meets The Smoker You Thought You Knew: The Rational Agent and New Cigarette Packaging Legislation in Australia', *Contemporary Drug Problems* 40 (1): 71–97.

Dennis, S. (2014), 'Explicating the Air: The New Smokefree (And Beyond)', The Australian Journal of Anthropology, forthcoming. Prepublication version. Available online: http://onlinelibrary.wiley.com./doi/10.1111/taja.12103.

Diprose, R. (2008), 'Biopolitical Technologies of Prevention', *Health Sociology Review* 17 (2): 141–50.

Douglas, M. (1966), *Purity and Danger*, New York: Praeger.

Dovey, K. (1999), *Framing Places. Mediating Power in Built Form*, London: Routledge.

Downes, S. (2014), The Q Brand Q Blog. Available online: http://qbrand.blogspot.com.au/2014/09/kmart-and-bwm-bowdlerise-classic-hit.html (Accessed 25 December 2014).

Dunning, B. (nd), Skepticblog website. Available online: http://www.skepticblog.org/author/dunning (Accessed 11 October 2014).

Eligter.com (2012) *Cigar Lighters, Cigarette Lighters, Zippo Lighters, Cigarette Cases, Ashtrays And Cigar Cutters*. Available online: http://www.elighters.com/cigarettes-cases.html (Accessed 30 January 2012).

Elliott & Shanahan Research (2009), 'Literature Review: Evaluation of the Effectiveness of the Graphic Health Warnings On Tobacco Product Packaging 2008', Unpublished report for the Australian Government Department of Health and Ageing.

Evelyn, J. (1661), Fumifigium: *The Inconveniencie of the Aer and Smoak of London Dissipated Together With Some Remedies Humbly Proposed.* London: Gabriel Bedel and Thomas Collins.

Flora, J. (2012), '"I Don't Know Why He Did It. It Happened By Itself": Causality and Suicide in Northwest Greenland', in J. Mair, A. Kelly and C. High (eds), *The Anthropology of Ignorance: An Ethnographic Approach*, 137–62, New York: Palgrave Macmillan.

Furey, A. (2012), Smokers' Rights vs. Scent-free Workplace *Ottawa Sun* 18 January 2012. Available online: http://www.ottawasun.com/2012/01/18/smokers-rights-vs-scent-free-workplace (Accessed 15 July 2014).

Gabriel, Y. (2008), 'Separation, Abjection, Loss and Mourning: Reflections on the Phenomenon of Organizational Miasma', Paper Presented at the Royal Holloway University of London ESRC seminar series: Abjection and Alterity in the Workplace, Seminar 1, University of Leicester, 28 May.

Germain, D., M. Wakefield and S. Durkin (2009), 'Adolescents' Perceptions of Cigarette Brand Image: Does Plain Packaging Make a Difference?', *Journal of Adolescent Health* 46 (4): 385–92.

Gilbert, E. (2008), 'The Art of Governing Smoking: Discourse Analysis of Australian Anti-Smoking Campaigns', *Social Theory & Health* 6 (2): 97–116.

Glasser, I. (2012), *Anthropology of Addictions and Recovery*, Long Grove: Waveland Press.

Global Advisors on Smokefree Policy (GASP) website, Available online: http://www.njgasp.org/emerging-trends-issues/thirdhand-smoke-concerns/ (Accessed 26 December 2014).

Global Smokefree Partnership (2008), *Global Voices: Working For Smokefree Air 2008 Status Report.* Available online: http://www.globalsmokefreepartnership.org/ficheiro/report.pdf (Accessed 1 July 2014).

Goldade, K., D. Burgess, A. Olayinka, G. Whemboula and K. Okuyemi (2012), 'Applying Anthropology to Eliminate Tobacco-Related Health Disparities', *See comment in PubMed Commons belowNicotine Tobacco Research* 14 (6): 631–38.

Goldberg, M., J. Liefeld, J. Madil and H. Vredenberg (1999), The Effect of Plain Packaging on Response to Health Warnings', *American Journal of Public Health* 89 (9): 1434–35.

Gusfield, J. (1981), *The Culture of Public Problems: Drink-Driving and the Symbolic Order*, Chicago: University of Chicago Press.

Haines-Saah, R. (2011), 'Pretty Girls Don't Smoke: Gender and Appearance Imperatives in Tobacco Prevention', in K. Bell, D. McNaughton and A. Salmon (eds), *Alcohol, Tobacco and Obesity: Morality, Mortality and the New Public Health*, 119–211, New York: Routledge.

Haines-Saah, R., K. Bell and S. Dennis (2014), 'A Qualitative Content Analysis of Cigarette Health Warning Labels in Australia, Canada, the United Kingdom, and the United States', *American Journal of Public Health*. Prepublication version. Available online: http://ajph.aphapublications.org/doi/pdfplus/10.2105/AJPH.2014.302362 (Accessed 23 December 2014).

Hall, R., K. Lopez and E. Lichtenstein (1999), 'A Policy Approach to Reducing Cancer Risk in Northwestern Indian Tribes', in R. Hahn (ed.), *Anthropology in Public Health: Bridging Differences in Culture and Society*, 142–62, New York: Oxford University Press.

Hammond, D., G. Fong, P. McDonald, R. Cameron and K. Brown (2003), 'Impact of the Graphic Canadian Warning Labels on Adult Smoking Behaviour', *Tobacco Control* 12: 391–95.

Hammond, D., G. Fong, R. Borland, K. Cummings, A. McNeill and P. Driezen (2007), 'Text and Graphic Warnings on Cigarette Packages: Findings from the International Tobacco Control Four Country Study', *American Journal of Preventative Medicine* 32 (3): 202–9.

Hammond, D., M. Dockrell, D. Arnott, A. Lee and A. McNeill (2009), 'Cigarette Pack Design and Perceptions of Risk Among UK Adults and Youth', *European Journal of Public Health* 19 (6): 631–7.

Hastings, G., M. Stead and J. Webb (2004), 'Fear Appeals in Social Marketing: Strategic and Ethical Reasons for Concern', *Psychology and Marketing* 21: 961–86.

Health Tap (nd), Health Tap website. Available online: https://www.healthtap.com/user_questions/771214 (Accessed 17 November 2014).

Heidegger, M. (1966), *Being and Time*, trans. J. Macquarie and E. Robinson, London: SCM Press.

Heidegger, M. (1971), 'Building Dwelling Thinking', in *Poetry, Language, Thought*, trans. A. Hofstadter, 145–61, New York: Harper and Row.

Hein, H. O., P. Suadicani, P. Skov and F. Gyntelberg, (1991), 'Indoor Dust Exposure: An Unnoticed Aspect of Involuntary Smoking', *Archives of Environmental Health* 46 (2): 98–101.

Hill, D. and T. Carroll (2003), 'Australia's National Tobacco Campaign', *Tobacco Control* 12: ii9–ii14. Available online: http://tobaccocontrol.bmj.com/content/12/suppl_2/ii9.extract (Accessed 19 October 2014).

Hunt, G. and J. Barker (2001), 'Socio-cultural Anthropology and Alcohol and Drug Research: Towards a Unified Theory', *Social Science and Medicine* 53: 165–88.

Ingold, T. (2007), 'Earth, Sky, Wind and Weather', *Journal of the Royal Anthropological Institute* 13: Supplement: S19–S38.

Ingold, T. (2008), 'When ANT meets SPIDER: Social theory for arthropods', in C. Knappett and L. Malafouris (eds), *Material Agency: Towards a Non-Anthropocentric Approach*, 209–15, New York: Springer.

Intergovernmental Committee on Drugs Standing Committee on Tobacco (2012), *National Tobacco Strategy 2012-2018*, Canberra: Intergovernmental Committee on Drugs Standing Committee. Available online: http://www. nationaldrugstrategy.gov.au/internet/drugstrategy/publishing.nsf/Content/ D4E3727950BDBAE4CA257AE70003730C/$File/National%20Tobacco%20 Strategy%202012-2018.pdf (Accessed 5 July 2014).

Interstate Road Transport Act 1985 (1985), Available online: http://www.comlaw. gov.au/Series/C2004A03169 (Accessed 10 November 2014).

Interstate Road Transport Regulations 1986 Cth., reg 51B (1986), Available online: http://www.comlaw.gov.au/Details/F2007C00044 (Accessed 15 November 2014).

Irigaray, L. (1999), *The Forgetting of the Air in Martin Heidegger*, trans. M. Mader, Texas: University of Texas Press.

Ivers, R. (2011), *Anti-tobacco Programs for Aboriginal and Torres Strait Islander People Resource Sheet Number 4*, Canberra: Australian Government Australian Institute of Health and Welfare.

Jackson, M. (1983), 'Thinking Through the Body: An Essay on Understanding Metaphor', *Social Analysis* 14: 127–48.

Kapferer, B. (2003), 'Introduction: Outside All Reason – Magic, Sorcery and Epistemology in Anthropology', in B. Kapferer (ed.), *Beyond Rationalism: Rethinking Magic, Witchcraft and Sorcery*, 1–30, New York: Berghahn Books.

Katz, J. (1999), *How Emotions Work*, Chicago: University of Chicago Press.

Katz, J. (2006), 'Ethical Escape Routes for Underground Ethnographers', *American Ethnologist* 33 (4): 499–506.

Kauffman, N. and M. Nichter (2001), 'The Marketing of Tobacco to Women: Global Perspectives', in J. Samet and S. Soon Yoon (eds), *Women and the Tobacco Empire: Challenges for the 21st Century*, 69–98, Geneva: World Health Organization.

Keane, H. (2002a), 'Smoking, Addiction and the Marking of Time', in J. F. Brodie and M. Redfield (eds), High Anxieties: *Cultural Studies in Addiction* 119–33, Berkeley: University of California Press.

Keane, H. (2002b), *What's Wrong with Addiction?* Melbourne: Melbourne University Press.

Keane, H. (2006), 'Time and the Female Smoker', in E. McMahon and B. Olubas (eds), *Women Making Time: Contemporary Feminist Critique and Cultural Analysis*, 94–115, Perth: University of Western Australia Press.

Klein, R. (1993), *Cigarettes are Sublime*, Durham: Duke University Press.

Klepeis, N., W. Ott and P. Switzer (2007), 'Real-time Measurement of Outdoor Tobacco Smoke Particles', *Journal of the Air & Waste Management Association* 57: 522–34.

Knauft, B. (1987), 'Managing Sex and Anger: Tobacco and Kava Use Among the Gebusi of Papua New Guinea', in L. Lindstrom (ed.), Drugs in *Western Pacific Societies: Relations of Substance*, 73–98. Lanham: University Press of America.

Kohrman, M. and P. Benson (2011), 'Tobacco', *Annual Review of Anthropology* 40: 329–44.

Kohrman, M. and S. Xiao (2008), 'Anthropology in China's Health Promotion and Tobacco', *The Lancet* 372.9650: 1617–18.

Kristeva, J. (1982), *Powers of Horror: An Essay on Abjection,* New York: Columbia University Press.

Kuper, A. (2004), 'Review of the book, Malinowski: Odyssey of an anthropologist 1884-1920', *London Review of Books* 26 (19): 29–30.

Lagan B. (1991), 'Grand Prix Row Smoulders On'. *The Sydney Morning Herald* October 29: 7.

Langer, M. (1989), *Merleau-Ponty's Phenomenology of Perception: A Guide and Commentary,* Tallahassee, FL: Florida State University Press.

Latour, B. (2010), 'A Plea for Earthly Sciences', in J. Burnett, S. Jeffers and G. Thomas (eds), *New Social Connections: Sociology's Subjects and Objects,* 72–84 London: Palgrave Macmillan.

Le Guerer, A. (1990), *Scent: The Essential and Mysterious Powers of Smell*, New York: Kodansha International.

Leclerc, A. (1979), *Au Feu Du Jour* (The Fire of the Day) Paris: Grasset.

Levi-Strauss, C. (1973), *From Honey to Ashes: Introduction to a Science of Mythology*, New York: Harper and Row.

Lucan, ([AD 65] 1896), *The Pharsalia of Lucan,* trans. E. Ridley, London: Longmans, Green and Co.

Luik, J. (1996), '"I Can't Help Myself": Addiction as Ideology', *Human Psychopharmacology* 11: S21–S32.

Lundin, S. (1999), 'The Boundless Body: Cultural Perspectives on Xenotransplantation', *Ethnos* 64 (1): 5–31.

Macauley, D. (2005), 'The Flowering of Environmental Roots and the Four Elements in Pre-Socratic Philosophy: From Empedocles to Deleuze and Guattari', *Worldviews: Environment, Culture, Religion* 9 (3): 281–314.

Macnaughton, J., S. Carro-Ripalda and A. Russell (2012), '"Risking Enchantment": How are we to View the Smoking Person?', *Critical Public Health* 22 (4): 455–69.

Mair, J., A. Kelly and C. High (2012), 'Introduction: Making Ignorance an Ethnographic Object', in J. Mair, A. Kelly and C. High (eds), *The Anthropology of Ignorance: An Ethnographic Approach*, 1–32, New York: Palgrave Macmillan.

Mair, M. and C. Kearins (2007), 'Critical Reflections on the Field of Tobacco Research: The Role of Tobacco Control in Defining the Tobacco Research Agenda', *Critical Public Health* 17 (2): 103–12.

Malinowski, B. (1954), 'Sorcery as Mimetic Imitation', in R. Redfield (ed.), *Magic, Science and Religion and Other Essays*, 70–84, New York: Doubleday.

Manning, E. (2007), *Politics of Touch: Sense, Movement, Sovereignty*, Minneapolis: University of Minnesota Press.

Marshall, M. (1981), 'Tobacco', in F. King and R. Craig (eds), *Historical Dictionary of Oceania*, 288–9, Westport: Greenwood Press.

Marshall, M. (2005), 'Carolina in the Carolines': A Study of Patterns and Meanings of Smoking on a Micronesian Island', *Medical Anthropology Quarterly* 19 (4): 365–82.

Marx, K. ([1848] 1969), *The Communist Manifesto. Vol. 1 of Marx/Engels Selected Works*, trans. S. Moore, Moscow: Progress Publishers.

Marx, K. ([1856] 1978), 'Speech at the Anniversary of the People's Paper', in R. Tucker (ed.), *The Marx-Engels Reader*, 2nd edn, 577–8, London: Norton.

Matt, G., P. Quintana, M. Hovell, D. Chatfield, D. Ma, R. Romero and A. Uribe (2008), 'Residual Tobacco Smoke Pollution In Used Cars For Sale: Air, Dust, And Surfaces', *Nicotine And Tobacco Research* 10 (9): 1467–75.

Matt, G., P. Quintana, M. Hovell, J. Bernert, S. Song, N. Novianti, T. Juarez, J. Floro, C. Gehrman, M. Garcia and S. Larson (2004), 'Households Contaminated By Environmental Tobacco Smoke: Sources of Infant Exposures', *Tobacco Control* 13 (1): 29–37.

Matt, G., P. Quintana, J. Zakarian, A. Fortmann, D. Chatfield, E. Hoh, A. Uribe and M. Hovell (2011), 'When Smokers Move Out And Non-Smokers Move In: Residential Thirdhand Smoke Pollution and Exposure', *Tobacco Control* 20 (1): 1–3.

Matteoni, F. (2010), *Blood Beliefs in Early Modern Europe*, Hertfordshire: University of Hertfordshire.

Mauss, M. ([1935]1979), 'Body Techniques in Sociology and Psychology', in *Essays by Marcel Mauss*, trans. B. Brewster, 97–123, London: Routledge & Kegan Paul.

Mayo Clinic (2014), Mayo Clinic Website. Available online: http://www.mayoclinic. org/healthy-living/adult-health/expert-answers/third-hand-smoke/faq-20057791 (Accessed 1 November 2014).

McDonald, R. (1992), *Shearers' Motel*, Sydney: Picador.

McFadden, M. (2004), *Dissecting Antismokers' Brains*, Pipersville: Aethna Press.

Merleau-Ponty, M. ([1945] 1962), *Phenomenology of Perception*, trans. C. Smith, London: Routledge and Kegan Paul.

Metherell, M. (2012), 'Big Tobacco Loses High Court Battle Over Plain Packaging', *The Sydney Morning Herald*, 15 August 2012. Available online: http://www. smh.com.au/opinion/political-news/bigtobacco-loses-high-court-battle-over-plain-packaging (Accessed 21 September 2014).

Ministerial Council on Drug Strategy (2004), *National Tobacco Strategy (2004) 2004-2009: The Strategy,* Canberra: Ministerial Council on Drug Strategy, Department of Health and Aged Services. Available online: http://www.who. int/fctc/reporting/Australia_annex7_national_tobaccostategy2004_2009.pdf (Accessed 14 October 2015).

Munafo, M., N. Roberts, L. Bauld, and U. Leonards (2011), 'Plain Packaging Increases Visual Attention to Health Warnings on Cigarette Packs in Non-Smokers and Weekly Smokers But Not Daily Smokers', *Addiction* 106: 1505–10.

Munro, C. (2007), 'Neighbours See Off Smokers In Tribunal', *Sydney Morning Herald*, 28 February. Available online: http://www.smh.com.au/news/national/ neighbours-see-off-smokers-in-tribunal/2007/02/27/1172338624538.html (Accessed 30 June 2014).

Mutti, S., D. Hammond, R. Borland, M. Cummings, R. O'Connor, and G. Fong, (2011), 'Beyond Light and Mild: Cigarette Branding Descriptors and Perceptions of Risk in the International Tobacco Control (ITC) Four Country Survey', *Addiction* 106 (6): 1166–75.

Nading, A. (2013), 'Humans, Animals, and Health: From Ecology to Entanglement', *Environment and Society: Advances in Research* 4 (1): 60–78.

National Expert Advisory Committee on Tobacco (1999), *National Tobacco Strategy 1999 to 2002-03: A Framework for National Action.* 1999, Canberra: Ministerial Council on Drug Strategy, Department of Health and Aged Services. Available online: http://www.nationaldrugstrategy.gov.au (Accessed 13 January 2015).

Nichter, M. and E. Cartwright (1991), 'Saving the Children for the Tobacco Industry', *Medical Anthropology Quarterly* 5 (3): 236–56.

Nichter, M. (2003), 'Smoking: what does culture have to do with it?', *Addiction* 98 (1): 139–45.

Nichter, M., G. Qunitero, M. Nichter, J. Mock and S. Shakib (2004), 'Qualitative Research Contributions to the Study of Drug Use, Drug Abuse, and Drug Use(r) Related Interventions', *Substance Use and Misuse* 39 (10–12): 1907–69.

Nichter, M., M. Nichter, P. Thompson, S. Shiftman and A. Moscicki (2002), 'Using Qualitative Research to Inform Survey Development on Nicotine Dependence Among Adolescents', *Drug and Alcohol Dependence* 68: 41–56.

Northern Territory Government Tobacco Control Act Tobacco Retail Displays (nd), 'Displays and Point of Sale: Banning Tobacco Displays'. Available online: http://www.health.nt.gov.au/library/scripts/objectifyMedia.aspx?file=pdf/52/95.pdf (Accessed 30 January 2015).

O'Loughlin, B. (2010), 'Peter Sloterdijk (2009) *Terror From The Air*, Trans. A. Patton and S. Corcoran. Los Angeles, CA: Semiotext(E)'. Available online: http://www.culturemachine.net/index.php/cm/article/viewFile/396/414 (Accessed 11 January 2015).

Orima Research (2013), *Department of Health and Ageing National Tobacco Campaign – More Targeted Approach – Phase 3 Culturally and Linguistically Diverse Audiences Component Final Report*, Sydney: Orima.

Parr, V., B. Tan, P. Ell and K. Miller (2011), *Market Research to Determine Effective Plain Packaging of Tobacco Products. Report Prepared for the Department of Health and Ageing*, Sydney: GFK Blue Moon Research.

Pearlman, J. (2012), 'Australia's new plain packaging "makes cigarettes taste worse"', *The Telegraph*, 30 November 2012. Available online: http://www.telegraph.co.uk/news/worldnews/australiaandthepacific/australia/9713249/Australias-new-plain-packaging-makes-cigarettes-taste-worse.html (Accessed 14 November 2014).

Peeples, L. (2011), 'Your Nose Knows: The Invisible Threat of "Thirdhand Smoke"'. *The Huffington Post,* 26 August 2011. Available online: http://www.huffingtonpost.com/2011/08/26/thirdhand-smoke-smoking-risks_n_938241.html (Accessed 23 July 2014).

Philip Morris International (Australia) website (nd), Available online: http://www.pmi.com/marketpages/pages/market_en_au.aspx (Accessed 6 July 2014).

Pottage, A. (2013), 'No (More) Logo: Plain Packaging and Communicative Agency', *U.C. Davis Law Review* 47 (2): 515–46.

Quitnow (2012), Quitnow Website. Available online: http://www.quitnow.gov.au/internet/quitnow/publishing.nsf/content/smokescreen-lp (Accessed 15 November 2014).

Rabinow, P. (2007), *Marking Time: On the Anthropology of the Contemporary*, Princeton: Princeton University Press.

Richardson, I. (2005), 'Techsoma: Some Phenomenological Reflections on Itinerant Media Devices', *The Fibreculture Journal* 6. Available online: http://six. fibreculturejournal.org/fcj-032-mobile-technosoma-some-phenomenological-reflections-on-itinerant-media-devices/ (Accessed 17 February 2015).

Rhodes, R. (2014), Comment to the 'To The Point' Page. *The Advocate*, 18 December 2014.

Room, R. (2003), 'The Cultural Framing of Addiction', *Janus Head* 6 (2): 221–34.

Russell, A. and S. Lewis (2011), 'Being Embedded: A Way Forward for Ethnographic Research', *Ethnography* 12 (3): 398–416.

Samson, B. (1980), *The Camp at Wallaby Cross: Aboriginal Fringe Dwellers in Darwin*, Canberra: Australian Institute of Aboriginal Studies.

Scollo, M. and M. Winstanley, eds (2012), *Tobacco in Australia: Facts and issues*, 4th edn, Melbourne: Cancer Council Victoria. Available online: www.TobaccoInAustralia.org.au (Accessed 30 July 2014).

Sloterdijk, P. ([1998] 2011), *Sphären I – Blasen, Mikrosphärologie (Spheres I – Bubbles, Micro-Spherology)*, Frankfurt am Main: Suhrkamp.

Sloterdijk, P. (2009), *Terror From the Air*, trans. A. Patton and S. Corcoran, Cambridge, MA: MIT Press.

Stafford, J., M. Daube and P. Franklin (2010), 'Second hand Smoke in Alfresco Areas', *Health Promotion Journal of Australia* 21: 99–105.

State of Western Australia (2006), *Tobacco Products Control Act,* Perth: State of Western Australia. Available online: http://www.austlii.edu.au/au/legis/wa/consol_act/tpca2006271/index.htl (Accessed 14 December 2014).

Stebbins, K. (1987), 'Tobacco or Health in the Third World: A Political Economy Perspective with Emphasis on Mexico', *International Journal of Health Services* 17 (3): 521–36.

Stebbins, K. (2001), 'Going Gangbusters: Transnational Tobacco Companies "Making A Killing" in South America', *Medical Anthropology Quarterly* 15 (2): 147–70.

Strange, H. and J. McCrory (1981), 'Bulls and Bears on the Cell Block', in J. Guillemin (ed.), *Anthropological Realities: Readings in the Science of Culture*, 257–73, New Jersey: Transaction Books.

Tan, Q. (2012), 'Smell in the City: Smoking and Olfactory Politics', *Urban Studies* 50 (1): 55–71.

Tate, C. (1989), 'In the 1800s, Antismoking Was a Burning Issue', *Smithsonian* 20 (4): 107–17.

Tavernise, S. (2014), 'In New Calculus On Smoking, It's Health Gains vs. Pleasure Lost', *New York Times*, 7 August 2014. Available online: http://www.nytimes.com/2014/08/07/health/pleasure-factor-may-override-new-tobacco-rules.html.

Thompson, L., J. Pearce and R. Barnett (2009), 'Nomadic Identities and Socio-Spatial Competence: Making Sense of Post-Smoking Selves', *Social and Cultural Geography* 10: 5, 565–81.

Tobacco Free Arizona website (nd), Available online: https://tobaccofreeaz.wordpress.com/2010/03/17/those-with-cancer-in-family-history-must-avoid-smokers/#more-1797 (Accessed 5 October 2014).

Tobacco.org (2009), 'Law Protects Against "Third Hand Smoke" as Well as Second Hand Tobacco Smoke', Tobacco.org website 6 January 2009. Available online: http://archive.tobacco.org/news/276822.html.

Tobin, L. (2011), 'Smokers Ignore Health Warnings', The Guardian 30 May 2011. Available online: http://theguardian.co.uk/education/2011/may/30/smokers-health-warnings-cigarette-packets (Accessed 21 September 2014).

UCTV Prime Cuts (2012), 'Clearing the Air of Thirdhand Smoke' 18 October 2012. Available online https://www.youtube.com/watch?v=G2vlk_b6UyE (Accessed 15 November 2014).

United States Department of Health and Human Services (2014), The Health Consequences of Smoking: 50 Years of Progress. A Report of the Surgeon General 2014. Available online: http://www.surgeongeneral.gov/library/reports/50-years-of-progress/index.html (Accessed 5 July 2014).

United States Public Health Service (1972), 'The Health Consequences of Smoking: A Report of the Surgeon General: 1972', Office of the Surgeon General. Available online: http://profiles.nlm.nih.gov/ps/access/NNBBPM.pdf (Accessed 29 August 2014).

United States Public Health Service (2006), 'The Health Consequences of Involuntary Exposure to Tobacco Smoke: A Report of the Surgeon General 2006', Office of the Surgeon General. Available online: http://www.surgeongeneral.gov/library/reports/secondhandsmoke/index.html (Accessed 8 October 2014).

Wakefield, M., D. Germain and S. Durkin (2008), 'How does Increasingly Plainer Cigarette Packaging Influence Adult Smokers' Perceptions About Brand Image? An Experimental Study', Tobacco Control 17 (6): 416–21.

Wakefield, M., L. Hayes, S. Durkin and R. Borland (2013), 'Introduction Effects of the Australian Plain Packaging Policy on Adult Smokers: A Cross-Sectional Study', BMJ Open 3:e003175.

Wayne, J. (2014), 'Why Smokers Must Be Shamed' The Huffington Post, 5 March 2014. Available online: http://www.huffingtonpost.co.uk/jemma-wayne/smoking-ban-uk-_b_4895623.html (Accessed 4 February 2015).

Weiss, G. (1999), Body Images: Embodiment as Intercorporeality, New York: Routledge.

Wells, R. (2011), 'Women Drinking, Smoking in Pregnancy', The Sydney Morning Herald, 15 November 2011. Available online: http://smh.com.au/lifestyle/life/women-drinking-smoking-in-pregnancy-20111114-1nfsh.html (Accessed 21 September 2012).

Wells, R. (2012), 'Does this Colour Turn You Off?', The Sydney Morning Herald, 17 August 2012. Available online: http://www.smh.com.au/national/does-this-colour-turn-you-off-20120816-24bf4.html (Accessed 21 September 2012).

What to expect.com (2012), What To Expect Parenting Website. Available online: http://www.whattoexpect.com/forums/australian-parents/archives/third-hand-smoke-141.html (Accessed 13 January 2014).

Williams, G., J. Popay and P. Bissell (1995), 'Public Health Risks in the Material World', in J. Gabe (ed.), Medicine, Health and Risk: Sociological Approaches, 113–32, Oxford: Blackwell.

Winstanley, M. (2012), 'Public Attitudes to the Tobacco Industry', in M. Scollo and M. Winstanley (eds), Tobacco in Australia: Facts and Issues, 4th edn, Melbourne: Cancer Council Victoria. Available online: http://www.tobaccoinaustralia.org.au/chapter-10-tobacco-industry/10-2-the-manufacturing-industry-in-australia (Accessed 11 September 2014).

Winter, J. (2001), *Sacred Tobacco, Silent Killer*, Oklahoma: University of Oklahoma Press.

Wogalter, M. and R. Rashid (1998), 'A Border Surrounding a Warning Sign Affects Looking Behavior: A Field Observational Study'. Proceedings of the Human Factors and Ergonomics Society 42nd Annual Meeting, Human Factors and Ergonomics Society, Santa Monica, California.

Wolfson, E. (2013), 'What Happens When You Quit Smoking?', *Healthline website.* Available online: http://www.healthline.com/health-slideshow/quit-smoking-timeline (Accessed 3 January 2015).

Wood, L., K. France, K. Hunt, S. Eades and L. Slack-Smith (2008), 'Indigenous Women and Smoking During Pregnancy: Knowledge, Cultural Contexts and Barriers to Cessation', *Social Science and Medicine* 66 (11): 2378–89.

World Health Organization (2011), 'WHO Report on the Global Tobacco Epidemic, 2011: Warning About the Dangers of Tobacco', Geneva: World Health Organization.

Wynne, E. (2012), 'Smokers are reporting plain packaged cigarettes taste worse than branded' ABC Radio Perth website, 30 November, 2012. Available online: http://www.abc.net.au/local/stories/2012/11/30/3645022.htm (Accessed 26 October 2014).

# Index

Aboriginal and Torres Strait Islander
    smokers   37, 80
Action on Health and Smoking   128
Action on Smoking and
    Health   22, 139
addict   16, 71, 79, 82, 84
addiction   12, 13, 16, 24, 38–9, 50,
    84, 130
    cultural functions of   38
    tobacco framed by   38
Adey, P.   128, 129
*Advocate* (newspaper)   149
affect   33
air
    as agent   101–4
    breath and   109–13
    classed   122
    difference in   127–8
    explication   104–9, 152
    history of   146–8
    infinite and pure, protection
        of   130–2
    legislation of   47
    public   122–4
    secondhand, explication of   115–17
    smoking to remember   163–4
    theoretical background of   99–101
Air Navigation Act (1920)   43
Air Navigation Regulations (1947)   43
American Anthropological Association
    (AAA)   121
Americans With Disabilities Act   22
Anderson, B.   31–3
anisotropic sense of smoker   55
anthropology   18, 23–4, 31, 70, 72,
    93–4, 169–72, 174 n.5, 176 n.4
    of air   104
    colonial   128–30
    public health and   11–12
    reformulation, of smoker   82–6
    smokefree   30

smoker and   16–17
of smoking   12–16
anti-smoking advertisements and
    campaigns   24, 25, 29, 39, 55,
    57, 62–5, 108, 109, 115, 118,
    123, 125, 152, 164, 171
    medical knowledge and   108
    *See also* graphic warnings
atmospheres   18, 20, 23, 25,
    29–35, 48–50, 53–4, 59, 68, 71,
    94, 98, 100, 103, 109, 111–12,
    129, 144, 147–8, 150, 154, 171,
    177 n.10
    cultural   80
    secessionary   128
    *See also individual entries*
atomterrorism   102
Australia: The Healthiest Country by
    2020 report   60
*Australian* (newspaper)   49–50
Australian Broadcasting Corporation
    (ABC)   48
Australian Broadcasting Tribunal   40
Australian Council on Smoking and
    Health   60
Australian Institute of Family
    Studies   65
Australian Olive Association   75

Ballantyne, C.   135, 147
Banzhaf, J.   22, 139
Barker, J.   70
Barnett, R.   61
Bell, K.   15, 38–9, 67, 117, 126, 135,
    137–8
Benson, P.   83
Benson and Hedges World Series
    Cricket (1988)   39–42
Berman, M.   100
Big Tobacco   16, 17, 37, 51, 72, 79,
    132, 171

bioethical agency   163
Bittoun, R.   142
Black, P.   12, 13
Blaine, D.   123
*BMJ Open*   50
body-altering perspective   165–6
Borthwick, F.   118, 155
boundary crosser, smoke as   21, 23
Brady M.   15
Braidotti, R.   163
Brandt, A.   18
breath and air   109–13
British American Tobacco Australia
      (BATA)   72–3
Broadcasting Act   41
Brochet, F.   157
Buttrose, I.   126

Calma. T.   80
cancer   22, 37, 39, 43, 54, 59, 72, 79,
      81, 90–1, 93, 98, 105, 106, 124–8,
      132, 136, 142, 148, 149, 160
Carnap, R.   116
Carroll, T.   62, 79, 105, 110
Cartwright, E.
      'Saving the Children for the
      Tobacco Industry'   14
Chapman, S.   18, 49, 52–3, 160
Choy, T.   100, 103, 104, 112, 132
classed air   122
Classen, C.   122, 140
Clift, K.   126
Cochoy, F.   71
Cohn, N.   143
colonial anthropology   128–30
Connor, S.   66–7, 123, 146, 155
Corbin, A.
      *Foul and the Fragrant*   124
culinary paradox   12
cultural atmosphere   80
Curtin University   147
      study   61–2

Daddo, C.   142
Daube, M.   49, 60, 62, 66, 116
Department of Health (Australian
      Government)   37
Department of Public
      Prosecutions   41

Diprose, R.   55, 164
disgust   61, 114–15, 120, 124–8,
      132, 149
Douglas, M.   127, 148
Dovey, K.   127
Downes, S.   35

elighter website   159
enclosed public place, meaning and
      significance of   44–6
Euclidean metaphor   54–5
Evelyn, J.   130–1
      'Fumifugium'   131
*Everybody Knows* campaign   125
'Every Cigarette Is Doing You Damage'
      campaign   79
exhalation   97–8, 151, 153
      *See also* miasmatic exhalation
exhaled mainstream smoke   114
explication, of air   25–6, 83,
      97–9, 101–2, 111, 113, 114,
      127, 129, 130, 151, 170, 172,
      178 n.3
      in cigarette advertising   152
      as finitude   146
      for ignorant agent   104–9
      scientific   115
      secondhand   115–17
      versions of   102–3

Farrell, L.   65
Flora, J.   94
fourthhand smoke   151–2, 157–60,
      164–6
      air explication in cigarette
      advertising and   152–5
      rational agent and travel agent
      and   166–7
      smoking to remember air
      and   163–4
      taste and   155–7, 161–3
Franklin, P.   116
Furey, A.   121

GfK Blue Moon   74, 75
Gilbert, E.   19, 108–9, 110, 151
Global Advisors on Smokefree Policy
      (GASP)   21–2
Graffis, R.   143

graphic warnings  65, 76–8, 84,
    90–1, 160
Gray, N.  41
Guillaumier, A.  160
Gusfield, J.  115

habitual body  110
Hagan, J.  110
Haines-Saah, R.  19
'happiness quotient'  84
Hastings, G.  77
Haywood, W. D.  36
Heidegger, M.  99–100, 150
    'Building Dwelling Thinking'  99
    *Poetry, Language, Thought*  99
Hill, D.  62, 79, 105, 110
*Huffington Post*  141, 143, 147
Hunt, G.  70

indigenous smokers  37, 80, 91
'Indigenous Woman'
    advertisement  81–2
Ingold, T.  100–1, 112
inhalation  17, 97–8, 104, 109–10,
    113, 124, 151, 177 n.1
Institute of Public Affairs
    (IPA)  51, 52
internal inconsistency, of
    smoking  90–3
International Tobacco Control Policy
    Survey  77
Interstate Road Transport Act
    (1985)  43
Interstate Road Transport Regulations
    (1986)  43
Investor State Dispute Settlement
    (ISDS)  73
Irigaray, L.  99–100, 109, 146, 150
    *The Forgetting of Air in Martin
    Heidegger*  99

Kapferer, B.  88–9, 92–3
Karlin, M.  41
Katz, J.  109, 153, 155, 167
Keane, H.  38–9, 54, 55
Kierans, C.  53
Klein, R.  109, 164, 166
    *Smoking is Sublime*  152
Knauft, B.  17

Kohrman, M.  15, 83
Kristeva, J.  22, 138

Langer, M.  110
Latour, B.  103
Leclerc, A.  152
Le Guérer, A.  118
licensing, of smokers  18
'looking behaviour' studies  76
Lundin, S.  163, 164

Macnaughton, J.  82, 83, 84
mainstream smoke  114
Mair, M.  53
'Make Smoking History'
    campaign  60
Malinowski, B.  85–6
Manly Council (Sydney)  46
Manning, E.  145
Markel, S.  112
Marshall, M.  13
    'Carolina in the Carolines'  14
Marx, K.  32, 100
Matt, G.  136, 137, 141, 147
Matteoni, F.  139–40, 143
McFadden, M.
    *Dissecting Antismoker's
    Brains*  147
*Medical Journal of Australia, The*  49
Merleau-Ponty, M.  56, 59, 110, 164
miasmatic exhalation  25, 114–15,
    136, 138, 147, 151
    air protection and  130–2
    cancer and  124–7
    colonial anthropology and  128–30
    condemnation of smokers
        and  120–2
    public air and  122–4
    secondhand air explication
        and  115–17
    smell and  118–20
miasmatic pollution  141–2
Ministerial Council on Drug Strategy
    (MCDS)  42, 78
Mitchell, W.  41
mobile tobacco contamination
    packages  137–8
modernity
    explication as foundation of  102

as shared condition 100
moral rightness 49–50
Morris, P. 73
Mosman Municipal Council
(Sydney) 46
mosquitoes and smoke, eradication
of 128–30
Munafò, M. 77
municipal councils 46–7

Nading, A. 129, 130
national campaign, on smoking 42
National Drug Strategy 37
National Expert Advisory Committee
on Tobacco 78
National Healthcare Agreement 30
National Preventative Health
Taskforce 51–2
National Tobacco Campaign (NTC)
(1997) 37, 105, 123
Artery, Lung, Tumour, Brain
(or Stroke), Eye and Tar
campaign 105–8
National Tobacco Strategy (NTS)
116, 117
1999–2003 78
2004–9 78
2011 79–80
2013–18 115
National Warning Against
(1972–1975) 42
neighbor smoke 47
New South Wales Consumer, Trader
and Tenancy Tribunal 47
Nichter, M.
'Saving the Children for the
Tobacco Industry' 14
nicotine 13, 14, 16, 21, 38, 39, 54,
58, 71, 79, 104, 135–6, 142,
144, 174 n.2
Non-Smokers' Movement of Australia
(NSMA) 41, 147–8

olfaction 26, 98, 115, 117–20, 124,
136, 139–40, 144–6, 155
power and 122
oppositionary pair
longevity and untimely death
and 53–60

public health and tobacco
companies and 50–3
right and wrong of 48–50
smoking time and time free of
smoking and 60–7
spatial states 67–9
other, olfactory perception of 140
out-boundedness, from body
site 153
outgassing 147
OxyGen website 148

Parslowe, F. 41
Pearce, J. 61
Peeples, L. 137
phenomenology 19, 25, 56, 59, 108,
167, 173 n.2, 178 n.4
Philip Morris International (Australia)
(PMIA) website 72
plain cigarette packaging 17, 29,
49–52, 60, 63, 71, 73–7, 154,
160–2
assessment via participants'
awareness regarding labels 76
Pottage, A. 71
present body 97, 110, 113, 152, 161
public health 15–18, 23–4, 71–3,
83–9, 91–4, 97, 104, 146, 160,
162, 164, 169–71
anthropology and 11–12
framing 128
goal 129, 174 n.5
interventions, and smoker
construction 36–9
messaging 125, 152
rational agent of 78–82
tobacco companies and 50–3
warning signs 67, 127, 135
public place legislation, nuances of
43–7

Queensland Cancer Council 126
Quitnow website 81, 106–8, 124

Rabinow, P. 31
Rashid, R. 76
rational smoker 16, 17, 24, 72, 107
case study of 86–8
Rhodes, R. 149

Room, R. 38
Rowe, J. 126
Roxon, N. 51, 74, 76

Samson, B.
  *Camp at Wallaby Cross, The* 12
Scollo, M. 37, 40–2
  *Tobacco in Australia* 38, 50, 114,
    117, 127
secondhand smoke. *See* miasmatic
    exhalation
sensing body 154–5
Serres, M. 117, 146, 153, 154, 155,
    166–7
sidestream smoke 114
Sloterdijk, P. 101–4
  *Terror from the Air* 101
smell 26, 36, 58–9, 98, 115, 121–2,
    124–6, 132, 134–5, 145, 155, 172
  miasmatic exhalation 118–20
  of stale cigarette smoke 137–8
  thirdhand smoke and 139–44
smokefree environments 42–3
Smoke Free Generation initiative 45
Smoke-Free Public Places Act
    (2003) 45, 67–8
'Smoking – who needs it?'
    campaign 42
sociality 118–20, 122, 132, 166
'Sponge'(television commercial) 107
Stafford, J. 116
Stead, M. 77
Stebbins, K. 13
'Stop Before the Suffering Starts'
    campaign 79
*Studio Ten* 126
'Suffering' campaign 79
Swedenborg, E. 123

'Tackling Indigenous Smoking' 80
taste 58, 76, 159, 160–1, 178 n.3
  with capital T 156–7
  with small t 155–6
Tate, C. 36
Taylor, P. 49
temporal disobedience, of
    smoke 66–7
thirdhand smoke 20–2, 25, 66–7,
    112, 127, 128, 151

history of air and 146–8
mobile tobacco contamination
    packages and 137–8
second law of
    thermodynamics 148–50
significance of 133–6
smell and 138–44
touch and 144–6
United States on 36
Thompson, L. 61
Tobacco.org 139
tobacco advertisement, legal
    definition of 35
Tobacco Advertising Prohibition Act
    (1992) 35, 37
Tobacco Control Act (2002) 46
tobacco control research 15
Tobacco Free Arizona (TFA)
    website 22, 128
Tobacco Plain Packaging Act
    (2011) 51
Tobacco Plain Packaging Regulations
    (2011) 51
Tobacco Products Control Act
    (2006) 33–4
tobacco smoke 20, 25, 78, 133–5,
    150, 176 n.2
  exhaled 26, 97
  exposure to 117, 121, 124, 126
  inhaled 98, 104, 107–8, 177 n.1
  outdoor 116, 125
  research on 106, 115
  residue 139 *see also* thirdhand
    smoke
  sensitivity to 22, 128
  types of 114
tobacco-specific nitrosamines 135
touch 132, 142, 167
  of thirdhand smoke 134, 136,
    138, 144–6
Trobriand Islanders 85, 86

UCTV 134
United Telecasters 41
universities, as smokefree places 47

'The War on Smoking' 21
Waverley Council (Sydney) 46
Wayne, J. 24

Webb, J.   77
Western Australia Cancer Council   60
'What to Expect' website   144–5
Williams, G.   85
Winickoff, J.   134
Winstanley, M.   37, 40–2
  *Tobacco in Australia*   38, 50, 114, 117, 127
Winter, J.
  *Sacred Tobacco, Silent Killer*   80
Wogalter, M.   76
Wolfson, E.   54
Wood, L.   91
Wooldridge, M.   105
World No Tobacco Day   107
Wynne, E.   160